SELF-ESTEEM, RECOVERY AND THE PERFORMING ARTS

ABOUT THE AUTHOR

Donna Douglass received her Bachelor of Arts in Music Therapy degree from the University of Pacific in Stockton, California, and her Master of Arts in Special Education from Arizona State University in Tempe, Arizona. She has worked many years in mental health as a clinician, administrator, and educator, specializing in the production of musical shows and plays. During her career, she founded two nonprofit organizations: the Salem Creative Arts Center in Oregon and *Project Arts* in Phoenix, Arizona. It was in the first program that she established *Theatre Extraordinaire,* her first musical theatre company for seriously mentally ill adults, followed by a second company of the same name in Phoenix. After relocating to Spokane, Washington, she founded *On Stage!,* a performing arts recovery program that included her third theatre company. It was the establishment of this program that offered the opportunity for an innovative university research study on the effects of the performing arts on skill building and work readiness.

Ms. Douglass' extensive experience includes working in nursing homes, day treatment centers, private and state hospitals, and prisons, as well as 1 year in South Vietnam in Special Services. She founded the music therapy program at Arizona State University and was an associate professor of music and director of music therapy at Willamette University in Salem, Oregon. During her career, Ms. Douglass has written numerous songs and musical plays for her theatre company productions and a book titled *Accent on Rhythm: Music Activities for the Aged.* Currently, she is on the adjunct faculty at Washington State University Spokane and two community boards: The Supported Education Enhancing Rehabilitation (SEER) Advisory Board and the Spokane County Substance Abuse Advisory Board.

SELF-ESTEEM, RECOVERY AND THE PERFORMING ARTS

A Textbook and Guide for Mental Health Practitioners, Educators and Students

By

DONNA DOUGLASS, M.A.

CHARLES C THOMAS • PUBLISHER, LTD.
Springfield • Illinois • U.S.A.

Published and Distributed Throughout the World by

CHARLES C THOMAS • PUBLISHER, LTD.
2600 South First Street
Springfield, Illinois 62794-9265

ISBN 978-0-398-08606-0 (hard)
ISBN 978-0-398-08607-7 (paper)
ISBN 978-0-398-08608-4 (ebook)

Library of Congress Catalog Card Number: 201003165

With THOMAS BOOKS *careful attention is given to all details of manufacturing and design. It is the Publisher's desire to present books that are satisfactory as to their physical qualities and artistic possibilities and appropriate for their particular use.* THOMAS BOOKS *will be true to those laws of quality that assure a good name and good will.*

Printed in the United States of America
MM-R-3

Library of Congress Cataloging in Publication Data

Douglass, Donna.
Self-esteem, recovery and the performing arts : a textbook and guide for the mental health practitioners, educators and students / by Donna Douglass.
p. cm.
Includes biographical references and index.
ISBN 978-0-398-08606-0 (hard)–ISBN 978-0-398-08607-7 (pbk.)
1. Self-esteem. 2. Mental illness. 3. Performing arts. 4. Mental health. I. Title.

BF697.5 S45D686 2011
616.89'165–dc22 2010030165

CONTRIBUTORS

Dennis G. Dyck, PhD.

Professor, Psychology and Neurosciences
Vice-Chancellor and Associate Vice Provost for Research
Washington State University Spokane
Spokane, Washington

David E. Martineau

Masters in Urban and Regional Planning (MURP)
Member, American Institute of Certified Planners. (AICP)
Portland, Oregon

To my parents–
For the gift of music
and the joy it has brought into my life

and

To the many people with psychiatric disabilities
from whom I have learned so much,
and whose resilience has proven recovery is possible,
even in the most difficult of circumstances.

FOREWORD

In my years as a clinical researcher, practitioner, and educator, I have seen many mental health systems attempt to create interventions that will lead to recovery of persons with psychiatric disabilities. Although some interventions have an impressive evidence base (e.g., family education and support, assertive community treatment), many programs struggle with finding ways to lead to significant positive changes in service users' quality of life and other areas of recovery. However, every now and then a program comes along that stands out. It looks different, and its outcomes are undeniable. This is the case with On Stage! and its predecessors, programs that appear unlike other mental health programs because they *are* unlike other mental health programs. As researchers try to identify new methods focusing on recovery (rather than symptom management and psychotherapy) for people with a serious mental illness, Ms. Douglass has discovered a unique approach, using the performing arts, that has proved to be an effective mental health intervention. In performing arts activities that develop self-esteem and resilience, participants find themselves in a normalized environment where they are, from day one, referred to as students, not patients or clients. Once enrolled in the program, many of these students find they finally have something to look forward to–a reason to get up in the morning. In classes and rehearsals that focus on performing, skill building and personal growth, students enjoy participating in activities that are motivating and personally satisfying–and fun. Although Ms. Douglass' approach to rehabilitation is not unassailable, there is a plausible theoretical framework provided, as well as preliminary findings that support the effectiveness of the program and its approach.

Ms. Douglass has taken it upon herself to write a book about her lifelong work, experiences, and approach to promoting normalizing and recovery-based experiences. Furthermore, it is about as readable and moving as a textbook can be. Consequently, I feel she has much to share with students, practitioners, family members, and users of mental health services. Written with a human touch, Ms. Douglass is not afraid to talk about her own experiences and how her work focuses on "one person at a time." She has done a considerable amount of research into understanding why and how her programs work. She has conceptualized, in a social learning framework, what it is about participating in a demanding performing arts program that is "healing and transforming," effectively describing how her approach to recovery fits into the social learning model. Specifically, her students build self-esteem and resilience through skill development and graded exposure in a group format that provides the opportunity for observational learning and reinforcement. Additionally, in a unique approach to reducing performance anxiety, students experience carefully constructed desensitizing experiences by performing first for each other and then gradually for small to large audiences. Ms. Douglass' approach is both intuitive and provocative–offering a hypothesis that the organization inherent in music and dance can promote healing and development in persons with neurocognitive and perceptual disabilities. She further touches on this subject in a discussion on the healing influence of music and movement on cognitive development and learning.

As most people know, mental illnesses are isolating conditions, in part, because of the misunderstanding and "stigma" associated with them. The performing arts programs created by Ms. Douglas provided destigmatizing experiences not only for users of mental health services, but also for providers, family members, and the community. Another unique aspect of her program was the partnership established with Whitworth University in Spokane involving service learning student volunteers in her productions. This program had two important functions: It provided normalizing role models for the users of mental health services, and it reduced stigma as volunteers learned that persons with psychiatric disabilities can be productive, talented, and accomplished. It was definitely a two-way street because both sides benefited from the experience.

Designed to be more than a description of an effective mental health recovery program, this book also provides practical tips and guidelines on how to implement a similar program in the community. Just as seen in her instruction methods with mental health service users, Ms. Douglass' teaching of practitioners is highly practical, hands on, and demonstrative. Program guides, member sign-in forms, and costume designs are all provided. This book is an invaluable guide to anyone interested in implementing a musical theatre program for people with psychiatric disabilities.

In closing, as someone who was fortunate to be found by the author in the "yellow pages" (see story #11) almost 15 years ago, I am indebted to what Ms. Douglass has taught and imparted to me personally. More significantly, her substantial contribution to the training of many students and providers has led to the achievement of recovery goals by students and the reduction of stigma in service providers. Finally, my hope is that this book will significantly enhance the dissemination of Ms Douglass' incredibly rich knowledge base, and thereby promote the recovery of many more persons afflicted with a mental health disability–"one life at a time."

DENNIS DYCK, PH.D.
Professor, Psychology and Neurosciences
Vice-Chancellor and Associate Vice Provost for Research
Washington State University Spokane
Spokane, Washington

PREFACE

Do not go where the path may lead–
Go instead where there is no path and leave a trail.
–Ralph Waldo Emerson

How do I start a program like yours? How do you motivate people to get involved? How do you help people deal with stage fright? How do you retain people in your programs? These are just a few of the questions I have been asked by family members, professionals, and others after they have seen the shows I have produced with casts of people with psychiatric disabilities. Then there are the questions I have asked myself: What is there about stage performance that keeps service users motivated and looking forward to the next show? What are the specific benefits of a performing arts experience? Finally, why does this approach to recovery work? This book has been written to answer these questions and to (1) introduce Self-Esteem in Recovery (SEIR), a recovery model created for people with a serious mental illness; (2) address the need for innovative programs promoting recovery; (3) provide a new recovery model for use in the arts therapies and related fields; and (4) offer a program that can be adapted for people with physical and developmental disabilities.

THE AUDIENCE

This book is offered as a new resource on recovery for two groups of readers interested in expanding their knowledge on recovery programs for people with a serious mental illness. The first group includes practitioners, educators, and students in mental health and related fields. Specifically, it is intended for *mental health practitioners* providing direct services in the arts and related fields and for activity directors interested in staging variety shows in long-term-care facilities; for *educators* looking for innovative resources to provide new insights and theories along with ideas for research; and finally for *entry-level students* in the areas of music and other arts therapies, recreation therapy, psychosocial rehabilitation, and psychiatric occupational therapy. Further, literature cited throughout the book provides a background and foundation for the theories and principles of the SEIR model. The second target group is for individuals or organizations desiring to establish a musical theater program within their communities.

THE FORMAT

Because this book is written for two distinct groups of readers, it is divided into two parts. Part I, *Background and Evidence,* is written as a text with two goals: (1) to *serve as a resource* for educators teaching introductory classes, and (2) to *provide background information* for those interested in starting a community musical theatre company for people with a serious mental illness and other disabilities. Chapter 1 is a brief history of the evolution of mental health practices in the United States. Also included is a literature review on self-esteem and a summary of a research study conducted by the author on the effects of the performing arts in recovery. Chapter 2 describes the history and development of the SEIR model and includes a description of The Recovery Wheel, an evaluation tool created by the author to assess progress on the eight SEIR goals. Chapters 3, 4, 5 and 6 provide information on how a SEIR program can be utilized to reduce stress, develop resilience, reduce performance anxiety, build cognitive skills, and promote stigma reduction.

Part II, *Getting Started,* is designed as a guide to anyone interested in implementing a musical theatre company for people with psychiatric disabilities. Created from the author's extensive experience in producing variety shows and founding theatre companies, this section describes the process that has led to many successful stage productions. In Chapter 7, the reader will find a guide describing a recruitment process and the first informational meeting. The remainder of the chapter describes how a show is created, from selection of a theme to preparation for opening night. (Because it is beyond the scope of this book to include, in detail, the methods designed to implement a SEIR program, a handbook on clinical applications of the model is being developed for this purpose.) Thus, with the information in this section and Part I, those interested in starting a community musical theatre company should have enough background to begin a project that will greatly benefit a wide range of people with disabilities.

SPECIAL FEATURES

After so many years of clinical work, the author has hundred of stories to tell about her students and their journeys, via her programs, to recovery. So included within the text are several of these success stories, some titled *One Life at a Time,* others told in short vignettes. In addition, there are descriptions of the unique experiences the author and her students have encountered during their "travels" together. For example, there was the incident when a portable stage collapsed during a performance and another when a cast member walked out 5 minutes before the curtain went up on a major event! Then there are the unique circumstances surrounding the founding of the author's two nonprofit organizations, Salem Creative Arts Center and Project Arts, and the most recent, On Stage!. Also of particular interest is the role the author's theatre companies played in reducing the stigma associated with mental illness. Specifically, it was not only the public performances that educated audiences, but, more importantly, the personal contact between community volunteers and cast members that seemed to have the most lasting effect. Finally, it is the author's hope that the content of this book will interest educators, clinicians, and students to consider pursuing research on the effectiveness of the performing arts and the SEIR model on the recovery of people with a serious mental illness.

D.D.

INTRODUCTION: A PERSONAL PERSPECTIVE

I am often asked two questions: Why did you decide on music therapy as a career? Why, when working with people with disabilities, has stage production and its related activities always been your intervention of choice? This brief autobiographical sketch may offer some answers to these questions and provide insight into the reasons for my pursuit of a career in mental health.

Music has always been an important part of my life due to my musical family and my mother's insistence that I take piano lessons and practice a lot! In the 1920s and 1930s, my parents played in a family dance band, with my mother on piano, Dad on trumpet, an uncle playing saxophone and clarinet, and another uncle on drums. I was told stories of how this small band of musicians would drive in a Model A Ford to various grange halls where they played for dances, often arriving home around 4:00 a.m. As a child, I remember watching musical variety shows at the local grange halls where my parents were frequent participants. Sometimes these events included those old-fashioned minstrel shows where the performers were in black-face, dark suits, and top hats.

The earliest recollection of my own stage experience is when, at around age 6, I sang a vocal solo titled *Alice Blue Gown* before an audience at a local grange hall. It is not surprising that I do not recall exactly how I felt about my performance. But I do remember my excitement over the wonderful costume created for this special occasion by a family friend: a fancy blue gown with lace and ribbons and a hat to match. How I loved that dress and the way I felt when wearing it, like a princess or perhaps even a queen, anxiously awaiting to hear the accolades from an adoring audience. Following my debut on the stage were many years of study in the performing arts that included lessons in classical piano, ballet, tap, and voice. During that time, I performed dozens of times on the piano in festivals and contests, always evaluated on my performances by one or more serious-faced judges sitting behind long tables and waiting, it seemed, for me to make a mistake. In retrospect, I realize that early on I began experiencing extreme performance anxiety brought about by two major fears: a lapse of memory and making a mistake. Although some students could perform in high-stress environments with seemingly little anxiety, I was not so lucky. Although my anxiety level varied according to the performance environment, any situation requiring a "perfect" performance would bring about all the signs of extreme nervousness: sweaty palms, racing heartbeat, and, on one occasion, knees that locked prior to walking onto a stage. (I was given a gentle push to get me started!)

Despite long hours of practice, repeated episodes of performance anxiety, and the memorization of innumerable music scores required for the many festivals, guilds, and other contests, I managed to complete 12 years of piano study before leaving for college. It was while in high school that I discovered three kinds of musical performance that gave me the greatest satisfaction and the least anxiety: accompanying vocal and instrumental soloists, playing in dance bands, and playing for musical theatre productions. In all of these situations, I knew that if I made a mistake, I had a chance to recover through improvisation and opportunities to keep going no matter what happened. Although I may have been somewhat nervous, the debilitating dread that was ever-present when I was playing classical music was not there.

Thanks to my mother, a piano teacher, I learned to play popular music at a time when this style of playing was strictly forbidden by my classical piano teacher, who, for some reason, thought playing popular music would interfere with my musicality in the performance of classical music. (I remember living in fear that she would hear of my wayward behavior!) However, I continued to pursue my interest in playing popular music, thus developing a skill that has proved to be invaluable throughout my career–and my life. (By the way, I eventually transferred to another piano teacher who was not at all critical of my performing with dance bands and other pop music groups.) Clearly then, the personal experiences I have had over the years, especially my constant struggle with performance anxiety, played a major role in the development of programs that focus on reducing anxiety and improving self-confidence and self-esteem. (I can only imagine what performing might have been like if someone had taught me techniques of stress reduction; i.e., deep breathing, positive thinking.)

Although the development of the recovery model described in this book was created recently, my interest in using the performing arts in the recovery process began years before the word "recovery" was associated with mental illness. With each production, beginning at Napa State Hospital in the 1960s, I witnessed dramatic improvements in self-confidence and self-esteem, outcomes that resulted in my continued interest in the therapeutic benefits of the performing arts. Over time I realized that, although "opening nights" are the highlight of any production, what happens during rehearsals and backstage can contribute to the participants' personal growth and well-being. For example, the camaraderie that develops among cast and crew can create what is frequently referred to as a theatre "family." Moreover, there is something very special about being part of a process where everyone involved works very hard toward a common goal, learning to deal with the stress caused by a bad rehearsal but coming together to experience the ultimate in emotional highs–a great opening night.

I believe adamantly in the healing power of the arts. It is this belief that provided the motivation behind the creation of the Salem Creative Arts Center (Salem, OR), Project Arts (Phoenix, AZ), and On Stage! (Spokane, WA). Further, I believe that every person, with or without a disability, is innately creative and only needs the opportunity to discover, develop, and express that creativity. Finally, I think every person with a disability should be given the opportunity to discover and utilize the strengths and abilities that will support their recovery and lead to successful achievement of their life goals. By combining my personal experience in performance with a background in providing music therapy and recovery services to people with disabilities, I believe I have created a recovery model that will help these persons experience what they truly deserve: to be treated with respect, accepted for who they are, and afforded opportunities to improve their quality of life and overall well-being. After all, people with a mental illness are people, too, just like you and me.

LESSONS LONG REMEMBERED

When working with people with a mental illness and related emotional problems, one learns early on the importance of keeping one's emotions under control, especially in a crisis situation. I learned two lessons during my training and later work experience that strongly influenced my ability today to "keep my head while everyone around is losing theirs." The first lesson occurred during my internship in 1959 at the Menninger Foundation in Topeka, Kansas. To create consistency in the way that employees responded and reacted to patients, a protocol known as *A Guide to the Order Sheet* was written with details on how to relate to patients in specific circumstances (Menninger Foundation, 1982). Sometimes referred to as "attitude therapy," a psychiatrist might, for instance, prescribe a "matter of fact" approach, indicating that the employee was to refrain from showing any emotional response or expressing any opinions when working with the patient. Another directive was "active friendliness," granting permission to interact with the patient in a relaxed, friendly manner. Although attitude therapy is no longer utilized at the Menninger Foundation, the lessons I learned from this unusual treatment approach were invaluable because it taught me to be more aware of my own behavior and how it could affect my relationship with my patients. (I also learned the importance of keeping my keys out of sight due to the intimidating effect they could have on patients: another Menninger protocol.)

I learned the second important lesson when I was activities director in a day treatment center. Our medical director, a psychiatrist and one of my most memorable mentors, was a compassionate man who taught his staff the importance of refraining from being "caught up" in the emotions of the moment. I will never forget the expression he used to describe how we should react: "Keep it in neutral" no matter what happens. Throughout my long mental health career, I never forgot those words, a lesson that helped a great deal, as reflected in the following two stories.

Story 1. In the mid-1960s I was employed as a classroom teacher in a school and treatment center for emotionally disturbed adolescents. Now why, you might ask, was I teaching academics when I had no formal training in the area? As it turned out, the agency hired me out of desperation: teachers kept leaving. In fact, a previous teacher left rather quickly after students set fire to the papers on her desk! At this point, the administration had decided that someone with a mental health background was needed to keep the students under control, so they hired me. (As it turned out, I wore two hats in that job: a classroom teacher and a music therapist.) An example of the importance of "keeping it in neutral" occurred when, in the former role, I entered the classroom and sat down at my desk. As I began pulling open the center drawer, there was a loud "bang" as caps (used in cap guns) exploded. The result was two runs in my stockings, one in each leg. Now I could have reacted in one of two ways: by freaking out and running from the room (students were waiting for this!) or demonstrating to the "culprits" that the act was no big deal, which is exactly what I did. I recall looking up from the damage to my stockings and saying, "Someone owes me for a new pair of nylons," and beginning the lesson of the day. Needless to say, my students were very disappointed in my reaction and hopefully realized that it would take more than a minor explosion to take me out of "neutral."

Story 2. This same agency, because of its volatile population, seemed to always be confronted with a crisis of some degree. An example is a situation that took place when I was wearing my music therapy hat. For weeks we had been rehearsing a variety show to be presented as a fundraiser for the school. Everyone was excited because this was the first time a show had been part of such an event. However, an incident during dress rehearsal the night before almost caused cancellation of all festivities. The house parent (I'll call him "Evan") of one of the residents got into argument that resulted in Evan threatening his wife with a knife. The police were called, and Evan was taken to jail. When students got the news, they were devastated. This man was greatly admired and respected by everyone, so it was not surprising that students wanted to cancel the next day's event. However, before they made that decision, I assembled the cast on stage and asked one question: What would Evan want you to do? The answer, of course, was that he would want the show to go on, and that is exactly what happened. And what a performance it was. Those students sang and danced their hearts out–for Evan, for the school, and for a public that, with their applause, showed their appreciation for an incredible show. Little did that audience know how close this event came to an unexpected cancellation. Here once again was another reason to "keep it in neutral," not give up and prove once again that no matter what happens, "The show will go on."

The preceeding stories are just two examples of how the early lessons in emotional control got me through some very stressful situations, including physical attacks by patients, bombs in Vietnam, and all of those stage shows where a last-minute crisis was a sure thing. So I offer this bit of advice to my readers: Take a deep breath (or more if necessary), stay positive, and, for your own sanity and those around you, Keep It In Neutral!

ACKNOWLEDGMENTS

This book is the product of three influential sources: the many service users who turned my vision of performing arts recovery programs into a reality, the insights I have gained from those willing to share their recovery stories, and the collaboration with colleagues at WSU Spokane. Although it is impossible to cite everyone who has contributed, I want to acknowledge those whose influence has been significant.

To Michael Smith, manager of the Bing Crosby Theatre where On Stage! presented its annual public performances. To the many community mental health agencies in Spokane, especially Family Service Spokane, the Evergreen Club, and Spokane Mental Health, who supported the On Stage! mission with their referrals, making it possible for us to fill our classes. To the National Alliance for the Mentally Ill (NAMI) in Spokane who featured the On Stage! theatre company at so many NAMI events. To the musicians in my combos who donated their valuable time so we could always have live music at our shows, with kudos to Loren Rux on trumpet, Brian Flick on guitar, and Ron Baer on drums. To the Westminster United Church of Christ for providing rehearsal space for 9 of the 10 years On Stage! offered its mental health services. And to Steve Cada, property manager for SAMCA, LLC, whose advocacy made possible a special lease agreement, allowing On Stage! to move into its own facility.

To my Project Arts staff, Donna, John, Alan, Kathy, Mary Ann, Pauline, Lynn, and Billie, and the Board of Directors who helped my vision of an arts recovery program for seriously mentally ill adults in Phoenix become a reality. To Stan Heddleston, MSW, whose advocacy for Project Arts resulted in our initial funding, and from whom I learned so much about supported education and recovery. To my students at Willamette University in Salem, Oregon, whose talents and energy made possible the success of my first musical theatre company for people with a serious mental illness.

A SPECIAL THANKS

In any major project, there are always people and organizations whose contribution to the project's completion has been invaluable. Writing of this book is no exception. So with deep appreciation and gratitude, I offer a special thanks.

To the Washington Institute of Mental Health Research and Training (WIMIRT) and Washington State University Spokane for providing office space, technical support, and use of library resources during this 3-year project. I especially appreciate the help received from Diane Norell, MSW, whose advice and counsel helped me realize that I had created a new recovery model and whose invaluable assistance played a significant role in the completion of this book. Also to Robert Short, PhD, for his patience and advice, and to Mason Burley who provided technical support during the many times my computer was less than cooperative. To Kathy Schwartz and Robert Pringle, librarians, for coming to my rescue when I encountered problems in my literature search. To two extraordinary graphic artists, Mark Mickelson, who created the book's illustrations from my very amateur designs, and Susan Lyons, who helped prepare the first draft of my manuscript. And finally to Brian Pitcher, Chancellor of WSU Spokane, who made possible my dream of On Stage! having its own facility.

To Dennis Dyck, PhD, Vice-Chancellor and Director of Research at WSU Spokane, who, as then director of WIMIRT, believed in my vision to establish a performing arts recovery program in Spokane. Instrumental in procuring the research funding that launched On Stage!, Dr. Dyck's advocacy and strong belief in our mission strongly influenced the continuation of our program, despite critical funding issues, for 10 years.

To Katherine Crow, choreographer extraordinaire, whose delightful, creative dance routines gave life to each and every On Stage! production and whose inherent ability to connect with our cast members built morale, lifted spirits, and helped each person to be successful. The messages she communicated to the cast–"There's no such thing as a mistake" and "It is ok to fail as long as the effort is made"–freed everyone to perform to the best of their ability.

To the Jim and Donna Simanton Foundation, whose yearly support enabled On Stage! to survive despite funding cuts and other fiscal challenges. And to Donna Simanton, who, after Jim's passing and the closure of On Stage!, continues to be a dear friend and champion of good causes.

To the many mental health service users whose loyalty and dedication were responsible for the success of my three theatre companies. Your willingness to work so hard for the many weeks it took to produce our shows is a tribute to the resilience of the human spirit and proof that recovery from a serious mental illness is possible.

To Donna White, a music therapist, my former student, and now a lifelong friend, who became my partner in implementing Project Arts in Phoenix. It was her valuable participation in and dedication to our mission that provided the support I needed to make this program possible. In addition, I will always appreciate the valuable assistance Donna offered when I was creating the first draft of this book in the mid-1990s.

To my publisher, Michael Thomas, whose belief in the value of my work made this book possible. Working with you has been a pleasure, and I am honored to be associated with your esteemed publishing house.

And finally, to each and every person who has contributed so much to this project, a line from one of our On Stage! show tunes seems to say it all:

"Hats off to you, my friends,
Hats off to you!"

CONTENTS

Page

Foreword ix
Preface xiii
Introduction xvii

PART ONE: BACKGROUND AND EVIDENCE

Chapter

1. HISTORY AND RESEARCH 5
   Mental Health Practices: The Evolution 5
   Toward a Recovery Model 15
   Self-Esteem: What Else Does the Literature Say? 18
   The Healing Power of the Arts: Is It Real? 21
   A Study on the Effects of the Performing Arts on the Recovery of Adults with a Severe Mental Illness 22

2. TOWARD A RECOVERY MODEL 33
   One Life at a Time 33
   Self-Esteem and Recovery (SEIR) 35
   History and Development of the SEIR Model 36
   The SEIR Model 37
   Model Structure 39
   The Recovery Wheel: Evaluating SEIR Goals 63

3. STRESS REDUCTION, RESILIENCE AND RECOVERY 66
   One Life at a Time 66
   Reducing Stress: The Ten Commandments 70
   Stress-Resistant Personalities 70

Stress Reduction and Resilience 75
Coping With Stress 78

4. REDUCING PERFORMANCE ANXIETY IN THEATRICAL PERFORMANCE 81
One Life at a Time 81
A Positive Approach 83
Anxiety: The Good and the Bad 84
A Desensitization Process: Small to Large Audiences 85

5. MUSIC, COGNITION, AND RECOVERY 94
One Life at a Time 94
Music, Cognition and Recovery 97
Cognitive Skills and Serious Mental Illness 101
Cognitive Skills, Functions, and SEIR Skill-Building Activities 104

6. STIGMA REDUCTION AND THE PERFORMING ARTS 120
One Life at a Time 120
A Historical Perspective 122
Advocacy for Change 125
Professionals and Families 130
Mental Health Service Users 132
Stigma Interventions 133
Performing Arts Interventions 134
Program Examples 136

PART TWO: GETTING STARTED

7. THE MUSICAL THEATRE COMPANY 153
Recruitment and Retention of Cast Members 154
The Informational Meeting 157
The First Theatre Company 159
Getting Organized 160
The First Production 162
Program Guides and Forms 165
Expecting the Unexpected: The Crisis Resolution Guide 167
The "Experienced" Theatre Company 168

Secrets to Success: Patience, Practice, and Perseverance 170
Publicity and Programs 173
Costumes 175
Sets and Props 178
Theme Shows 179

Appendix A: Program Guides 185
1. Cane Construction Guide 185
2. Crisis Resolution Guide 186
3. Dance Routine: *I'm a Yankee Doodle Dandy* 189
4. Personality Characteristics of the Successful Teacher/Therapist . . . 191
5. Program Boilerplate 193
6. Program Sample 194
7. Program Rules and Guidelines 195
Appendix B: Forms 197
1. Confidentiality Statement and Consent Form 197
2. Member Enrollment Form 199
3. Member Information Form 200
4. Member Sign-In Form 201
5. Pre-Performance Self-Evaluation 202
6. Post-Performance Self-Evaluation 205
7. Theatre Company Contract 206
References 209
Index 221

ILLUSTRATIONS

Page

Tables

Table 1 On Stage! Research Study: Assessment Summary. 25
Table 2 Recovery Wheel Assessment Example. 64
Table 3 Characteristics of Stress-Resistant and Stress-Prone Personalities 72
Table 4 On Stage! Cast and Crew Analysis 138
Table 5 Publicity Timeline. 173

Figures

Figure 1 History of Psychotropic Drug Development 9
Figure 2 SEIR Model: Toward Self-Esteem, Self-Efficacy and Recovery. 40
Figure 3 SEIR Model: Detailed 41
Figure 4 Building Stress-Resistant Personalities: Performing Arts Intervention 74
Figure 5 Cognitive Skills, Functions and SEIR Interventions 106
Figure 6 Learning Process: Dance Routines 116

Case Examples

1. "David" Schizophrenia. 19
2. "Dan" Schizophrenia 42
3. "Michael" Schizophrenia 44
4. "Audrey" Schizophrenia 35
5. "John" Major Depression 58
6. "Maria" Schizophrenia 76
7. "Ellen" Severe Anxiety Disorder. 91

8. "Ken" Schizophrenia 108
9. "Robin" Bi-Polar Disorder 139
10. "Emily" Major Depression 145
11. "Maxine" Schizophrenia 164

Stories

1. The Beginning 7
2. Changes 13
3. The "Chatter Factor" and More 46
4. The Unexpected 49
5. Adapting: The Key to Success 53
6. Stress Resistance and Resilience 80
7. Einstein and the Violin 97
8. King George and the Power of Music 100
9. Stigma Busting 122
10. Project Culture: Talent Unplugged 131
11. It's in the Yellow Pages 137
12. University Students: Changing Attitudes 140
13. It's a Family Show 142
14. Let's Celebrate! 144
15. Come Hear the Music 148
16. Be Ready for Anything 167
17. Hats Off! 168

SELF-ESTEEM, RECOVERY AND THE PERFORMING ARTS

Part One

BACKGROUND AND EVIDENCE

Chapter 1

HISTORY AND RESEARCH

MENTAL HEALTH PRACTICES: THE EVOLUTION

> Recovery from mental illness is not the same as cure. It means regaining control over one's life if not one's illness. It means leading a useful, satisfying life even though symptoms may reoccur.
>
> –William A. Anthony

The ethical treatment of people with a serious mental illness has been a major concern of mental health advocates for decades. However, it was not until the 1950s that significant advances in psychiatric medicine began to change treatment approaches, offering hope to the thousands of patients confined in state institutions. Because these changes led to the evolution of mental health treatment as known today, it seems important that readers know how scientific research has promoted treatment innovations. Knowing this may further the understanding and appreciation of the role the recovery movement has played in the lives of service users today. Therefore, a brief overview of the topic is presented here, in which the author has taken the liberty to use her experience in mental health as the basis for dividing the history of psychiatric treatment into three categories of practice: *Confinement, Deinstitutionalization, and Recovery.*

Confinement

Ancient Theories

Confinement and mistreatment of the mentally ill has a long and disturbing history, beginning when society became convinced that victims were to blame for their illnesses. Prior to this time, the causes of mental illness encompassed a wide range of theories ranging from the compassionate to the ethereal. Divided into three categories by the author, some of these beliefs are summarized below:

- **Biological Malfunctions.** According to the Egyptians (about 4,000 years ago), all diseases had physical causes, and the heart was responsible for the symptoms of mental illness; Hippocrates and the Greeks believed that depression originated from "black bile."
- **Outside Forces.** Aeschylus, a Greek playwright, theorized that demon possession explained the cause of mental illness; in early Egypt, the loss of status was believed to be the cause.
- **Psychic Functions.** Galen, a surgeon from Greece considered psychic functions of the brain to be the cause of mental illness. Others who believed in related theories were Homer ("God's taking the mind away"), Socrates ("Mental illness was heaven-sent"), Aristotle ("Melancholia is the cause"), and the Bible (Mental illness originates from despair and cognition).

Treatment for the aforementioned theories encompassed a wide range of approaches, including faith, exorcism, music, diet and exercise, confrontation, humor, entertaining stories, and diversion. In some cases, no treatment was used because practitioners believed the illness was "heaven-sent" and therefore an act of God (Bipolar World, 2009).

Although most of these ancient theories may seem nonsensical when considering what is known today about the etiology of mental illness, it should be noted that people with mental illness during ancient times were usually treated with compassion and not vilified for having a mental disease. Furthermore, some theorists had the right idea as they searched for medical reasons to explain the origin of mental illness. Unfortunately, as the 20th century began, changes occurred that would significantly alter the direction of mental health treatment for decades to come.

Evolution in Treatment: An Overview

During the 18th and 19th centuries in the United States, people with a mental illness were placed into over-flowing institutions and asylums that were little more than warehouses, with negligible treatment and therapy. Moreover, since the beginning of the 19th century, the number of people with severe mental illness had been increasing, and by 1955, 4 out of 1,000 people were in mental institutions.[1] Especially disturbing was the use of the term "warehousing" to describe the holding of patients for indefinite amounts of time with little hope for release. In the meantime, as psychiatrists argued about the cause of mental disorders, there were no effective treatments available to help the chronically mentally ill. Furthering the stigma already associated with mental illness, derogatory words such as "nut house," snake pit," and "bug house" were employed to describe mental institutions. (The author recalls, when working at a state hospital in the early 1960s, how patients were sometimes referred to as "inmates" and long-term hospital workers described as "bughousers.") Unfortunately, the deplorable conditions in early institutions would continue until the mid-20th century, when, after decades of wrongful confinement, mistreatment, and unspeakable abuse, people with a mental illness would no longer be subjected to treatments once considered traditional practice. Instead, a revolutionary discovery would take place, changing the direction of mental health treatment well into the future.

Story 1: The Beginning

In the early 1960s and straight out of internship, I was employed as a music therapist in a state hospital. Suddenly I was confronted with the reality of mental health treatment at that time: 5,600 patients living in a facility that was, for the most part, self-sustaining. Patients worked without pay on a farm that grew food, while others were assigned to services that supported the running of the hospital. Due to this large patient population, many activities were designed to be recreational as opposed to therapeutic. This explains why I was placed in charge of producing the many variety shows given by patients to entertain the hospital community. Thus was the beginning of my show production experience. It was while rehearsing for one of these events that I worked with "Sara," a most unforgettable

1. It is interesting to note at this point that "cross cultural and historical studies indicate that chronic mental illness is a recent phenomenon of Westernized countries." Indeed, the World Health Organization recently conducted studies showing the "rate of recovery from severe mental illness is much better in third world countries than in Western industrialized countries" (Fisher & Ahern, 2009).

patient. A talented singer very excited about being on stage, she attended rehearsals regularly and seemed to be looking forward to her performance. However, on the day of the production, Sara disappeared, something she apparently did now and then. Why she chose this particular time to "elope" I can only speculate. Perhaps it was stage fright or maybe the side effects from the lobotomy she had undergone years earlier. Who knows? What I do know is this: Sara loved to sing. And when belting out one of her torch songs, all symptoms of her mental illness seemed to disappear as her audience clapped and cheered in response to her remarkable performance.

Development of Antipsychotic Drugs

If a catch phrase were to be used to describe the progress in psychiatric biochemistry over the past five decades, we might say, "We've come a long way, baby!" It is due to the development of these new antipsychotic drugs that people recovering from a serious mental illness are no longer hindered as much in their recovery by the debilitating side effects of earlier medications. In fact, the lives of many people have changed so dramatically that they can now look forward to the future with hope and expectation, rather than despair and apprehension. This remarkable progress in mental health treatment involves a long line of scientists diligent in their determination to find the cause of and treatment for mental illness. To give the reader a timeline regarding the milestones in psychiatric drug development, a brief history of these events is presented here. In addition, a timeline on drug history can be found in Figure 1. The source of this information is the book *Better Than Prozac* by Samuel H. Barondes, MD (2003a), renowned in his field for his research in psychopharmacology and psychiatric genetics.

History of Psychotropic Drug Development

Prior to 1950, Phenobarbital, an anticonvulsant and sedative, was widely used to quiet psychiatric patients. Although an effective sedating agent, the drug had two disturbing side effects: Patients slept for days, and it was addictive. Yet psychiatrists of the day showed little interest in the negative effects of Phenobarbital or in drugs of any kind, accounting for the lack of drug development up to this time. Then,

Figure 1

HISTORY OF PSYCHOTROPIC DRUG DEVELOPMENT

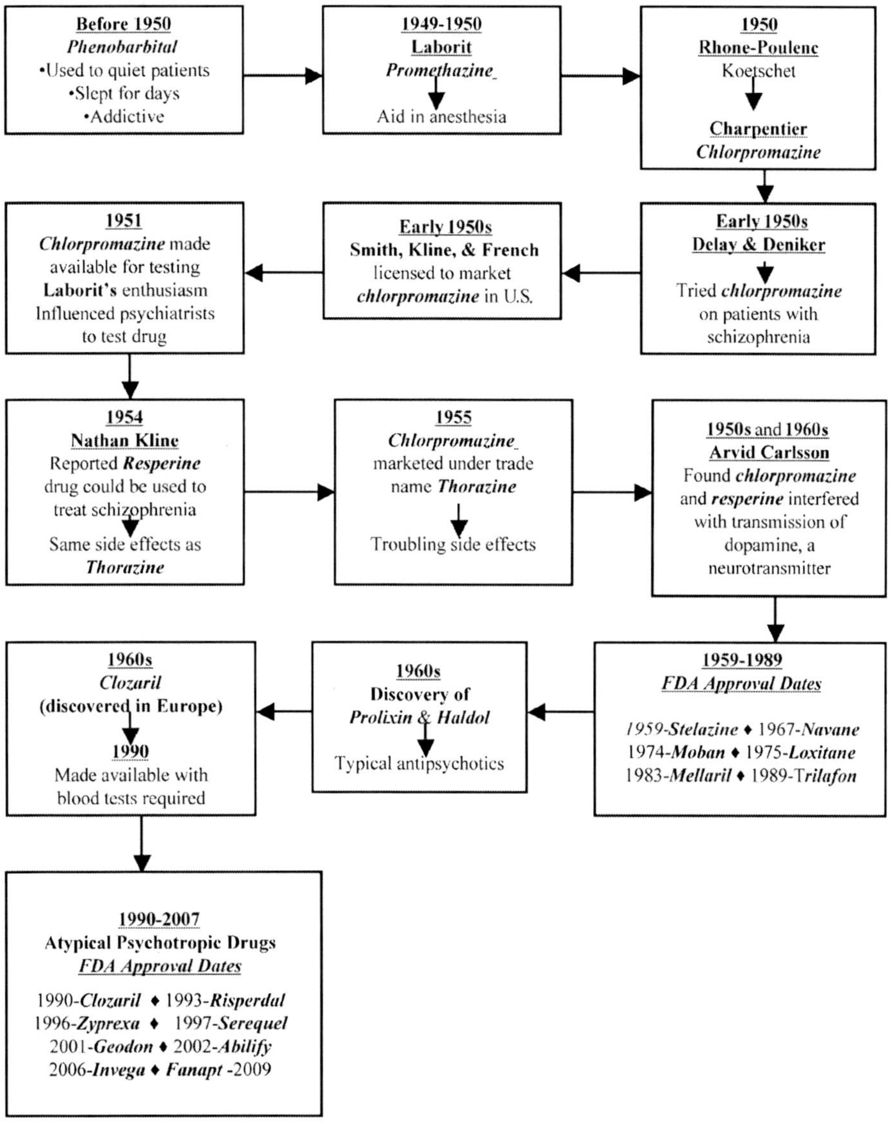

Figure 1. History of psychotropic drug development.

beginning in the early 1950s, a chain of scientific discoveries set in motion a process that eventually resulted in the astounding discovery of a new psychotropic medication. The circumstances involved were similar to that of many scientific breakthroughs: discovery of a new drug while in pursuit of a cure for a completely different disease or condition. Such was the circumstance that led to the discovery of the first antipsychotic medication.

In the 1930s, the drug promethazine was found to have both sedative and antihistamine properties, thus presenting the possibility that, because of its calming effect, this drug could be used to treat psychiatric disorders. However, due to its addictive nature and short-term effectiveness, psychiatrists of the time were not enthusiastic about using promethazine to treat their patients. Then in 1943, a Swiss chemist, Albert Hoffman, made a legendary discovery. While making a chemical variant causing uterine contractions, he found this drug had a hallucinatory effect when inhaled or ingested. Hoffman soon realized he had inadvertently discovered a mind-altering drug that "changed the perception of common objects, intensifying their colors and altering their shapes." Unknowingly, he had created a recreational drug later to be identified as LSD. Although a medical benefit of LSD was never found, Hoffman's discovery led to renewed interest in searching for new pharmaceuticals to treat mental illness.

THE MIRACLE DRUG

In 1952, Henri Laborit, a surgeon in Paris, accidentally discovered that promethazine relieved surgical shock when used in accordance with anesthesia. In the process of using this drug, he also discovered (to his surprise) a noticeable decrease in anxiety and an indifference in patients' response to pain. Realizing he had found not only an adjunct to anesthesia but a possible use of promethazine in psychiatric treatment, Laborit wrote an article about his findings for a medical journal, catching the attention of Pierre Koetschet at Rhone-Poulenc, a French chemical company. Koetschet then suggested that Paul Charpentier, an assistant director of the company, begin "tinkering" with the chemical structure of promethazine, an experiment resulting in the discovery of chlorpromazine. Charpentier then enlisted two French psychiatrists, Jean Delay and Pierre Deniker, to test the drug in clinical trials at a local psychiatric hospital. Accordingly, in the early 1950s, after thousands of psychiatric patients had been successfully treated in Europe, the remarkable outcomes of these tests captured the attention of psychiatrists in the United States. Consequently, by 1955, chlorpromazine was approved by the Food and Drug Administration (FDA) and marketed under the name Thorazine by the pharmaceutical company Smith, Kline, and French.

Clearly, the discovery of Thorazine gradually reduced the use of inhumane treatment to treat mental illness. Even with its debilitating side effects,[2] this antipsychotic medication was considered to be a miracle drug, significantly reducing the use the unacceptable treatment practices. Indeed, the age of psychopharmacology had begun. Nevertheless, it would take a decade or more before this dramatic treatment breakthrough began to decrease the traditional practice of confining patients in institutions.

The New Antipsychotics

Although Thorazine is no longer the "drug of choice" for the treatment of schizophrenia, its discovery along with imapramine (used to treat depression) in the 1950s were "landmark events not only because of the relief they provided to so many people, but also because they encouraged a search for other types of psychiatric drugs" (Barondes, 2003a). The *first generation* of these new medications are now referred to as "typical antipsychotics" and, although offering relief from hallucinations and delusions, caused debilitating extrapyramidal side effects[3] along with negative symptoms (apathy, withdrawal) (Meltzer, Park, & Kessler, 1999). To complicate treatment even further, many of these side effects made it necessary for patients to also take side-effect medicines, causing even more side effects, including dry mouth, constipation, fatigue, and memory loss. Thus, as the search for new drugs to treat mental illness continued, it was the hope of all concerned that a medicine to reduce or eliminate many of these side effects could be discovered.

Then in 1954, another drug, respirine, was discovered by Nathan Kline, a New York psychiatrist and proved to have the ability to treat schizophrenia. However, respirine was not as successful as Thorazine in treating the symptoms of schizophrenia, producing the same Parkinson-like side effects. In the meantime, as the search for a psychotropic

---

2. Thorazine produces side effects known as *tardive dyskinesia,* a condition in which patients exhibit involuntary grimacing and uncontrolled body movement.
3. The most debilitating of these effects is tardive dyskinesea, but drowiness, dizziness, muscle stiffness, tremors, restlessness, and weight gain may also occur.

drug with fewer side effects continued, Arvid Carlsson, the Swedish pharmacologist responsible for identifying dopamine as a neurotransmitter,[4] made another historical discovery: Thorazine and respirine interfered with the function of dopamine.[5] This discovery set the stage for further research into the role neurotransmitters play in the etiology of psychiatric disorders.

While the quest for new psychotropics continued in the 1960s and beyond, a new antipsychotic, Clozaril, was discovered in Europe in the 1960s. Although effective in decreasing the extreme side effects of the typical antipsychotics, the drug was eventually taken off the market due to its effect on the loss of white blood cells (granulocytes), a reaction resulting in infection. Over time, however, Clozaril was reinstated as an effective treatment, provided people taking the medication had a blood test monthly to check their white blood cell count. Consequently, because of its favorable characteristics[6] this new psychotropic gained approval by the FDA in 1990. Encouraged by the favorable effects of Clozaril, scientists proceeded to develop other drugs now classified as *atypical,* thus establishing the second generation of antipsychotics, medications that have become the treatment of choice today. Although not entirely free of side effects, none of these new drugs is nearly as debilitating as those caused by the typical antipsychotics.

DEINSTITUTIONALIZATION

With the discovery of more effective psychotropic drugs, the focus of mental health treatment began to move away from hospitalization and long-term care to community treatment centers and recovery. Shortly after the approval of Thorazine, reduction in hospitalization rates began. Consequently, between 1955 and 1994, public mental hospital beds in the United States were reduced by 91% (Thesen, 2001). Not surprisingly, the impact of this new treatment was brought to the attention of the U.S. Congress, resulting in the passing in 1963 of the Community Mental Health Center Act, thus establishing a national system of care. Around this same time, an increased use of psychotherapy and other

4. Neurotransmitters are the chemicals that nerve cells use to communicate with each other.
5. Dopamine is aneurotransmitter that helps regulate movement and emotion.
6. Clozaril produces minimal extrapyramidal side effects and improves sociability and "zest for life."

treatments (Palmer, 2000), along with new medications, resulted in a new treatment practice that better prepared patients for transition from in-patient to community-based care. Consequently, state institutions began releasing patients into their communities, where they were expected to receive the mental health services needed. However, the Community Mental Health Center Act, originally designed to serve non-psychotic patients and well intended, did not prepare social service agencies for this deinstitutionalization[7] of patients with psychotic disorders. These unforeseen circumstances resulted in these agencies being unprepared to serve the thousands of patients newly released into the community (Cook & Wright, 1995). Therefore, without the services needed to survive, many service users "were at a high risk of re-hospitalization due to lack of food, shelter, clothing and community supports" (Palmer, 2000). Later on, other efforts were made to improve psychiatric treatment, including the creation of the President's Commission on Mental Health in 1977 and in 1980 the passing of Mental Health Systems law. But politics interfered with implementation of the latter, nullified by an administration focused on cutting the federal budget (Hinshaw & Cicchetti, 2000).

Story 2: Changes

It was the late 1960s, when I was hired as activities director in a day treatment center located in central California. At a time when massive discharges from state hospitals had just begun, I recall vividly the impact this sudden change in mental health policy had on the Center's programming plans. Originally designed to serve those who had recently experienced an acute episode of mental illness, the Center now had to focus on re-designing its program. These changes meant meeting the needs of those with cognitive deficits and poor social and daily living skills. Dealing with hygiene problems became a daily occurrence as the staff began learning to cope with service users who had just left a hospital environment that promoted dependence and compliance. Of course, there was occasionally a humorous incident that provided a bit of relief from a sometimes stressful environment. I recall one in particular: Our agency nurse had become very impatient with the coffee maker be-

7. "Deinstitutionalization" is the term used to describe the release of patients from state institutions into the community.

> cause, in her view, it was doing its job much too slowly. So in frustration she began talking to the pot, telling it to "speed it up." This comment was overheard by a service user standing nearby, who remarked: "Oh, do you talk to coffee pots, too?" Yes, "things they were a'changin'," our small center just one example of what was occurring in mental health systems across the country.

Meanwhile, as advocates in Congress were fighting to establish a national mental health system, advocacy organizations were increasing their efforts to raise funds for improving services and educating the public in the process. However, it seemed there were never enough dollars to implement the well-intentioned efforts of those who passed the laws and regulations. Adding to this funding dilemma was what seemed to be the never-ending stigma attached to mental illness (Chapter 6). Fueled by the print and broadcast media that sensationalized any crime where a mentally ill person was involved (Stuart, 2006) and by a public whose knowledge of mental illness was limited, there seemed to be little anyone could do to notably alter the view of the general public. Then came breakthroughs in brain research that would significantly change the direction of mental health treatment and at the same time begin to, hopefully, decrease the stigma associated with mental illness.

RECOVERY

With a significant decrease in the number of people with a serious mental illness in hospitals, the focus of mental health treatment has changed from in-patient treatment to new community-based recovery approaches. Pioneering this effort was William A. Anthony, who is responsible for the rise of the psychosocial rehabilitation movement. When describing the focus on recovery as a revolution in vision, Anthony (1992) stated: "I believe that much of the chronicity in severe mental illness is due to the way the mental health system and societies treat mental illness and not the nature of the illness itself." With this new "vision" and the advancements in medicine and other treatment modalities, the direction of mental health treatment at last had turned away from confinement toward recovery.

Although this major shift in treatment methods has resulted in improvements, "much remains to be accomplished" (Garske & McReynolds, 2005). Still, the focus on recovery (a new "practice") has further motivated mental health advocates in their efforts to educate the public about the latest developments in psychiatric medicine and psychosocial rehabilitation. To this end, advocacy groups like the National Alliance for the Mentally Ill (NAMI) and organizations comprised of service users work diligently to educate the public about mental illness, focusing on stigma reduction and parity in health care (Hinshaw & Cicchetti, 2000).[8] As a result of these efforts, a significant gain was made when federal legislation for mental health parity was passed in October 2008 (Lynch, 2008). Although rightly heralded as a major breakthrough, this legislation, unfortunately, did not provide the funds needed to expand recovery programs. Consequently, continued funding cuts in community services have resulted in increased re-hospitalization rates and other costly interventions (emergency rooms, jails), a situation that could have been avoided had preventative community programs been available. Clearly, then, there is an urgent need, now more than ever, for cost-effective community recovery programs designed to meet the needs of a special population too long disenfranchised, stigmatized, and ignored.

TOWARD A RECOVERY MODEL

> Recovery is a process, beginning with diagnosis and eventually moving into successful management of your illness. Successful recovery involves learning about your illness and the treatments available, empowering yourself through the support of peers and family members, and finally moving to a point where you take action to manage your own illness by helping others.
>
> –National Alliance on Mental Illness

Despite the challenges still ahead, service users have benefited significantly from the results of the new brain research and focus on recovery. It is a fact, however, that some individuals respond more rapidly to treatment than others depending on their diagnosis. For example, 80% of those with bipolar disorder respond more promptly to treatment that includes psychotherapy, support, and education about the illness, while

---

8. In the Surgeon General's Report on Mental Health, parity is described as the effort to treat mental health financing on the same level as financing for general health services (1999).

individuals with major depression have a 65% chance of a timely response when medication is combined with other treatments. Even those with schizophrenia, the most serious of mental illnesses, have a 50% to 60% chance of recovery over time if they receive the medications and ancillary services they need (National Alliance on Mental Illness, 2008).

Contributing to these recovery rates are the following innovative programs that have significantly improved recovery outcomes:

- *Assertive Community Treatment,* a team approach designed to provide comprehensive, community-based treatment and rehabilitation to persons with serious and persistent mental illnesses.
- *Cognitive Behavioral Therapy* (CBT), a form of psychotherapy focusing on changing thoughts in order to change behaviors and emotions.
- *Multi-Family Education,* a method that trains families and persons with illness to work together to achieve overall recovery goals, including reduction of relapse and re-hospitalization, development of social networks for both families and service users, and lessening of the burden placed on families.
- *Clubhouses,* psychosocial programs that helps service users stay out of hospitals while achieving their social, financial, and vocational goals.
- *Supported Education,* a program offering service-users access to resources that will help them pursue their post-secondary educational goals.

All of these services provide opportunities for the acquisition of skills necessary for independent living and an improved quality of life. Accordingly, when given the opportunity to enroll in these programs, many people with psychiatric disorders have become productive members of their communities, supporting the "notion that people with a severe and persistent mental illness can lead a meaningful life while managing the illness (Rodgers, Norell, Roll, & Dyck, 2007). Still,

The task is not to become normal. The task is to take up your journey of recovery and to become who you are called to be. (Deegan, 1997)

due to lack of funding, numerous individuals do not have access to these programs and are struggling to obtain the basic services they need (i.e., housing, food, and health care). In addition, those whose goals include employment find the lack of services in vocational training and education further barriers to recovery.

RECOVERY AND SCHIZOPHRENIA

Although the mental health services described above have significantly changed the lives of many service users, there is one psychiatric disorder that does not have the success rate of others: schizophrenia. As of this writing, individuals with this disorder have only a 30% recovery rate (National Alliance on Mental Illness, 2008), the result of numerous challenges not experienced by individuals with other mental illnesses (i.e., deficits in social skills, social performance, and interpersonal skills). These liabilities significantly limit opportunities for finding work and participating in social and other activities supporting recovery (Garske & McReynolds, 2005). Furthermore, even though the development of atypical medications[9] reduces positive symptoms[10] and, to a lesser degree, negative symptoms,[11] many people with schizophrenia remain challenged by the disabling effects of the negative symptoms, thus impeding their chances for recovery.

In a study addressing self-esteem in persons with schizophrenia, researchers found that, although service users may have successfully decreased their positive symptoms, they still may struggle with mood disorders. However, often ignored and consequently untreated, these disorders can result in "profound consequences on social participation and on well-being" (Sorgaard et al., 2002). The authors of this study noted further that positive self-esteem and self-confidence were related to service users' satisfaction with leisure activities, an important aspect in the development of social skills and expanded social networks. In another study exploring the relationship of negative beliefs about mental illness to depression and anxiety, the authors found that negative

9. Atypical medications are new antipsychotic medications with fewer side effects than earlier medications and are now used as first-line treatment.

10. Positive symptoms reflect a reduction or loss of normal function, are easily observed, and include hallucinations, delusions, and disorganized speech and behaviors.

11. Negative symptoms reflect the reduction or loss of normal skills, including lack of motivation, inability to express normal feelings, depression, anxiety, and isolation.

symptoms in people with psychosis "are often under-recognized, under-diagnosed and under-treated," suggesting that psychological therapies could play an important role in emotional recovery by focusing on treating affective disorders and improving self-esteem (Karatizias, Gumley, Power, & O'Grady, 2007). Consequently, the lack of attention to negative symptoms and the failure of traditional treatment to alleviate them can find service users caught in a system offering little hope for recovery (Berge & Ranney, 2005; Gureja, Harvey, & Herman, 2004; Knut et al., 2002).

It is far beyond the scope of this book to address all of the issues that would be involved in changing the nation's current mental health system. In the author's opinion, however, a start would be to re-direct the millions of dollars currently funding expensive services into community recovery programs that focus on providing *all* the assistance needed to help service users achieve independence. Then, with recovery as a priority, perhaps the United States could move more quickly toward establishing a mental health system that truly meets the needs of all people with a serious mental illness.

SELF-ESTEEM: WHAT ELSE DOES THE LITERATURE SAY?

Research into the importance of self-esteem in well-being has been extensively documented. Even as early as 1890, William James, in the first psychology textbook, proposed that "the tendency to strive to feel good about oneself is a fundamental aspect of human nature" (Leary, 1999). For decades since the introduction of the James text, interest in self-esteem has continued and is reflected in many publications since that time. In an article on self-esteem and mental health promotion, the authors proposed that "positive self-esteem is associated with mental well-being, adjustment, happiness, success and satisfaction" and serves as a buffer when a person is faced with potentially destructive influences (Mann, Hosman, Schaalma, & deVries, 2004). These authors also stressed that self-esteem plays a major role in a person's ability to cope with life's circumstances, concluding that "low self-esteem can become a permanent barrier to recovery if not seen as one of the core variables in designing mental health programs" (Mann et al., 2004). Another factor that proved to play a significant role in building self-esteem is social support. With a strong support network, individuals are better able to develop a sense of well-being, resulting in changes including improved stress management, feelings of stability and self-worth, and an enhanced sense of self-efficacy (Rogers, Anthony, & Lyass, 2004; Shahar & Davidson, 2003).

Because numerous studies have substantiated the importance of self-esteem in life satisfaction and well-being, it should not be difficult to understand the important role it plays in the recovery of people with a mental illness. In a study by Roe (2003) on self-esteem and functioning after hospitalization, the author emphasized the importance of helping service users sustain positive self-esteem as they cope with the challenges of transitioning into the community. To this end, Roe suggested that self-esteem can be improved through treatment and should be considered an important treatment goal. Other studies have explored the relationship among self-esteem, anxiety, and depressive disorders, finding that low self-esteem can result in depression, anxiety, heavier use of psychiatric services, and a poor quality of life (Karatizias et al., 2007; Shahar & Davidson, 2003). Further indications of the importance of good self-esteem can be found in a study where Hall and Tarrier (2003) explored the use of Cognitive Behavioral Treatment (CBT) as an adjunct treatment in psychosis, with results establishing that improved self-esteem decreased psychotic symptomology and improved social functioning.

It would seem, then, that because self-esteem plays a significant role in positive rehabilitation outcomes, life satisfaction, and an improved quality of life (Kunikata, Mino, & Nakajima, 2005; Markowitz, 2001; Sorgaard et al., 2002; Torrey, Mueser, McHugo, & Drake, 2000), it should be considered a core variable in any recovery plan. Evidence supporting this premise was established in the research study described later in this chapter, in which the effectiveness of the performing arts on the rehabilitation of seriously mentally ill adults was evaluated. The results show significant improvement in work-readiness skills and self-confidence as well as in life satisfaction, quality of life, and overall well-being (Douglass, Martineau, & Dyck, 1997).

Case Example 1: "David"

David's recovery had reached a standstill. Diagnosed with schizophrenia, hospitalized several times, and now living with family, his deficits in social and interpersonal skills along with his paranoia prevented him from pursuing a recovery program. Although a member of a clubhouse that prepared service users for the work force, David's tendency to isolate coupled with a lack of interest in clubhouse activities precluded him from moving forward in his recovery. It was not until he heard about *Theatre Extraordinaire,* the *On Stage!* musical theatre company, that he showed an interest in joining a group of any kind. As it turned out, he had a history of participation in theatre activities, a natural acting talent, and a strong singing voice, making him an ideal candidate for the theatre company. David worked hard to overcome his fear of social situations and his paranoia but was reluctant to talk about his mental illness. However, as he became more comfortable in his new environment and more trustful toward staff, he began to share his paranoid thoughts, providing opportunities for him to receive the support needed to overcome his fears. In the supportive environment of *On Stage!,* David had finally found a place where he could work on overcoming some of the barriers to his recovery (social and interpersonal skills, trust). Eventually the self-esteem he gained through many successful experiences on stage gave him the courage to volunteer at a non-profit agency serving the developmentally disabled. At this facility, he taught some participants to read, receiving praise for his work and the support he needed to further his recovery. Although initially resistant to pursuing vocational training, David has now returned to the clubhouse where he is working as a cashier in the thrift store. So after 9 years in *On Stage!* and 3 years without the program, David has demonstrated that, given time, support, and opportunities to be successful, a person with a disorder as severe as schizophrenia can achieve self-efficacy and a significantly improved quality of life.

Unfortunately, despite its importance and the role it plays in recovery, there seem to be few community programs where improving self-esteem is of primary concern. Yet by addressing this issue early in the recovery process, persons with a serious mental illness could notably increase their opportunities for making significant progress toward their recovery goals. With this concept in mind the author's program, Self-Esteem in Recovery (SEIR), is presented as a model to be considered when creating a recovery program designed to improve self-esteem and, consequently, self-efficacy.

THE HEALING POWER OF THE ARTS: IS IT REAL?

> The power of music to integrate and cure–is quite fundamental. It is the profoundest nonchemical medication.
>
> –Oliver Sacks, *Awakenings*

> It is known that, as with musical notes, everything in the universe, including the planets, the galaxies, and our own bodies, vibrates. Our very thoughts, organs, and bones vibrate. These vibrations can be measured in terms of frequencies, just like a musical note. One idea behind healing with sound is to use frequencies (musical notes) to help harmonize our body and thoughts. So, when ever you hear a sound that is pleasing to you, you can be sure that it's frequency is harmonizing with or bringing harmony to your mind and body–Rhythm itself has the ability to loosen, free and set things in flow–Playing or dancing to pleasing rhythms helps the mind and body reach a state of flow (a zone in which a succession of goals or activities are being accomplished effortlessly). (Nidamboor, 2010)

Since antiquity, philosophers, physicians ,and people in a variety of professions have wondered at the healing power of music. What characteristics and qualities does this art form possess that can have such a profound effect on the psyche and the emotions? The answer to this question is addressed, in part, in the quotation above, where Nidamboor offers reasons for the harmony that music, particularly rhythms, can bring to the mind and body. Of particular importance is his reference to the role that rhythm plays in establishing "flow." (For further information on this topic, the reader is referred to a book titled *Flow: The Psychology of the Optimal Experience* by M. Csikszenthihalyi.) It is this state of effortless performance that has been exhibited over and over again in this writer's work with people with a serious mental illness. Specifically, it is the structure of the music that was observed to have facilitated the learning of many songs and dances and the rhythm of the music that "set things in flow." The combination of these two music characteristics worked together in the rehearsal process, enabling service users to attain a state of emotional freedom and well-being. Moreover, for many, their first performance experience was the beginning of a recovery journey in which the performing arts would continue to play a major role in promoting life satisfaction and well-being. Yes–music can heal, and when combined with dance and theatre, the results can be astounding.

In 1997, when the research team began a literature search to include in the research proposal launching the On Stage! project, studies on the effect of the performing arts on recovery were not to be found. This discovery was not surprising because most research was focused, as it is today, on the therapeutic use of the arts rather than the ways in which the arts might be used in recovery. The author proposes there were several reasons for this circumstance: Because the recovery movement was quite new at the time, little consideration had been given to the role the arts might play in recovery; the effects of the arts on recovery would be difficult to measure, and no evaluation instrument was available that would accurately assess the benefits of arts experiences in recovery. Clearly, then, the time had come to explore and document, for the first time, the effects of the performing arts on the recovery of people with a serious mental illness. To this end, results of the study presented below demonstrated what this writer had known all along–that the performing arts can play a significant role in helping service users achieve their recovery goals.

A STUDY ON THE EFFECTS OF THE PERFORMING ARTS ON THE RECOVERY OF ADULTS WITH A SERIOUS MENTAL ILLNESS

Principal Investigator: Dennis Dyck, PhD
Project Director: Donna Douglass, MA
Research Assistant: David Martineau, MURP, AICP

Background and Need Statement

Over the past several years, approaches to rehabilitating adults with serious and persistent mental illness (SMI) have focused on helping consumers build skills to help prepare them for entry/re-entry into the workplace. Supported education programs have been designed to provide such experiences by assisting persons with mental illness to participate in post-education opportunities in the community. Although supported education programs have helped a number of participants with psychiatric disabilities experience educational and vocational successes (Mobray, Bybee, & Shriner, 1996), a common problem is that a significant number of persons targeted by such programs do not possess the entry skills required to benefit from them and/or do not have the confidence and self-esteem necessary to vigorously pursue vocational or educational goals. The pre-requisite entry skills to succeed in supported education/occupational programs include: attention, concentration and memory skills, social skills, impulse control, frustration tolerance and responsibility for one's own behavior, following directions, accepting constructive criticism, co-operating within a group, willingness to risk failure, and task completion.

A well-known approach to teaching independent living skills has been developed by Liberman and colleagues (Liberman & Phipps, 1987; MacKain & Wallace, 1989). It is noteworthy that this approach (e.g., Social and Independent Living Skill Modules) relies extensively on the use of modeling, behavioral rehearsal, and role-playing in a small-group format as a teaching tool. Although important gains have been reported, particularly in such areas as conversational skills as well as symptom and medication management skills, unfortunately the gains made in the training setting often fail to generalize to the community (i.e., skills acquired in one setting often do not transfer readily to other settings). This failure to generalize may stem from the fact that skills programs are frequently not integrated into the day-to-day community of the participant. It seems reasonable that to promote such generalization, programs need to provide total community integration and normalization experiences, which also build self-confidence.

The present report evaluates a program, which is based on well-established behavioral principles such as modeling, behavioral rehearsal, and role-playing. Moreover, the program takes place in the community and is designed to promote normalization and community integration. In short, a program has been developed over a number of years by Donna Douglass, which uses participation in the performing arts to teach the supported education/employment entry skills. These skills include improvement in self-discipline, accepting supervision, interpersonal communication, risk-taking, concentration, and socialization. Personal development is also an important factor as students work toward improving self-concept, group cohesion/unity, energy level and quality of life while decreasing anger and depression. Evaluation of the aforementioned areas was conducted as well as an assessment of work- and school-related activities.

Methods

The program was evaluated using a pre- versus post-test design. The emphasis in this pilot project was to implement the program and generate preliminary data on the program effectiveness. It should be noted that the project director has been providing musical theatre programs to consumers with SMI for more than 35 years but until now has never had the opportunity to formally evaluate the outcomes of the program. The primary outcome measures include a pre-post assessment of eight work-readiness skills (i.e., risk-taking, self-confidence, responsibility, supervision, concentration, group unity, communication skill, and group involvement; Work Readiness Skill Assessment wheel, Douglass). A related assessment included a summary of changes in functioning, work- and school-related activities, and quality of life as compiled by the instructor from information provided by case managers and the students themselves. Self-reported mood changes as measured by standardized depression and anger scales were assessed before and after the program. Finally, qualitative information on the program was provided by the students through focus group and related interview formats. Data collection included the use of structured self-report surveys, focus groups, personal observations and testimonies, case manager interviews, audio/video documentation, and attendee comments following theater performances. See Table 1 for a detailed list of all assessments administered.

General statistical methods were used to describe and analyze the data. Pre- versus post-changes on the pre-designed self-report survey instruments were analyzed with paired t-tests. Alpha was set at .05 using a one-tailed test.

Results

The On-Stage! program consists of two sets of participants–those enrolled in the Introduction to Musical Theater Class (n=13) and the Musical Theater Company (n=10). Although the results are presented separately in the appendix, for the main analysis, the classes were combined to improve statistical power. Seventeen persons provided both pre- and post-test survey data (Class n=9, Theater Company n=8).

Table 1
ON STAGE! RESEARCH STUDY: ASSESSMENT SUMMARY

Quantitative Pre and Post Tests	*Descriptions of Assessments*	*Completed By*
Work Readiness Assessment Wheel (WRAS)	Assesses eight work readiness areas; risk-taking, self-confidence, self-discipline, supervision, concentration, group unity, socialization, and interpersonal skills	Project participant
Group Interaction and Self-Confidence Surveys	Nonstandardized surveys adapted for evaluation of program	Project participant
Anxiety Scale	Standardized instrument (Spielberger)	Project participant
Beck Depression Scale	Standardized instrument (Beck)	Project participant
4-Dimensional Scale of Functioning	Records participants level of functioning (Comtois & Ries)	Participant's Case Manager
FAACT	Assesses participant's quality of life (Lehman)	Project Director in interview with each participant
Quantitative Information	*Description*	*Completed By*
Case Manager Surveys	A structured interview with case managers developed specifically by project director and conducted at end of evaluation period	Project Director
Focus Groups	Conducted with all participants at end of evaluation period	Washington Institute Staff
Videotaping	Used for immediate feedback for students and to document student progress	On Stage! Staff
Testimonials	Taken from participants and those who attended performances	On Stage! Staff

Survey Results

Work-Readiness Skills

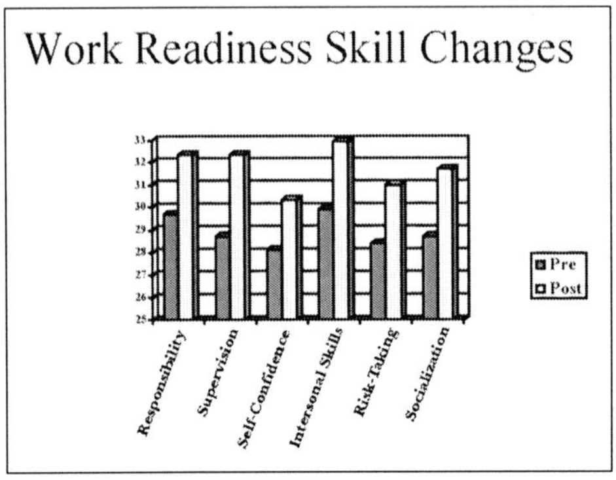

The Work-Readiness Skills Assessment survey (WRSA; Douglass, Martineau, & Dyck, 1997) was designed to measure variation in occupational readiness abilities among persons with psychiatric disabilities. In examining the results obtained on this measure, it is apparent that almost all of the work-readiness areas showed improvement. Indeed, six of the eight variables showed significant improvement (all ps <.05; one tailed). As shown in the figure, significant improvements were seen in willingness to accept responsibility, accepting supervision, self-confidence, interpersonal skills, risk-taking, socialization, daily activities, and quality of life. Although the predictive validity of the WRSA has yet to be established, the fact that six of the eight areas tapped by this instrument showed statistical improvement is a promising indicator of the program. A summary of how each of the variables is defined is provided below:

- *Responsibility:* refers to the participant's level of commitment and self-discipline and ability to complete assignments on time and to meet deadlines.
- *Supervision:* refers to the participant's willingness to accept constructive critical feedback, level of openness and receptivity to instruction, and degree of comfort requesting assistance.
- *Self-confidence:* refers to the participants' degree of belief in their ability to succeed, self-presentation skills, and ability to give themselves credit for achievements.
- *Interpersonal skills:* refers to the participant's communication skills (listening and expressive), including non-verbal (postural) and eye contact.
- *Risk-taking:* refers to the participants' willingness to take risks where there is a reasonable chance of success but also the risk of failure. It also refers to the ability to learn from mistakes.

- *Socialization:* refers to the participants' ability to exercise patience and to show consideration for others in a group setting.

Follow-up of the program participants in the following year will provide further evidence of the long-term effects of the program as well as evaluate the predictive validity of the WRSA (i.e., participants with higher scores on the WRSA would be expected to more frequently participate in future work and educational activities relative participants with lower WRSA scores).

Other Survey Results

Other results indicated that both depressed mood and state anger were lower after the program, although only the anger measure reached significance. Further, overall quality of life was reported to be significantly improved for participants as was the quality of their friendships following the program.

Work Placement Results

The effect of the program on more conventional work/school outcomes was summarized by the instructor after interviewing participants as well as their respective case managers. The results indicate that six (29%) participants had an *active* educational/vocational placement following the program, with another five (24%) currently *planning* for a placement. Taken together, this represents over half of the class. When these results are placed in context, they are truly remarkable. The context is that the program only ran for 6 months and the State employment figures indicate that only 15% of persons served by the public mental health system are employed (Stegner, personal communication). On a more sobering note, it is noteworthy that seven students have high potential for a placement (33%) but do not have a plan to translate that potential into reality. This signals the need for additional vocational/educational linkages and planning to be integrated within this program.

Focus Group Results

Following the end of the program, separate focus groups were conducted with students in the Theater Class and the Theater Company.

This yielded qualitative information on how the program was experienced and is summarized below. Qualitative statements below typify the self-reported improvements attributed to the program. For participants in the Theater Class, these included the following: improved physical fitness, health and well-being, the realization of personal goals and objectives, improvements in making commitments, improved self-confidence and the ability to accept mistakes, improved social interactions, coming to terms with their illness, and improved relationships with their case managers.

Case Manager Interviews

Following the completion of the program, case managers for 11 students provided information on changes in functioning, interests and activities related to work/school, and medication status. The following are brief profiles summarized from selected case manager reports.

S.M., diagnosed with Mixed Bi-Polar Disorder, improved her coping skills and ability to handle stress, reducing significantly her number of angry outbursts. Since starting On Stage!, she has enrolled in computer classes and, although some of her medications were increased, demonstrated a decrease in depression and anxiety and an improved self-confidence. She also has become less hesitant to offer her own ideas regarding her treatment.

L.T., diagnosed with Schizophrenia, Paranoid Type, showed improvement in self-esteem, self-confidence, motivation, and ability to cope with stressful situations. She is less depressed and anxious and has decreased case manager contacts and appointments. Although prior to enrolling in On Stage! she had tried two jobs and failed, she began volunteering at the clubhouse greenhouse and now works at a local chain store 18 hours per week. Another significant change was her increased desire for family reunification. L. T.'s paranoia decreased some, although she still hears voices and had one medication increased as a result.

F.C., diagnosed with Major Depressive Disorder, showed improvement in self-presentation skills, posture, personal appearance, and self-confidence, as well as a decrease in anxiety level. She demonstrated more interest in work-related activities, is attending classes at a local community college, and is focusing more energy into productive activities. In addition, her medications are in the process of being lowered. Her case manager feels the combination of medications and On Stage! are responsible for reducing F.C.'s symptoms.

O.L., diagnosed with Mixed Bi-Polar Disorder, demonstrates improved appearance, posture, and self-presentation skills. Also her ability to deal with stress and self-confidence has improved as her anxiety has decreased. Addionally, she has had some reduction and other changes in medications. Although she used to stay home a lot, O.L. is now getting out more and has begun enjoying using the Internet on her own computer. She is considering courier work in a Temporary Employment Program with a local mental health center and has done some volunteer work.

H.S., diagnosed with Bi-Polar Disorder, decreased her dependency on her case manager and showed improvement in emotional stability, self-esteem, confidence, and problem-solving skills. She also demonstrated a decrease in paranoid thinking and had one medication decreased. She has discussed the possibilities of work or school with her case manager, stating she now has something to look forward to.

SUMMARY AND RECOMMENDATIONS

Over the past several years, approaches to rehabilitating persons with serious and persistent mental illness have focused on helping consumers build skills that will prepare them for entry/re-entry into the workplace. Although communities have developed programs to assist such persons (e.g., supported education/employment), there are few opportunities in the community that are available for consumers who do not possess the basic skills for these preparatory programs and/or lack the self-confidence to pursue a vocational or educational goal. Although skill-building programs have been described in the psychiatric rehabilitation literature, they often fail to promote community integration. This is essential given that mental illness isolates and stigmatizes such persons as well as their families. The program evaluated in this proposal used participation in the performing arts as a tool for promoting basic skill development, personal development, and community integration. The rationale for the program is summarized in the introduction and developed more fully in the paper written by Donna Douglass titled "Self-Esteem Building and the Performing Arts." The results reported here indicate that in a 6-month period, a number of students made significant gains in skill development, self-confidence, and motivation. The survey results clearly support the improvement of work-readiness skills. In addition, decreased anger, depressed mood, and improved quality of life were observed. These results were confirmed by case managers and were elaborated by the students in the focus group. The latter results provide an indication of the wide-ranging impact of the program that is not readily quantifiable. It is clear that many of the students developed a sense of pride and self-respect that they had not recently enjoyed. As well, a result that the evaluation did not capture is the pride that family members took in their family member's accomplishments. Although difficult to measure, the enthusiastic response of the public to the performances of the group suggests that the program has community integration and de-stigmatizing impacts.

There are two caveats to keep in mind when interpreting the results. First, the design did not include a control condition. Thus, it cannot be assumed that a matched group of consumers who was given the same amount of attention would not have shown similar improvement. Second, the evaluation focused on short-term gains and does not speak to the program's long-term benefits. Subsequent evaluations should include an attention control condition and administration of follow-up assessments to determine the program's long-term impacts.

Notwithstanding the aforementioned caveats, we believe the results of the evaluation are both promising and instructive. We therefore make the following recommendations:

1. The program needs to be expanded to include consumers who are in-patients, particularly those in the state hospitals who are preparing for community re-entry.
2. The program needs to be expanded to include the development of individualized and tailored educational/work plans. This will require additional staffing and integration with supported education and work programs.
3. The program needs to continue to be carefully evaluated to continue to refine and improve the curriculum.

In summary, we believe that this program is an innovative approach to rehabilitation and recovery. As such, it makes an important contribution to the normalization of persons with SMI. It is a strength-building approach and complements other rehabilitation and recovery initiatives undertaken by the Mental Health Division.

PRIMARY FINDINGS

- Participants have improved their skills and abilities in the following areas: self-discipline and commitment, working effectively with others, socialization and communication, accepting supervision and dealing with stress.
- Participants have experienced personal growth through improved self-confidence and experiences that require risk, improved physical fitness, feelings of belonging, group cohesion, and the development of patience and empathy toward others.
- Participants have developed a more positive attitude by recognizing and dealing with self-defeating behaviors. This change in attitude has been achieved through learning to be less critical toward themselves and others, frequent successful experiences, using mistakes as learning tools rather than an excuse for self-criticism, and recognizing the achievements of others.
- Participants have increased their community support network by forming friendships within the program that continue off-site and participation in mainstream community activities (i.e., church choirs, advocacy groups, theatre activities).
- Performances by Theatre Extraordinaire, the program's musical theatre company, have educated the public about mental illness by performing at conventions, community events, and the Bing Crosby Theatre (formerly the Metropolitan Center for the Performing Arts) in downtown Spokane.

POLICY IMPLICATIONS

From participant and mental health staff testimony and observations of On Stage! staff, it is known that participants in On Stage! use less case management time and have reduced their frequency of hospitalizations and involvement with the criminal justice system. Participants in On Stage! also have a higher quality of life.

Chapter 2

TOWARD A RECOVERY MODEL

ONE LIFE AT A TIME

When Melissa began her journey with On Stage!, the symptoms of her depression seemed an insurmountable barrier to her recovery. When asked to describe the problems she faced when joining Theatre Extraordinaire, she said she was very shy with a low self-esteem and an inertia that left her lethargic and unmotivated. She further stated that her inexperience in working with others and her poor motor coordination contributed significantly to her lack of self-confidence. Diagnosed with dysthymia with major depressive episodes, Melissa also struggled with symptoms from a mild cerebral palsy that made dancing with the company very difficult for her. Yet despite these challenges, she was determined to become a member of Theatre Extraordinaire.

Melissa's performing arts experience began in elementary school, where she participated in choral groups and other creative arts activities, continuing to do so through high school. Following graduation, she ceased her involvement in the performing arts and did nothing further in this area until age 40, when she heard about On Stage!. Thinking the program might offer her once again the opportunity to pursue her passion for the theatre, she enrolled in Theatre Extraordinaire. Although shy and anxious about appearing on stage again, Melissa brought with her a strong determination to succeed. Her sense of humor, friendly personality, and ability to interact positively with others were assets that helped her to be readily accepted by her peers in the company. It was not long before it became evident Melissa was a talented comedic actress.

From the beginning, one of the staff's major challenges was to deal with Melissa's self-defeating behaviors, specifically her tendency to compare herself to others. She seemed unable to give herself credit for her special talents in the areas of comedy and improvisation. For example, she wanted very much to perform vocal solos that were beyond her abilities despite the fact that her vocal talents were best utilized in comedy songs. It was when she began comparing her voice to others and expressing to this writer that she didn't have any talent that she would threaten to leave the company. It would take a great deal of support and encouragement from staff and the cast to convince her to stay. Then, as her self-confidence improved, Melissa's threats to leave decreased significantly, and her courage to participate in more dance routines increased. As she learned to focus on her strengths and abilities and to use positive affirmations when self-critical thoughts began to surface, her level of participation increased, and she began taking lead roles in the company's plays and sketches. It was in a roaring 20s play that she had her first opportunity to demonstrate her wonderful comedic talent. Cast as a gangster's girlfriend, Melissa brought down the house with her performance of a song titled "Hey, There, Big Boy!"

Melissa's Recovery Outcomes

Although her road to recovery was sometimes a bumpy one, Melissa's self-confidence gradually began to improve. Contributing to this improvement were two major factors: learning to view mistakes as part of the learning process and reducing self-criticism. She also learned to focus on recovering after a mishap rather than dwelling on the missteps she had made. This realization helped Melissa to be less self-critical, giving her the courage to take the risks necessary for reaching her recovery goals. As time went on and her confidence improved, she began participating in the company's plays and sketches. With acting as her forte, she was given major roles in which her comedic talents brought applause and laughter from her audiences. This recognition of her special abilities further enhanced Melissa's self-confidence, improving her self-esteem.

After several months in On Stage!, the skills and self-confidence she had acquired began to generalize to Melissa's everyday living. She gradually gained enough confidence to enroll in music classes at a community college and begin volunteering with a local community theatre. She also enrolled in Middle Eastern dance classes, performing with fellow students in recitals and other events. In addition, she became employed as an actress and stage manager in a local community theatre company–a far cry from a person fearful of appearing on stage. Not only had Melissa conquered her fear of failure and criticism, but she also had become a role model and an inspiration to her fellow On Stage! cast members and other mental health consumers. After 5 years, Melissa left the company to pursue other interests and increase her volunteer hours with some nonprofit organizations. Perhaps her success story is best summarized in this single phrase from the company's theme song: "You've come a long way, baby!"

SELF-ESTEEM AND RECOVERY (SEIR)

> Recovery from mental illness is not the same as cure. It means regaining control over one's life if not one's illness. It means leading a useful satisfying life even though symptoms may reoccur.
>
> –William A. Anthony

What is recovery for someone with a severe mental illness? Is it a cure? Is it a process? Is it even a possibility? In seeking answers to these questions, the reader will find that a lot has changed since the days when a diagnosis of mental illness was seen as a life-long sentence in a mental institution. The goal of treatment at that time was to stabilize patients, keep them at a "maintenance" level, and accept the fact that this condition was the best to be hoped for. It was not until the late 1980s that researchers challenged the belief that mental illness was chronic, thus introducing the concept that recovery from psychiatric disorders was possible. Since then, with science and research to support its efforts, the recovery movement has significantly changed the lives of many people with psychiatric disabilities.

Of course, the meaning of recovery may vary from one person to the next. For instance, one individual's goal may be to become a community volunteer, while another may work toward full-time employment. However, although individual goals may differ, the overall meaning of recovery is the same for all: an improved quality of life that includes self-actualization,[12] life satisfaction and well-being, personal empower-

12. Self-actualization is the achievement of one's full potential through creativity, independence, spontaneity, and a grasp of the real world.

ment[13] and community reintegration.[14] In summary, the following description of the recovery process seems to say it all.

> Recovery–does not mean the illness has gone into complete remission. It means that over time, through what for many is a long and difficult process, individuals come to terms with their illness, learn first to accept it and then move beyond it. They learn to believe in themselves as individuals, learn their strengths as well as their limitations and come to realize that they have the capacity to find purpose and enjoyment in their lives. (Further), recovery–requires a belief by (persons) with the illness and those around them" that recovery is possible. How far and how quickly each individual recovers will vary widely, and it is important to recognize and value every step, no matter how small. (Rethink, 2009)

HISTORY AND DEVELOPMENT OF THE SEIR MODEL

The creation of the SEIR model evolved from the author's work with the seriously mentally ill spanning almost five decades. Although early experiences in a variety of hospitals and out-patient programs contributed significantly to her future work, there were four programs that influenced the model's development, the first three founded by the author: *the Salem Creative Arts Center (SCAC), Project Arts, On Stage!,* and *Transitions.* These programs are described below with further information in Chapter 6.

The first program, SCAC, was a nonprofit organization serving people with a serious mental illness, founded by the author during her tenure as Director of Music Therapy at Willamette University in Salem, Oregon. The primary purpose of SCAC was to support Theatre Extraordinaire, the first musical theatre company for service users in the Salem community. It was the overwhelming success of her initial experience with this musical theatre company that convinced the author to further explore the development of recovery programs utilizing the performing arts as a primary intervention.

---

13. Personal empowerment "asserts that ultimate control over the life of the person with psychiatric disabilities belongs solely to that person" (Corrigan, Mueser, Bond, Drake, & Solomon, 2009).
14. Community integration "is the affirmative vision specifying that the public is responsible for helping people achieve their life goals." (Corrigan, Mueser, Bond, Drake, & Solomon, 2009).

The second nonprofit organization founded by the author was Project Arts, located in Phoenix, Arizona. This program included visual and performing arts classes, a musical theatre company (another Theatre Extraordinaire), and an ABE (Adult Basic Education) and GED (General Education Diploma) course of study. The third program, On Stage! (Chapter 7), provided one of the most significant contributions to the development of SEIR: an opportunity to research the effects of the performing arts on recovery. The results of this study and evidence from the author's experience created the foundation for the SEIR model. Finally, an organization called Transitions, also located in Phoenix, was a supported education program designed on an established model that prepares service users for entry into higher education. As program coordinator, the author collaborated with Transition's founder in developing an innovative curriculum focusing on self-esteem building and community integration. Classes and other services (education counseling and coaching) were offered in two venues: Phoenix Community College and a site within the community. Although not a performing arts program, Transitions provided the author with valuable experiences, insights, and information on recovery that contributed to the development of SEIR.

THE SEIR MODEL

Knowing the important role that self-esteem and self-efficacy play in the recovery of people with a serious mental illness, the author focused on these two areas when designing the SEIR model. Consequently, during a literature search to find support for the methods used in the model, an article on the benefits service users can experience in community arenas caught her attention. In this article, Sells et al. (2006) identified the following nine themes that should be included in recovery programs: Understanding and Acceptance, Fun and Enjoyment, Role Shifting, Meaningful Routines, Employment, Spirituality, Esteem, Anger, and Integrative Aspects. Coincidentally, the author found that eight of these themes are present in any SEIR program as described below:

- **Understanding and Acceptance.** SEIR students become members of a peer group that serves, for many, as a family offering support, safety, common interests and trust-building activities.

- **Fun and Enjoyment.** SIER activities offer opportunities for fun and enjoyment by encouraging students to enjoy themselves more by taking life less seriously, looking for humor in stressful situations, and joining friends/peers in non-mental health-related community activities.
- **Role Shifting.** By participating in rewarding activities involving interactions with community volunteers, SEIR students experience positive shifts in how they view their roles and those of others.
- **Meaningful Routines.** An important aspect of recovery is becoming involved in productive activities that provide motivation to get out of bed in the morning and become part of a daily routine. As SEIR activities become part of this routine, students can find themselves looking forward to attending classes or rehearsals that help them feel there is a purpose to their day.
- **Employment.** Becoming employed is often a major goal for people with psychiatric disabilities. However, frequently many of these individuals are unprepared to enter the workplace because of deficits in work-readiness skills. SEIR offers activities that build these skills by encouraging students to view the program as they would a job (i.e., arriving on time, notifying instructors of reasons for absences, following through with commitments, and learning to accept constructive criticism).
- **Esteem.** Because good self-esteem is necessary for students to achieve their recovery goals, it is the core of the SEIR model. Every aspect of the program provides opportunities for success, supporting students as they strive to reach the eight core goals of the program. These successful experiences play a significant role in helping students achieve these goals, leading to improved self-esteem, a major step toward recovery.
- **Anger.** Uncontrollable anger is a behavior that can prevent service users from successfully integrating into any social or employment environment. This behavior is especially problematic when a SEIR student arrives at a rehearsal, angry from the way he/she had been treated by a caregiver or frustrated from an experience with stigma. In this situation, SEIR staff can help this student by first acknowledging that he/she has a reason to be upset but that remaining angry is unproductive, does not solve the problem and can seriously interfere with his/her recovery. Then, after reminding the student that the control of emotions is a requirement for

participation in the program, ask the student to join the rehearsal when his/her anger is under control.

- **Integrative Aspects.** When the experiences from the positive environment (arena) of the program, its activities, and fellowship become integrated, service users can experience a sense of affirmation as to who they are apart from their mental illness. SEIR activities offer many opportunities for students to realize they are not a mentally ill person, but a person who happens to have a mental illness, thus affirming their identity, individuality, and role in the community.

To begin a recovery process incorporating the aforementioned themes, the SEIR model features self-esteem as the core variable leading to the promotion of self-efficacy. Although some researchers may view self-efficacy as a precursor to self-esteem (Garske & McReynolds, 2005), it is this writer's view that in order for people with disabilities to achieve self-efficacy, they must first develop confidence in themselves. Only then will their self-esteem begin to improve along with a belief in their ability to succeed at any given task (self-efficacy). However, these changes do not come easily for people with a mental illness who are not always encouraged or supported by mental health professionals to try new activities due to the risks involved. Because this overprotectiveness can lead to dependence, compliance, and powerlessness, service users can find themselves without the self-confidence needed to take risks and learn new skills. Accordingly, a SEIR program uses a step-by-step method in which service users are afforded numerous opportunities to experience success, thus promoting self-esteem and self-efficacy. This approach, the foundation of the SEIR model, can help people with a serious mental illness (and other disabilities) believe in themselves and their ability to reach their recovery goals. A note of reference: When discussing the SEIR model, service users may also be referred to as students, cast members, or performers.

MODEL STRUCTURE

The SEIR model design is comprised of three components: *goals*, *process*, and *behaviors*. Figure 2 shows the relationship of these components to each other, specifically how the development of *goals* leads to

Figure 2

SEIR MODEL: TOWARD SELF-ESTEEM, SELF-EFFICACY, & RECOVERY

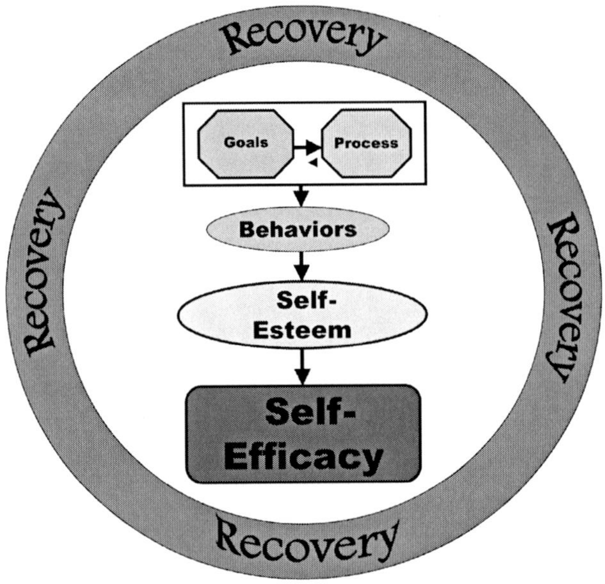

Figure 2. SEIR Model: Toward self-esteem, self-efficacy, & recovery.

process (method) that in turn results in *behavior* changes. The arrow from the component box indicates that by progressing through these three components, students build *self-esteem* that eventually leads to *self-efficacy*, which then can improve even further the level of *self-esteem*. Figure 3 denotes the eight categories of each component, all selected because they apply directly to performing arts activities as documented and experienced by the author. The five elements surrounding the red oval identify some of the benefits experienced by the achievement of *self-efficacy*. How all elements of the SEIR model work together to achieve its purpose is described below.

COMPONENT ONE: GOALS

After developing and administrating performing arts programs in a wide variety of facilities over the years, the author has seen hundreds of people with a serious mental illness benefit from experiences in music therapy groups, music education classes, and stage productions.

Figure 3

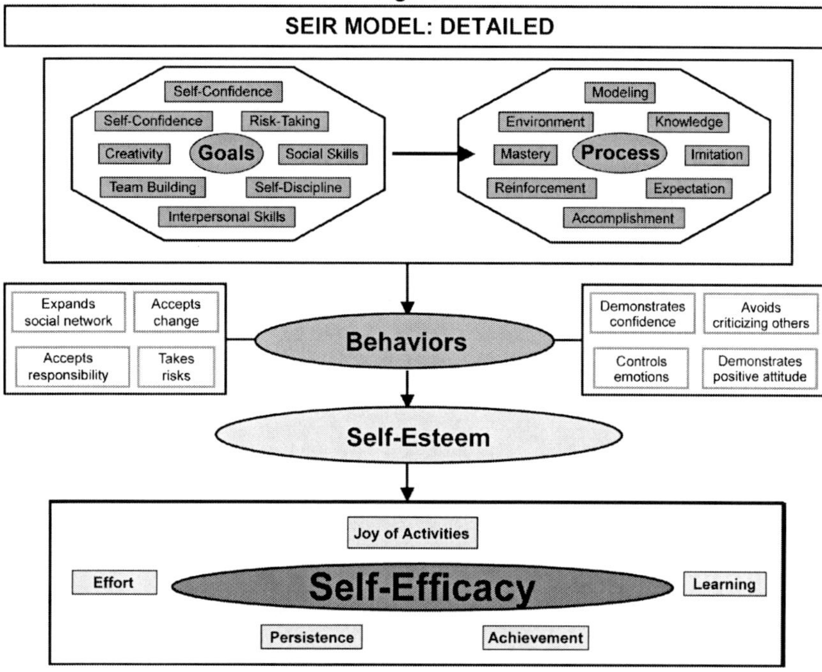

Figure 3. SEIR Model: Detailed.

Although the opportunity to formally evaluate the effectiveness of her programs prior to 1996 did not present itself, the author was convinced early in her career that participation in the performing arts played a significant role in the recovery of people with a mental illness. When finally the opportunity to evaluate the effects of these experiences on recovery outcomes presented itself (Douglass, Martineau, & Dyck, 1997), eight goals were identified on which to base this research. Over time, these goals were revised and are described below, along with the objectives for each. *The Recovery Wheel* described later in this chapter can be used to evaluate students' progress toward these goals.

Goal 1. Self-Confidence

Objectives

- Experience frequent success
- Recognize, not deny, achievements
- Give self credit for successes

- Develop a positive attitude
- Avoid negative self-talk
- Be recognized for accomplishments
- Learn new skills
- Help others learn new skills

> On Stage! has given me confidence and self-worth. It has brightened my life to the point where I no longer walk with my head down.
>
> –Company member

Although they may have taken the first steps necessary to begin their recovery (acceptance of disability, medication stabilization, etc.), many students find themselves "stuck" in a place seeming to offer little, if any, hope for recovery. In these circumstances, they can easily become discouraged, lose motivation, and just stop trying. It is probable, then, that their situation will not change until they have gained the confidence needed to deal with the many challenges they are yet to face during the recovery process. In an effort to address this critical issue, the SEIR model is designed to build self-confidence with a curriculum offering numerous opportunities for success. As students realize progress toward their recovery goals is possible, they will develop a belief in themselves, their abilities, and, foremost, their chances to be successful.

Case Example 2: "Dan"

Dan, a young man with schizophrenia, was living in a group home and working in a recycling center when he joined Theatre Extraordinaire. Because at one time he had to drop out of school due to severe memory impairment, he was convinced he would never be able to memorize the lines in a play in which he had a major role. Dealing with poor self-esteem and lack of self-confidence he seemed unable to refrain from saying "I can't remember" or "I know I can't do it." However, after working with his fellow cast members for a few weeks, his confidence gradually improved, as did his ability to remember his lines. When the curtain went up on opening night, he knew most of his lines but carried a script on stage to give him that boost of confidence needed to deal with opening night "jitters." As his confidence improved even more, Dan eventually did not need a script and went on to participate in other productions totally "scriptless." His remarkable progress can be attributed to two major influences: a young man playing opposite Dan who possessed many qualities Dan admired (confidence, talent, compassion) and a cast and staff who gave him continued support and encouragement during the rehearsal process. The outcomes of Dan's performing arts experience (improved self-confidence, belief in his strengths and abilities) gave him the opportunity to move forward in his recovery. Over a period of several months and after a series of performances, his self-esteem significantly improved as did his belief in himself and his future.

Goal 2. Teram-Building Skills

Objectives

- Work cooperatively with others
- Learn to trust
- Learn to "go with the flow"
- Praise others
- Be enthusiastic
- Volunteer for work assignments
- Accept ideas from others
- Contribute ideas in planning session
- Offer help to others when needed

> I've seen people opening up. Here we've come together. We're a group. Some of us are close. We've gained a lot of good friendships.
>
> –Cast member, SCAC

Successful transition into community living for people with a serious mental illness can require, along with other basic skills, the ability to work effectively as a team member in a variety of situations. Specifically, participation in vocational training or education programs can involve working closely with fellow students in small groups where flexibility, enthusiasm, and good communication are necessary. Yet as important as they are in everyday living, opportunities for people with psychiatric disabilities to develop these team-building skills can be limited. To this end, SEIR offers, in its musical stage productions, a unique approach when learning to work more effectively with others. As cast members and backstage assistants, students learn they must depend on each other, leading to the development of unity and trust. At the same time, students who participate in publicity and other non-performance activities become more self-confident when they realize how their participation has contributed to a successful production.

Case Example 3: "Michael"

Michael was an angry and frustrated young man when he was referred to the On Stage! program by his case manager. With a history of delinquent behavior, a defensive attitude, and little, if any, concern for others, he needed to find some direction in his life and a way to improve his confidence and self-esteem. Within a short time in the program, it became obvious that underneath the hostile and rebellious behavior was a creative energy that, when re-directed into his performance, electrified audiences. As a member of Theatre Extraordinaire, he had the opportunity to focus the energy previously expressed through his destructive behavior into meaningful and productive activities. He developed his dance and vocal skills and learned to play the guitar with tutoring from a fellow cast member. Performances before small and large audiences gave Michael the recognition and acceptance he desperately needed to improve his self-confidence and give him hope. During the rehearsal process, his ability to work with others improved significantly as he became more tolerant of those who learned less quickly than he and more patience with a sometimes very slow rehearsal process. Because he learned new material so quickly, staff often placed Michael in leadership positions where he could help others. For example, he would assist the choreographer in rehearsals by demonstrating dance steps and leading dance lines. As his confidence improved, he was given musical roles that highlighted his natural talents and magnetic personality. After several years with the theatre company, Michael enrolled in a local community college where he received a certificate in visual art studies.

Goal 3. Interpersonal Skills

Objectives

- Be a good listener
- Express ideas and opinions clearly

- Be open to others' viewpoints
- Stay in control of emotions
- Listen to opinions of others
- Maintain good eye contact
- Think carefully before speaking
- Express feelings appropriately

> On Stage! has built up my self-esteem, and given me a new outlook on life, and I've made a lot of food friends.
>
> –Company member

Many people with special needs have poor interpersonal and communication skills that interfere with the development of relationships. Participation in a program designed around SEIR goals provides students with opportunities to explore and experience new ways of relating and communicating. For example, during a wrap-up session at the end of a class or rehearsal, students are encouraged to share with others their feelings about their learning experience. What did they learn? What did they do well? What can be improved? Consequently, participating in this discussion can yield two benefits. First, students learn to express themselves appropriately within a group, and, group members reluctant to speak out may develop the courage to share their feelings. Another time when good interpersonal skills play an important role is during the rehearsals just prior to a performance. It is then that emotional control is critical, for anxieties are high and tempers can flare as performers worry about whether they will be ready to perform. In preparation for this highly stressful situation, performers learn techniques in anxiety reduction (i.e., deep breathing, anger management, and assertive communication) early in the rehearsal process. It is through the development of these skills that students learn how to work well with others, both within and apart from the SEIR program.

Goal 4. Self-Discipline

Objectives

- Accept responsibility for behavior
- Manage time effectively
- Follow through with commitments

- Complete assigned tasks
- Arrive on time
- Listen attentively
- Perform needed tasks without being told

I really loved being cared about like I mattered in the group, that I wasn't replaced because I misbehaved. I also learned there were consequences to bad behavior, but I wasn't rejected because of it.

–Cast member, On Stage!

Story 3: The "Chatter Factor" and More

Membership in a musical theatre company necessitates a strong commitment and a willingness to do whatever it takes to create a successful stage production. Moreover, participation in a show requires all cast members to accept specific responsibilities and realize the importance of each person's role in the success of the production. While most members accept their given roles, petty jealousies can occur if, for example, a member feels he/she should have been given a role assigned to someone else. This situation is especially difficult to resolve if that member feels entitled to a role because of seniority and becomes even more problematic if he/she lacks the ability to perform in the given role. Usually this problem can be resolved by assigning the member to another role that is less demanding. However, on a rare occasion this approach can fail, resulting in a threat by the member to leave the company. All staff can do at this point is to assure the member that he/she would be missed, but that it is the member's decision.

Another problem, one that the author found to be the most challenging, were members of the On Stage! theatre company who began talking to others the minute there was a break in a dance routine or when staff was giving verbal instructions. Even correcting these individuals in front of their peers was effective only for a short time. This lack of self-discipline was not only disruptive and time-wasting but also demonstrated a disrespect and disregard for others. It was out of sheer frustration that my assistant director and I finally found the answer to our dilemma in one word: *silence.* Specifically, on each occasion where the "chatter factor" came into play, the instructor leading the activity would stop whatever she was doing, stand still, and say nothing. What followed was indeed amazing. The talking would continue until someone noticed the instructor was just standing and staring at the group. One by one, members began quieting each other until there was total silence, at which point the instructor would say "thank you" and proceed with the activity. Soon peer pressure helped to control this disruptive behavior, resulting in less time wasted and a reduced stress level for all concerned.

Goal 5. Creativity

Objectives

- Adapt to any situation
- Accept new ideas
- Realize there is more than one right answer
- Use imagination
- Be comfortable with the unknown
- Be open and receptive to learning
- Be a flexible thinker
- Be a skillful problem solver

> On Stage! has helped me improve my dancing and singing and my self-confidence and esteem. It has also helped me to get along with people in a group.
>
> –Company member, Project Arts

In today's workplace, employers are seeking individuals who are flexible thinkers with new ideas, unafraid to use their imaginations when solving problems. In the same way, classroom instructors who recognize creativity as an important characteristic in well-rounded and well-educated people will appreciate students who are open minded and imaginative and have a good sense of humor. However, too often people with disabilities do not have access to activities that will develop their creative abilities. Therefore, one of the primary goals of any SEIR program is to provide opportunities for creative expression (i.e., chorus, dance routines, and short skits). Because often the immediate response to an offer to participate in one of these activities is "I'm not creative," students are encouraged to eliminate these words from their vocabularies and to think more positively about their creative potential.

Consequently, as attitudes begin to change and confidence improves, some students may choose to become involved in the planning process of a stage production, offering ideas for dance routines, costuming, set design, and writing sketches. Realizing their ideas will be considered and possibly adapted into a production can result in even more improvement in self-confidence. Moreover, successful experiences in problem solving can build skills that lead to a heightened interest in becoming involved in community activities where these newly discovered skills can be utilized.

Goal 6. Self-Presentation Skills

Objectives

- Be comfortable before a group
- Speak clearly
- Look at audience
- Stand tall
- Project voice
- Think positively

> On Stage! has helped me build the confidence I need to speak in front of an audience by teaching me ways to control my anxieties.
>
> –Cast member

Whether in a classroom or on the stage, appearing before others can produce performance anxieties that are difficult to manage if not controlled. The author has developed a method for addressing this issue, a desensitization process that begins with performances before peers, focusing on frequent opportunities for students to experience success (Chapter 4). During this process, students learn many skills, including how to project their voices, speak clearly, develop a good posture, and maintain eye contact. These skills and many others enhance the chances of a successful performance before any kind of audience. Performers also develop an important cognitive skill that allows them to "think on their feet" and improvise their way out of an unexpected incident, a situation all too familiar to anyone who has ever been in a position of appearing before others.

Story 4: The Unexpected

The place was a resort hotel in Phoenix, Arizona; the occasion a major fundraising event for Project Arts. The featured entertainment for the evening was a performance by the organization's musical theatre company that included an energetic rendition of a western hoedown. Although the cast had rehearsed on the portable stage one or two times, the members had no idea what was about to happen. All was going well when suddenly some boards in the middle of the stage separated. Seemingly unaffected by this unexpected event, the cast kept on dancing, moving around the gap in the platform and finishing the dance as though nothing had happened. What was truly amazing was the fact that I was at the piano a few feet from the stage, unaware of what was taking place on stage! So why did these dancers know what to do in this unexpected situation? Because from the beginning they were taught that no matter what happens, keep going. They had learned to "think on their feet," thus averting a potentially disastrous incident. This special skill not only saved the day at this performance but demonstrated just one of the many ways the performing arts can promote the development of self-presentation skills that can generalize to any situation in students' daily lives.

Goal 7. Risk-Taking

Objectives

- Be willing to take risks
- Be unafraid to fail
- Be willing to say "I don't know"
- Be willing to try something new
- Have courage to stand up for beliefs
- Be comfortable introducing self to strangers
- Be unafraid to make mistakes
- Be comfortable in new situations

It's kind of nerve-wracking. I'm kind of scared, but it's helped me be around a lot of people . . . and I need that.

–Company member, SCAC

Often people with disabilities, especially those with a serious mental illness, express a desire to try something new but find they are facing two major problems: fear of failure and fear of making a mistake. Unless they can discover a way to overcome these barriers, learning the new skills necessary for reaching their recovery goals can be very difficult. Therefore, a SEIR program focuses on guiding students through a series of steps addressing the aforementioned fears, a process that builds the courage needed to take risks. During this procedure, students learn two important dynamics: how to *re-direct negative self-talk* that usually follows a mistake ("I can't do it") toward positive self-talk ("I'll try again") and how *mistakes can be seen as building blocks* toward a specific goal. In accordance with the latter, students also learn how to recover from mistakes without calling attention to themselves. To this end, the author's choreographer introduced the concept that "there is no such thing as a mistake" during a performance. Consequently, this positive approach helped students gain the confidence needed to recover from their mistakes, a skill that helped reduce the fears associated with an appearance before any kind of audience.

Goal 8. Social Skills

Objectives

- Walk away from escalating arguments
- Avoid interrupting others
- Avoid isolating self from others
- Control emotions
- Initiate conversations
- Avoid attention-getting behaviors
- Recognize personal boundaries
- Enjoy being around others

> My self-esteem wasn't too good when I got there. It taught me how to motivate myself–how to perform tasks regularly, and it taught me social skills. It was a life-saver.
>
> –Cast member, Project Arts

Individuals with special needs often have limited involvement in social activities or any group situation that necessitates interacting with others, circumstances that can lead to isolation, compromising recovery. For these persons, the supportive social environment in a SEIR program provides opportunities to practice social skills that eventually lead to an increased comfort level in group situations. As they become more at ease, students begin initiating conversations with their peers, gradually gaining enough confidence to participate more actively in group discussions. SEIR also offers a safe environment where students can make new friends with whom they can choose to socialize apart from the program. Then, as their social skills and confidence improve, students may also develop interest in joining community groups where they can meet new people, thus expanding their social networks.

Summary. As SEIR students begin the process of working toward their recovery goals, noticeable changes begin taking place. Negative attitudes become positive, improved social skills result in more friendships, and successful experiences improve self-confidence, resulting in two significant outcomes: improved self-esteem and enhanced self-efficacy. These areas of personal growth and skill development are just some of many ways in which the SEIR experience supports students in their ongoing efforts to be successful. Once students begin to experience progress toward their goals, other changes begin to develop, providing even further life satisfaction and well-being.

COMPONENT TWO: PROCESS

> People's beliefs about their abilities have a profound effect on those abilities. Ability is not a fixed property; there is a huge variability in how you perform. People who have a sense of self-efficacy bounce back from failures; they approach things in terms of how to handle them rather than worrying about what can go wrong.
>
> –Albert Bandura

Social Learning Theory and Modeling

It was not until the author decided to write this book that she seriously began thinking about the why of her method: *Why* did it work? After all, during her many years in clinical work, she had learned all she felt she needed to know: *what* to do and *how* to do it. The necessity for explaining the why never presented itself. That is, until she realized that, in order to clearly explain the SEIR model, it would be necessary to identify a theory on which to explain the why. It was this challenge that eventually led to the answer: Albert Bandura's social learning theory. After comparing the principles and methods of Bandura's work to the methodology of SEIR, several ways were identified in which the Bandura theory could be applied to improving self-esteem and promoting self-efficacy in a SEIR program. The application of this theory to SEIR methods will be described in detail in this chapter. However, so the reader will better understand why the author decided to use Bandura's work as the rationale on which to base her model, a brief overview of his social learning theory is presented here.

Social learning theory, in general, is based on the premise that learning occurs within a social context, suggesting that people learn from one another (Ormrod, 1999; Walker, 1981). Although there are many individuals in the fields of psychology, education, and sociology who have developed theories around this concept, it is Albert Bandura who is considered the main architect in the field (Ormrod, 1999). In Bandura's (1977) words: "Social learning theory approaches the explanation of human behavior in terms of a continuous reciprocal interaction between cognitive, behavioral and environmental determinants." In other words, human behavior (personality) is a continuous interaction among cognitive (mental), behavioral, and environmental influences. For example, a person participating in an activity will learn not only from verbal instructions (cognitive) but from the actions of others as well (behavioral), while another observer, noticing the actions of another participant elicit praise from the instructor, may imitate that behavior in order to receive similar recognition (environmental). The term used to describe this process is *modeling,* defined as learning from the example of others.

Social Learning Theory Principles

Bandura's social learning theory functions on three principles:

- The highest level of learning through modeling is achieved in two ways: organizing and rehearsing the modeled behavior symbolically, and overtly performing the behavior.
- Individuals are more likely to adopt a modeled behavior if that behavior results in outcomes valued by the observer.
- Individuals are more likely to adopt a modeled behavior if the

model possesses characteristics similar to those of the observer, is admired by others, and demonstrates a behavior that has functional value to the observer.

In applying these principles, Bandura theorizes more effectively than others about two things many people would consider the "strong suit" or "work horses" of the human personality: *observational learning* and *self-regulation* (psychological processes) (Boeree, 2006).

Observational Learning

By observing the actions of others and the results of those actions, people form ideas of how new behaviors are performed and later use this information as a guide (Bandura, 1977). Bandura further stipulates that, in order for individuals to successfully model the behavior of others, four conditions are necessary. The first two, *attention* and *retention* (cognitive skills), are required for individuals to learn and later apply new information. Because these conditions frequently offer a major challenge to people with disabilities, especially those with thought disorders, some performers in a SEIR program may require extra rehearsal time to learn a simple dance sequence. For instance, Dance Steps A and B may be quite easy to learn in isolation but when combined may require many repetitions before the complete sequence is retained. The third condition, *motor reproduction* (cognitive skill), is required for learners to execute movements by observing others. As in the first two conditions, this one can present a significant challenge to those with any kind of physical disability. Thus, in SEIR, a special effort is made to accommodate the needs of the physical challenged by adapting physical exercises and dance steps so no one will be excluded from any activity.

Story 5: Adaptation: The Key to Success

The cast of T*heatre Extraordinaire* was in the process of learning a new dance routine requiring execution of the grapevine step, a move involving the crossover of one foot behind the other. Most of the cast members were able to eventually learn this challenging move; however, those in the back row with motor coordination problems were unable to learn this step even though they could follow the dancers in front of them. The company's choreographer, being very skilled at adapting her choreography to the abilities of her students, recognized the problem immediately. The grapevine step was changed to a simple side step for the second row while the front row performed the grapevine. This adaptation gave dancers in the back row the confidence they needed to continue working on the routine, motivated by the knowledge that their instructor was willing to do whatever was necessary to help them have a successful performance experience.

The fourth condition presented by Bandura is the *motivation* to acquire the modeled behavior. For those with disabilities, this circumstance poses a significant challenge, especially to those grappling with symptoms of psychiatric disorders. Also affected are individuals who have experienced frequent failures in their recovery efforts. Here again the importance of short-term goals is emphasized so SEIR students can experience success within a brief time period. Furthermore, students with motivation challenges are encouraged to participate in physical activities that will help relieve their depression while increasing their energy levels. Specifically, dance exercises and line and folk dances are used to help students improve their fitness level (especially endurance) in an experience that is both joyful and energizing.

Modeling

In his theory, Bandura has identified several types of modeling that can be used in the learning process, including *observational, performance, imitation, vicarious,* and *symbolic.* All of these have been incorporated into SEIR methodology:

- **Observational Modeling,** a method where observers can learn new information without demonstrating new behaviors, is often the first step in the SEIR learning process. When observing a rehearsal or class that includes students with similar characteristics to those of the observers, potential students can be influenced by the successful performance of the models. Upon seeing these models master a two- or three-step dance sequence, observers may think, "If they can do it, so can I," a revelation that can lead to the confidence needed to enroll in the program and proceed to the next step in the learning process.

- **Performance Modeling** employs successful performance as the principal agent of change. This approach involves structuring the environment so participants can experience success and is descriptive of the process used in SEIR. In a supportive milieu offering many opportunities for achievement, SEIR offers a clear example of how performance modeling can be successfully utilized with people with a serious mental illness or other disabilities. Of particular importance is the role that stage performance plays in this learning model.

Case Example 4: "Audrey"

When Audrey joined Theatre Extraordinaire, the On Stage! musical theatre company, she was very shy and extremely fearful of appearing before an audience. Diagnosed with schizophrenia and recently discharged from a residential treatment program, she was faced with many challenges, especially in her struggle with poor social skills and low self-confidence. However, she loved to sing and was determined to give membership in the company a try. First, she began learning the dance routines in the safety of the back row where she could follow other dancers. After a short time, she moved into the second row, never believing she would ever be one of those "special" people in front. Then one day she was asked if she would like to try a place in front row. Hesitant at first but finally conceding to give it a try, Audrey rehearsed for the first time in the front line, performing very well. As her self-confidence improved, she was selected to perform in numbers that featured two or three company members. She eventually asked if she could sing a solo in one of the company's variety shows, evidence that her self-confidence had significantly improved. Motivated by her success in SEIR, Audrey began to work even harder toward her recovery goals. With the confidence and courage developed during her tenure with Theatre Extraordinaire, she became involved in her church choir and, accordingly, began to show interest in developing more skills, thus preparing her for the next major step in her recovery: independent living.

- **Imitation,** defined in psychology as the performance of an act whose stimulus is the observation of other groups or individuals, is another form of modeling employed in SEIR. Especially helpful to new students, imitating the movements of others during both exercise and dance routines decreases the anxiety usually associated with learning new skills in the company of others. Frequent repetition of these movements gradually reduces the need to imitate fellow cast members, leading to improved confidence in the ability to succeed.

- **Vicarious Modeling** takes place when observers "are easily aroused by the emotional expressions of others" (Bandura, 1997). To illustrate, when potential SEIR students observe an activity that includes people they know, emotional reactions can be the result. Consequently, these reactions can be enhanced if performers have the same emotional and/or physical challenges as the observers, and if the activity being performed reminds observers of a time in the past when they experienced the same feelings in a similar situation. For example, while observing the performance of a dance routine that uses a familiar song, an observer may recall a time when he/she performed to that same song in a high school musical. This association can heighten even further the observer's interest in joining a program where once again the feelings of joy and excitement accompanying a stage performance can be experienced.
- **Symbolic Modeling** occurs when the model is observed is some other medium (i.e., movies, television, videotape). The author has found this method especially effective when recruiting new SEIR students. By showing videotapes of rehearsals and performances, observers see both the SEIR learning process and the successful performance of the models, offering yet another way to help students decide whether they wish to join the program.

Stage Performance

In a SEIR program, three types of modeling (observational, imitation, and performance) are incorporated into the learning process in two stages: rehearsals, then performances. In the rehearsal stage, the aforementioned modeling categories are utilized to help students acquire the necessary performances skills. For instance, a student having difficulty visualizing his/her relationship to others in a dance routine can benefit from watching others perform, whereas another student may gain more confidence by placement in the second row where he/she can learn through imitation. In addition, rehearsals also play an important part in decreasing performance anxiety, and for many, anxiety in general. Again, modeling can play an important role. For instance, a student who has experienced a noticeable decrease in anxiety can serve as a role model to others whose anxieties have prevented them from performing. Now, with increased confidence, those who previously felt they were too anxious to try anything new can work to overcome their fears, knowing there is a good chance for success. Thus prepared with the skills and confidence needed for a successful performance outcome, students whose anxieties were a barrier to their recovery are ready to perform.

Self-Regulation

Self-regulation, the second "workhorse" of the personality, occurs when individuals, using their own ideas of what is appropriate or inappropriate behavior, change their behavior accordingly. Using this process, sometimes referred to as self-directed change, students learn to regulate their behavior by rewarding themselves after reaching a desired goal (Ormrod, 1999). In his discussion on this topic, Bandura uses the term "self-contracts," whereas this author has coined the term "contingency self-management" in describing a self-managed, self-rewarding process where individuals make a contract with themselves to change a behavior using rewards as an incentive. For example, SEIR students often find it difficult to follow a set schedule for completing homework assignments (learning dance steps and lyrics) due to poor time management skills and a tendency to procrastinate. Having these individuals create their own self-contracts can reduce dependence on others to make decisions for them, take control of the change process, and accept responsibility for their behaviors. If these students are motivated to change, this contingency self-management approach can be very effective, resulting in improved study habits, self-discipline and confidence in their chances to be successful.

Self-Efficacy

Self-efficacy, the belief in one's capacity to succeed, has long been considered a characteristic found in individuals who are successful, satisfied with their accomplishments, and have an overall sense of well-being. Having a strong sense of self-efficacy helps those with confidence approach difficult tasks as challenges, become more deeply involved in activities, set challenging goals, and uphold a high commitment to achieving them. When confronted with failure, they recover more quickly, taking responsibility for setbacks by acknowledging deficits in knowledge or skills. Accordingly, a person's level of self-confidence and belief in his or her abilities influence whether or not a positive outcome is anticipated (Pajares & Schunk, 2001).

In describing self-efficacy as it relates to social learning theory, Bandura identifies several precepts that can be directly applied to SEIR methodology. Following is a description of these and an example of each as applied in a SEIR activity.

- Change occurs when cognitive processes interact to recall an event in which individuals have experienced success, thus enhancing their chances for achieving mastery in a new and challenging behavior. (SEIR students preparing for their first performance may recall a time when they were successful in performing on another stage show. This memory in turn can promote the belief that they are capable of achieving success in a new but related situation.)
- Chances for a successful outcome are increased when individuals believe that a certain behavior will lead to the desired outcome (outcome expectancy). Chances for a successful outcome are enhanced if individuals believe they can successfully perform the behaviors required to achieve that outcome (efficacy expectation). (If SEIR students hold two beliefs–that rehearsing dance steps can lead to mastery and that they possess the ability to learn those steps–then their chances for a successful performance are greatly improved.)

It would seem, then, that if facilitating self-efficacy can enhance chances for success in a general sense then promoting self-efficacy in people with a serious mental illness could have the same results. Thus is the premise on which the SEIR model was created.

Case Example 5: "John"

John was an accomplished guitarist and performer when a major depression and alcoholism sent him into a downward spiral, leaving him homeless, living in his car, and struggling to survive. One day he happened to notice a flyer announcing the formation of a musical theatre company in a new recovery program for people with a serious mental illness. He immediately called for information and soon became a member of Theatre Extraordinaire. After a short time, the sadness and depression that had been ruling his life gradually began to lessen, replaced by a happiness he had not experienced in a very long time. Satisfaction with his new life had resulted in an improved self-confidence and motivation for this talented individual to find adequate housing, refrain from drinking, and again feel contentment in his life. When asked about his experience in this unique recovery program, John never hesitated to say: "It saved my life."

COMPONENT THREE: BEHAVIORS

> Change is the law of life. And those who look only to the past or present are certain to miss the future.
>
> –John F. Kennedy

It is often said there are only two sure things in life: *death* and *taxes.* Although this may be true, it seems that one more word could be added to these certainties: *change.* After all, if dying and paying taxes are unavoidable and mankind is resolved to accept them as inevitable, then surely change can be considered in the same way. Think about it. Can you imagine anyone going through life without experiencing some degree of modification in their habits, behaviors, or circumstances? Unlikely, to say the least. Of course there are always those who, satisfied with the status quo, spend a lifetime resisting the slightest alteration in their life-style or situation. Refusing to even consider modifications in attitude or behavior, these individuals seem to deny themselves a chance for a better future and an improved quality of life. Considering this further, the ability to view and accept change while looking toward the future could be an important predictor regarding the successful achievement of lifetime goals. Accordingly, by accepting this premise and the words of JFK as true, the importance of helping people with a serious mental illness and other disabilities develop feelings of hope, expectation, and belief in the future seems apparent.

Although the type of change required will vary from one individual to the next, for many it is making changes or adaptations in behavior that can present the most difficult challenge. Knowing this, it should not be surprising that people with a serious mental illness are faced with a much higher level of difficulty when confronting changes that may significantly affect their recovery. For example, some service users may be so fearful of trying a new treatment approach that they will reject any changes that may improve their chances for recovery. Therefore, helping these individuals recognize and decrease this fear and other barriers that block their progress is a primary focus of any SEIR program.

EFFECTIVE INTERVENTIONS

It is now well known that mental health treatment without a focus on recovery is not the most effective way to help service users regain their self-confidence and self-esteem. Moreover, unless supported by community-based interventions, individuals receiving only therapy and medications will have difficulty making significant progress toward their recovery. In fact, even those fortunate enough to be in recovery programs can become frustrated because of the slow advancement toward their recovery goals. Consequently, there is a need for interventions that focus on building self-confidence and self-esteem, ensuring that students experience, within a short period of time, small successes leading to noticeable progress toward recovery. To this end, SEIR programs promote:

- Improvement in self-confidence within 2 weeks of enrollment.
- Changes in behavior through activities that are both challenging and fun.
- Activities with positive outcomes, helping students set aside their emotional and personal problems for a brief time.
- Teaching students to recognize their strengths and abilities.
- A feeling of belonging in groups offering social and emotional support.

It is all of these components working congruently that help students stay motivated, especially when they realize success is possible. This realization can then inspire them to work even harder as each success rewards them for their commitment and perseverance.

After setting goals and becoming involved in the SEIR process of personal development and skill building, over time, students change their behaviors in many ways. Accordingly, the author has identified the following eight behaviors as having changed significantly due to students' involvement in her programs: expanded social networks, acceptance of change, increased risk-taking, acceptance of responsibility, demonstration of confidence, avoidance of criticizing others, control of emotions, and demonstration of a positive attitude.

Social Networks

Students expand their social networks by:

- Developing friendships within the program, leading to socialization with these new friends and others outside of the program.
- Volunteering at hospitals and/or nonprofit organizations.
- Joining community groups (i.e., church choirs, activist organizations).
- Enrolling in supported education or vocational training programs.

Change

Students learn to readily accept change by:

- Learning to perform previously learned skills in new ways.
- Acknowledging there can be more than one right answer to a problem.
- Learning to let go of old behaviors and attitudes that are inhibiting recovery.
- Accepting last-minute changes in venue, dance routines, or other activities.

Risk-Taking

Students develop the courage to take risks by:

- Participating in new activities despite fear of failure.
- Performing before an audience of strangers.

- Sharing feelings or expressing opinions within a group.
- Initiating conversations with group members they do not know.
- Volunteering to help on committees.

Responsibility

Students learn to accept responsibility by:

- Following policies and procedures of the program.
- Taking responsibility for behaviors, not blaming others.
- Following through with commitments.

Confidence

Students demonstrate improved confidence by:

- Volunteering to perform a solo in a small vocal ensemble or to appear as a featured soloist.
- Auditioning for a role in a short sketch.
- Volunteering to speak to a community group about the benefits of a SEIR program.
- Acknowledging both their strengths and limitations.
- Demonstrating improved posture and good eye contact.

Criticism

Students learn to avoid criticizing others by:

- Developing an understanding that the need to criticize others usually originates from poor self-esteem and feelings of inferiority.
- Improving self-confidence.
- Learning to forgive others for their mistakes.
- Accepting that no one is perfect.

Emotions

Service users will demonstrate the ability to control their emotions by:

- Recognizing when a situation is escalating and walking away.
- Learning to control anger with deep breathing exercises and/or

by leaving the activity space for a short time.
- Talking with staff before emotions escalate.
- Identifying the source of angry feelings that could be due to an incident unrelated to the current situation.

Attitude

Students will demonstrate a positive attitude by:

- Using positive self-talk.
- Avoiding self-criticism.
- Avoiding criticism of others.
- Believing in their ability to be successful.

In summary, it is the author's position that Bandura's social learning theory provides a theoretical base for the success of any SEIR program. Application of the theory's three principles are evident throughout the SEIR learning process as students organize, rehearse, and perform the modeled behavior in program activities; adopt modeled behaviors they value; and adopt behaviors modeled by someone admired and with characteristics similar to those of the observer. All of these processes work together within the SEIR model's three components, offering each student the opportunity to work toward independence and an improved quality of life. Accordingly, the following chapters on stress reduction, cognitive skills, and stigma reduction are intended to show how these three components work together to promote self-esteem and self-efficacy in people with a serious mental illness. As these changes begin to occur, students become more motivated to learn, are persistent in their efforts, and experience joy in every successful experience.

THE RECOVERY WHEEL: EVALUATING SEIR GOALS

During the author's clinical career, she has used several standardized self-assessment instruments to evaluate student progress toward therapeutic goals (i.e., improving self-esteem and self-confidence or reducing depression). Although helpful in assessing progress in some areas, the author found it difficult to find evaluation tools targeting specific recov-

Table 2
RECOVERY WHEEL ASSESSMENT EXAMPLE

SELF-CONFIDENCE	*TEAM BUILDING*	*INTERPERSONAL SKILLS*
I know that:	When working on a group project:	In a conversation with others:
1. __ I am a positive thinker.	1. __ I willingly cooperate with others.	1. __ I am a good listener.
2. __ I can learn new skills.	2. __ I am comfortable sharing my ideas when solving problems.	2. __ People easily understand what I am saying.
3. __ I feel good about myself even when I make a mistake.	3. __ I can trust others I work with.	3. __ I do not judge situations or others without knowing all the facts.
4. __ I can accept praise from others without embarrassment.	4. __ When something does not turn out as planned, I can adjust and "go with the flow."	4. __ I am able to help solve problems without losing control of my emotions.
5. __ I am a worthy person with the right to be respected.	5. __ I tell others in the group when they are doing a good job.	5. __ I listen to the opinions of others with an open mind.
6. __ I have a good chance of succeeding in whatever I choose to do.	6. __ When working with others, I approach the group's activities with energy and enthusiasm.	6. __ My eye contact is good when talking with someone.
7. __ I do not worry about what others think of my opinions and ideas.	7. __ I willingly volunteer for work assignments.	7. __ I think carefully before I speak.
8. __ I give myself credit for my achievements.	8. __ I offer help to others when I can.	8. __ I find it easy to express my feelings.
TOTAL POINTS:	TOTAL POINTS:	TOTAL POINTS:

Legend: 5 = Always 4 = Often 3 = Sometimes 2 = Seldom 1 = Never ery goals (self-discipline, risk-taking, team-building skills) that were appropriate for a wide range of abilities. For example, a lengthy self-assessment in any category may be inappropriate for service users whose cognitive deficits interfere with comprehension and concentration. Recognizing this, the author developed a self-assessment instrument easily understood, of reasonable length, simple to administer, and designed for immediate feedback to the test taker. Moreover, this instrument is intended for use not only in performing arts recovery programs but in related disciplines as well. An example from this assessment can be found in Table 2. The complete instrument will be included in a handbook currently in development.

Chapter 3

STRESS REDUCTION, RESILIENCE, AND RECOVERY

ONE LIFE AT A TIME

When considering her remarkable road to recovery, it is difficult to imagine that Eleanor at one time in her life had been suicidal, depressed, aggressive, and hospitalized several times. Diagnosed at age 23 with bipolar disorder and borderline personality disorder, she was hospitalized in five different facilities that same year, twice for attempting suicide and once under court order. Prior to the onset of her illness, she had completed 2 years of college and was working in a nursing home with plans to save money to complete her college education. When she finally had the funding she needed, she became ill and was hospitalized for depression and an attempted suicide. Refusing to accept her illness, she made several attempts to finish college after this, three times while married and three times after a divorce. During those 13 years, she tried counseling but refused medications, a behavior that resulted in hospitalizations in three different facilities. Then, after losing their adopted baby due to her abusive behavior, her husband finally divorced her, taking their other two sons with him. Filled with rage, she spiraled into a deep depression. Yet, despite these traumatic events and her ongoing struggle with the symptoms of her illness, Eleanor managed to complete a Bachelor of Arts in Applied Psychology just 10 months before enrolling in On Stage!.

Although some of her symptoms were under control due to medication, it was Eleanor's aggressive and sometimes violent behavior that was the primary barrier to her recovery. Even after her transition into the community, she continued to struggle to control her aggression, but she seemed unable to do so for any significant length of time. On one occasion, she was sent to jail for a week for trying to outrun a police car at a roadblock. After this incident, she was returned to the state hospital from which she had escaped the month before. At another time, the author witnessed Eleanor's attempt to assault a mental health employee when the employee said something that triggered Eleanor's anger. In fact, her case manager and other staff were so afraid of her that two people had to be in the room and the door left ajar when she was present. It seemed there was no intervention, medical or behavioral, that could break her chain of aggressive behavior.

Despite Eleanor's difficulty in keeping a job, she did achieve, at one time, success as a member of a professional music group. It was this interest in music that, shortly after hearing of a new program called On Stage!, she asked to be considered for enrollment. During her intake interview, although appearing sullen and depressed, she said she wanted to try the program so she could begin once again to play her guitar and become involved in performance. Consequently, she enrolled in the *Introduction to Musical Theatre* class, completing the 12-week course. Then, at the class's graduation celebration, she surprised her fellow class members by performing a song written especially for them. Titled *They Kept Urging Us On,* she later gave a repeat performance at the theatre company's first public show in 1997. Now a permanent member of Theatre Extraordinaire, Eleanor had taken yet another major step on her incredible journey toward recovery.

Eleanor's On Stage! Outcomes

> I always felt like I was oozing with evil and anger and now I feel so different, like I am really kind and caring, especially at work and at home. I am still socially awkward, but I understand that, since I was a misfit for so many years. All I could think about was hurting people and killing them in many different ways. And when I couldn't see how to do that, I would turn on myself and want to die. I was very much in that space while beginning in On Stage!, as I was so depressed I could hardly get out of bed. That's when your phone calls to come to rehearsal were so crucial to my getting out into the functioning world. (Eleanor)

Upon enrollment in On Stage!, Eleanor presented with several behaviors challenging her ability to integrate into the On Stage! community. These included poor interpersonal and social skills, poor impulse control, inability to take instructions, difficulty accepting constructive criticism, and impatience with others. The author recalls one incident in particular when Eleanor, for no apparent reason, lay down on the floor during a rehearsal. It was the actions of Katherine, the company's choreographer, who, instead of telling her to get up as others had done in the past, knelt down to speak with her. With words of encouragement and concern for her well-being, Eleanor was given the support she needed to stand and continue rehearsing. Later, when asked about this unusual behavior, she explained that she "would lie down when she was feeling overwhelmed, that the floor was something solid to hang on to." Consequently, it was the patience and caring of the On Stage! staff, working closely with her mental health team, that helped Eleanor overcome the many challenges she confronted daily.

Among many of Eleanor's talents was her ability to write songs that expressed her feelings about something that was happening in her life. In the following lyrics from a song written for students and cast members, she tells how her On Stage! experience affected not only herself but others in the company as well.

A Whole Lot Better

Verse 1
We came into this company, kind of shy with fears,
And hesitant to try to sing and dance,
Uncoordinated, lacking social skills,
And trusting people-we just took a chance.

Chorus
And we've grown with each other, not alone,
Finding the self we've never known,
Building confidence and pride.
And we'll try, no telling just how far we'll fly;
Whether we sing and laugh or cry,
We're feeling better deep inside.

Verse 2
Performances are scary, most of us agree,
With that no-such-a-good-feeling in our gut.
Palpitations, sweaty palms, some go completely blank,
But we go out and sing no matter what!

Chorus
And we've grown with each other, not alone,
Finding the self we've never known,
Building confidence and pride.
And we'll try, no telling just how far we'll fly;
Whether we sing and laugh or cry,
We're feeling better deep inside.

In an interview about 3 years after leaving the program, the author asked Eleanor to describe the benefits she had received as a result of her On Stage! experience. She responded with a long list that included learning to: work with a team; get along with others, "even those I don't like"; make new friends to meet outside of class time; encourage others who hesitated; take instruction and constructive criticism; and try new things. Of particular importance was learning the consequences of her aggressive behavior that, at one time, prevented her from performing with the company because she had to spend two nights in jail. She said she "was crushed" from having to miss that Christmas performance, learning from this experience that she needed to change–and change she did. Reflecting on this incident, she stated: "I really loved being cared about like I mattered in the group, that I wasn't replaced because I misbehaved. I also learned there were consequences to bad behavior, but I wasn't rejected because of it."

Today, Eleanor is married, receiving no public mental health services, seeing a counselor to help her deal with stress, and taking a minimum of medication. She is certified as a nursing assistant, working full time at a mental health residential treatment center, and has received a raise in recognition for outstanding performance in her job. She stated that she really "likes being on the other side of the glass" and always wondered what it would be like to help people like herself, and now she knows.

REDUCING STRESS: THE TEN COMMANDMENTS

All the world's a stage, and all the men and women merely players; they have their exits and their entrances, and one man in his time plays many parts.

–William Shakespeare

Whether it is "butterflies" in the stomach prior to giving speech, stage fright before a performance, or fulfilling expectations at work, everyone is subjected most of their lives to the stress of performance expectations. This view, so aptly expressed in the Shakespearean quote above, seems to be saying that in every aspect of our lives we are "on stage" and, consequently, subject to the stress associated with "performance." Certainly, then, the advantage of learning techniques to reduce anxieties associated with stress seems clear. However, those who have not seriously considered the consequences of high anxiety levels in general may be unaware of the importance that stress managements plays in their everyday lives. Thus, the intent of the following discussion is to enlighten the reader about this issue and the critical role stress reduction and resilience play in the recovery of people with a serious mental illness. In addition, the reader will find placed throughout the narrative "food for throught" in the "Ten Commandments for Reducing Stress in Your Life" (Lotus Girl, 2009).

1. Thou Shalt Not Be Perfect, Or Even Try To Be.

STRESS-RESISTANT PERSONALITIES

In studies on stress reduction and stress-resistant personalities, researchers agree that learning to cope with stressful events is essential in maintaining a healthy life-style. In particular, Kabasa, Maddi, and Courington (1981) found that the characteristics of stress-resistant individuals consisted of the following three components:

- A **commitment** to one's work and social relationships (investing oneself in solutions).
- A **belief** in one's ability to influence and control life's events (taking control of situations, rather than running from them).

- An **ability** to view change as a challenge rather than a problem (seeing opportunities rather than problems).

Equally important was the authors' suggestion that these three components "were not mutually exclusive but were inextricably intertwined aspects that bear a considerable resemblance to each other," together forming a "personality-based hardiness" (Kabasa, 1981; Kabasa & Puccett, 1983). In other words, it takes a combination of committing to a goal, taking control of life's events, and seeing challenges as opportunities to create a truly stress-resistant person. Further, there seems to be a concensus that stress-resistant people are: self-confident, energetic, ambitious, easy-going, slow to anger, minimally competitive, minimally pressured by time, and optimistic with a good sense of humor and good self-esteem. In addition, these individuals seem to understand the importance of regular aerobic exercise and adequate rest (Anderson, 2007; Holohan & Moos, 1985; Miller, 2009; Student Affairs, TCU, 2009).

2. Thou shalt not try to be all things to all people.

Considering the previously described characteristics of stress-resistant personalities and the struggles with stress that many people with a mental illness confront daily, it is not difficult to understand why service users develop stress-prone personalities that inhibit their recovery. Therefore, due to the importance of this issue and in preparation to describe her SEIR intervention program for reducing performance anxiety, the author has identified some specific characteristics observed in her students, and then compared them to those of stress-resistant individuals (Table 3). Then, in Figure 4, a graphic depicts the various ways in which the performing arts can intervene to promote the development of a stress-resistant personality. (The process for reducing many of the symptoms associated with stress in service users is addressed in Chapter 4.) Certainly, the obvious differences in the stress-resistant and stress-prone personalities should be considered as interventions are developed to reduce the anxiety levels of people with psychiatric disabilities.

3. Thou Shalt Sometimes Leave Things Undone That Ought To Be Done.

Table 3
CHARACTERISTICS OF STRESS-RESISTANT AND STRESS-PRONE PERSONALITIES

General Characteristics: Stress-Resistant Personalities

• Self-confident • Good self-esteem • Energetic • Ambitious
• Even disposition • Slow to anger • Low Competitive Level
• Minimally Pressured By Time • Optimistic • Good Sense of Humor

Specific Characteristics: Stress-Resistant and Stress-Prone Personalities

Components	Stress-Resistant Personalities	Stress-Prone Personalities: Service Users
COMMITMENT	• Have strong social support	• Tend to isolate due to lack of comfort in social situations
	• Are motivated to achieve and endure	• Lack confidence required for risk-taking and personal growth
	• Have clear sense of values, goals, and capabilities	• Have symptoms that interfere with ability to think clearly about the future
	• Share feelings with others	• Are fearful of disclosing feelings and/or have poor communication skills
	• Actively participate in groups with family and friends and in other social events	• Are often estranged from family and have no close friends
	• Are helpful to others	• Have minimal interest in others, often due to focus on self and dealing with symptoms of illnesses
CONTROL	• Are easy-going	• Experience extremely high anxiety levels from stress and other symptoms of disorders
	• Use coping strategies	• Avoid dealing with stressful events by denying the problem, retreating or minimizing event's importance

Table 3–*Continued*

CONTROL *(continued)*	• Feel influential, not helpless	• Feel powerless due to low self-esteem and low level of self-efficacy
	• Have minimal psychological reactions to stressful events	• Overreact to stressful events due to high anxiety levels and lack of coping skills
	• Have internal locus of control: Believe events determined by self	• Have external locus of control: Believe events are determined by powerful others, fate, or chance
	• Seldom wary	• Worry excessively about situations or events over which they have no control or about circumstances they could control but do not have skills to do so
CHANGE	• Have positive attitudes toward change	• Refuse to see how change can be a positive influence in recovery, resisting anything that will mean leaving their "comfort zone"
	• Find meaning in stressful life events	• Become too overwhelmed by anxiety to view stressful events as anything but negative experiences
	• Are creative problem solvers	• Lack creativity required for approach to problem solving
	• Look for more than one right answer to solving a problem	• Are unable to see more than one right answer to a problem
	• Are open-minded, critical thinkers	• Are inflexible thinkers, lacking ability to consider points of view other than their own

Figure 4

Building Stress-Resistant Personalities with Performing Arts Interventions

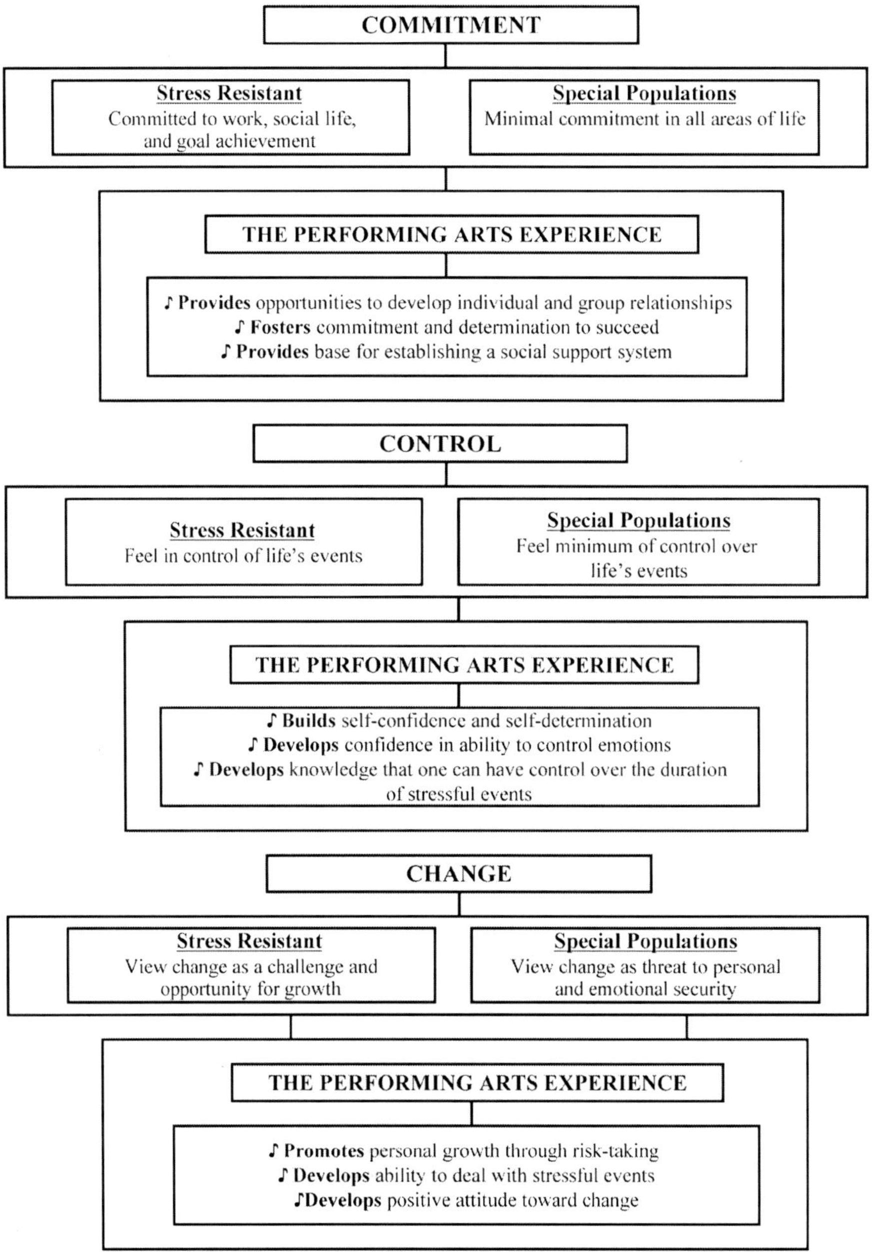

Figure 4. Building stress-resistant personalities with performing arts interventions.

STRESS REDUCTION AND RESILIENCE

Stress Reduction

So why are high levels of stress so prevalent in people with mental illness? Part of this answer may be found in the belief by many that service users are incapable of making decisions, taking risks, and learning from their failures. Consequently, these people develop an overdependence on others in all aspects of daily living. After all, many of them have experienced repeated and lengthy hospitalizations where most decisions are made for them, offering little opportunity for the development of strategies that prepare them for independent living. Moreover, even after transition into community treatment, this dependent relationship can continue to be fostered by a mental health system based on a therapeutic/medical model promoting a protective and relatively stress-free environment. Further, professionals working in this "old" model often discourage risk-taking activities fundamental to the development of personal growth and eventual independence. Consequently, service users can become discouraged, resulting in the loss of motivation and belief in their chances for recovery. This view is reflected in a keynote address on recovery and empowerment delivered at an international conference by Patricia Deegan (1997), mental health advocate and service user. Her perspective on how the mental health system can foster anxiety and other psychiatric symptoms by dehumanizing and disempowering service users is reflected in the following comments:

4. Thou Shalt Not Spread Thyself Too Thinly.

> Almost everything you do gets understood in reference to your illness. You used to have days when you had "ants in your pants" but now they say you are agitated. You used to feel sad sometimes but now you are said to be depressed. You used to disagree sometimes but now you get told you lack insight. You used to act independently but now you get told that your independence means you are uncooperative, non-compliant and treatment resistant. You used to take risks. You learned from your failures. It was part of growing and learning. But now that you have been labeled with a mental illness the dignity of risk and the right to failure have been taken from you. No wonder you get angry.

Although Deegan's address was given more than a decade ago, her message is relevant today because it speaks to a problem encountered by many service users in their struggle for independence: finding a balance between the normal dependence in a healthy relationship and the overdependence that can be fostered by caregivers, both professional and familial. Fortunately, the recovery model, with its focus on a service user-driven system, strives to develop this balance in strength-based programs that help individuals build the skills necessary for independent living. Thus, by promoting self-determination and self-efficacy rather than overdependence on others, people with a mental illness now have opportunities to work in partnership with caregivers in a process leading to the achievement of each person's recovery goals.

5. Thou Shalt Learn To Say No.

Resilience

Resilience: The capacity to recover from extremes of trauma and stress.

Case Example 6: "Maria"

Diagnosed with schizophrenia and living alone, Maria was found by her family in a catatonic state totally incapacitated and in need of hospitalization. She was admitted to a state hospital and told by her psychiatrist that she would never be capable of living on her own. Eventually her family intervened, and Maria was transferred to a supervised living facility in the community, but still given very little hope for recovery. Yet when she heard about a new arts program for people with a mental illness, she asked for an interview and enrolled in two classes: *Beginning Art* and *Introduction to Musical Theatre.* After completing the theatre class, she joined *Theatre Extraordinaire,* the program's musical theatre company, while continuing to take art classes. She began performing with the theatre company, moving from the back to the front row in dance routines and displaying her art at the program's community art shows. Maria's remarkable progress can be attributed to the benefits she received from the program (improved self-esteem) and her determination and belief that she could succeed in whatever she chose to do (self-efficacy). After several months in the program, Maria enrolled in a local community college, eventually receiving a certificate in clerical studies.

Regardless of whether one believes resiliency to be a personality characteristic or an acquired skill, it cannot be denied that the ability to overcome problems and challenges in daily living is essential if one is to enjoy a successful and satisfying life. Yet despite its importance, the term "resiliency," in this writer's experience, is seldom, if ever, mentioned when planning mental health interventions. Nonetheless, Maria is just one of many who have demonstrated their resilience as they struggle to overcome the adversities associated with their mental illnesses. Now leading independent, productive lives, the determination of these individuals (like those in the stories throughout this book) to survive is, indeed, a tribute to the resiliency of the human spirit. So why is not more attention paid to a characteristic so necessary if anyone is to surmount the obstacles encountered in everyday living? Some researchers have asked this same question.

6. Thou Shalt Schedule Time For Thyself And Thy Supportive Network.

Although there seems to be more interest in resilience as a concept in mental health treatment, its prevalence in clinical practice is not yet evident. In an article on the subject, Atkinson, Martin, and Rankin (2009) stressed the importance of the role of resilience in recovery: "Fostering resilience is central to the paradigms of strengths-based practice and recovery models within the mental health field." Other researchers seem to agree with this concept, suggesting that learning to overcome adversity is fundamental to good mental and physical health (Tusai, Puskar, & Sereika, 2007; Rutter, 2007; Tugade & Fredrickson, 2004). Moreover, seemingly related to the importance of fostering resilience is the emerging positive psychology movement, originated by Martin E. P. Seligman with an "aim–to begin to catalyze a change in the focus of psychology from preoccupation only with repairing the worst things in life to also building positive qualities" (Seligman &

7. Thou Shalt Switch Off And Do Nothing Regularly.

Csikszentmihalyi, 2000). In describing further the scope of this movement, the authors stated:

> Whatever the personal origins of our conviction that the time has arrived for a positive psychology, our message is to remind our field that psychology is not just the study of pathology, weakness and damage; it is also the study of strength and virtue. Treatment is not just fixing what is broken; it is nurturing what is best. Psychology is not just a branch of medicine concerned with illness or health; it is much larger. It is about work, education, insight, love, growth and play. And in this quest for what is best, positive psychology does not rely on wishful thinking, faith, self-deception, fads or hand waving; it tries to adapt what is best in the scientific method to the unique problems that human behavior presents to those who wish to understand it in all its complexity. (Seligman & Csikszentmihalyi, 2000)

It would seem, then, that the positive approach advocated by this emerging movement underscores the importance of creating interventions focusing on strengths and abilities, a methodology that seems complementary to the mental health recovery movement. Indeed, by paying more attention to helping service users develop coping mechanisms, the outcome can be individuals who are stress-resistant, resilient, and better prepared to deal with life's daily challenges. Finally, perhaps this song title, "Pick Yourself Up, Dust Yourself Off, and Start All Over Again," best describes, in just a few words, what this writer feels is the most important characteristic of a resilient personality: a positive attitude. Featured in "Swing Time," a 1936 film made during the Depression, this tune was written to inspire hope in its listeners and encouragement to not give up despite the dire circumstances. It is not surprising the songs' message is relevant even today.

8. Thou Shalt Be Boring, Untidy, Inelegant And Unattractive At Times.

COPING WITH STRESS

When pursuing the development of a more stress-resistant personality, researchers in the field have suggested the following strategies: (1)

laugh often; (2) focus on the positive; (3) exercise often; (4) look for creative solutions; (5) develop strong social supports; (6) get plenty of rest; (7) re-evaluate the pace of your life; (8) set realistic goals; (9) reward yourself for successes; (10) learn to deal with your anger in a healthy way; (11) be aware of your emotional state; (12) avoid negative self-talk; (13) view mistakes as learning experiences; (14) take responsibility for your decisions; and (15) learn to relax (Anderson, 2007; Landis, 2009; Seaward, 2004). Of course, people who have learned these coping strategies and have incorporated them into everyday living may take for granted their ability to deal with life's everyday stressors. However, for people with a mental illness, incorporating any of these behaviors into their daily lives can be challenging, to say the least, and in most cases present significant barriers to recovery. Thus, the importance of providing innovative interventions for stress reduction seems critical if service users are to achieve their recovery goals.

9. Thou Shalt Not Even Feel Guilty.

So what would a mental health program designed to promote resiliency and reduce stress include? After considering the 15 strategies listed above and the personality characteristics deemed to be important in developing resilience, this writer recommends that a stress-reduction program offer opportunities for service users to learn the importance of:

1. Incorporating humor into their lives by learning to laugh at themselves and not take life so seriously.
2. Focusing on the positive by avoiding negative self-talk.
3. Exercising regularly to reduce stress.
4. Developing coping mechanisms to deal with stress.
5. Taking controlled risks that develop courage and help to create a "hardiness" toward dealing with stressful events.
6. Developing strong social supports by making new friends and joining social activities.
7. Setting realistic goals.
8. Avoiding overcommitment by learning good organizational skills.
9. Rewarding themselves for successes.
10. Learning impulse control and dealing with anger in a healthy way.

11. Viewing mistakes as building blocks to learning.
12. Accepting responsibility for behaviors and decisions.
13. Relaxing and getting plenty of rest.
14. Understanding that no one is perfect.

Generally speaking, there seems to be an agreement among researchers and others that people with stress-resistant personalities have a better chance at achieving their life goals than those who have not developed stress-reduction strategies. Consequently, by studying the characteristics of stress-resistant individuals, mental health interventions can be created that focus on developing these same characteristics in people with a mental illness. Also, it has been noted that, when designing clinical interventions, more attention should be paid to the role that resilience plays in dealing with life's adversities because it is the resilient person who can "bounce back" from unexpected stressful events. Finally, the positive psychology movement underscores the importance of "nurturing what is best," thus emphasizing the value of recognizing that service users have strengths and abilities that, if fostered, can lead to significant strides toward recovery.

10. Especially Thou Shalt Not Be Thine Own Worst Enemy, But Be Thine Own Best Friend.

Story 6: Stress Resistance and Resilience

When On Stage! had to close its doors in 2006, the staff of a Spokane mental health service provider presented me with a certificate that read, in part: "In appreciation for your belief in people and their resiliency." Needless to say, I was deeply moved and so pleased to know there was a provider out there who truly believed in the strengths and abilities of people with a serious mental illness and their ability to become more stress-resistant and, consequently, more resilient. My belief in this resilience grew stronger every day as I witnessed a woman with an alcoholic husband, another with a severe anxiety disorder, a man who constantly battled voices in his head and a woman whose depression had isolated her from the world as they began to believe in themselves and their abilities to overcome adversity. All they needed was a chance, and they found it in a program called On Stage!.

Chapter 4

REDUCING ANXIETY IN THE THEATRICAL PERFORMANCE

ONE LIFE AT A TIME

Sandy was 51 and diagnosed with schizoaffective disorder when she began attending Theatre Extraordinaire rehearsals with a friend who was a cast member. Although depressed and suffering from low self-esteem and equally low self-confidence, Sandy brought with her a great sense of humor, a characteristic that seemed to be her defense mechanism for dealing with the many challenges of her disorder. Her ability to see humor in almost any situation was evident when, after attending rehearsals for several weeks, company members began calling her their "groupy," and she laughed at her new "identity." It was her humor and friendly manner that endeared her to her peers as she was welcomed into the company. However, she made one thing perfectly clear from day one: There was no way we were going to get her "on that stage!" Yet when asked if she would like to help off-stage at rehearsals and performances, she did not hesitate to take on this new role, seeming to enjoy being referred to as the company's "techie."

Sandy had been working with the company for about 2 years when there was an unexpected turn of events: She told the author she would like to join the company as a performer. When asked what had brought about this decision, Sandy said she was tired of being depressed and socially isolated and had decided to do something about it. Moreover, she felt that the only way to move forward in her recovery was to find an activity that "gave me a good reason to get up in the morning," and that joining the company would provide the motivation she needed. So to the surprise of everyone and despite her fear of being on stage, she began participating in rehearsals.

Now an official cast member, Sandy put her heart and soul into learning the company's dance routines. She began by participating in warm-up exercises at the beginning of each rehearsal, then shortly afterward joining the second row to learn the company's signature song and dance routine, "We've Come a Long Way, Baby." Despite her inexperience, she learned dance steps quickly and was soon able to sing while dancing, a skill often requiring weeks or months of training for many cast members. Then, after just a few rehearsals, it was discovered that Sandy had a most unusual range to her voice: She sang low enough to be placed with the tenors or baritones! (Since the male section could always use one more voice, Sandy was a welcome addition.)

By the time the company began rehearsing for its Christmas program, Sandy had gained enough confidence to ask if she could sing "O Holy Night" as a solo. After a successful performance in her first Christmas show, her level of participation and enthusiasm increased significantly. Nevertheless, she had made it very clear that she was not interested in being anywhere but in the back row of the company's dance routines. However, later on her attitude would change when staff and fellow cast members urged her to move beyond her comfort zone and join the front row. And so she did. Then, as her confidence improved, so did her level of participation, evidenced by her volunteering for specialty numbers in which she performed as a soloist and with small groups. In addition, she possessed a talent for improvisation, often engaging in humerous exchanges with a show's emcee. There is no doubt this special woman was a performer at heart and an audience favorite. Sandy continued to perform with Theatre Extraordinaire until the program was discontinued 5 years later.

Sandy's On Stage! Outcomes

Perhaps the most important role that membership in Theatre Extraordinaire played in Sandy's recovery was the support she received from her theatre "family." The rehearsals offered a safe environment where she could progress at her own pace, receive praise for her accomplishments, and be given encouragement when she made mistakes and wanted to quit. As her self-confidence grew, so did her belief in herself as she recognized the value of her talents and the role she played in making the company's successful productions possible.

Soon Sandy began participating in the company's original skits proving to the amazement of all that she was a talented comedic actress. Evidence of this talent was highlighted when one day before rehearsal she stood next to the piano and began singing the lyrics to a song that was "in her head." Eventually this improvisation resulted in the following lyrics, set to music by the author and performed by Sandy at the company's final public performance.

I Am Terrific

Tempo: Soft shoe

I am terrific------ to be specific:------ I'm just wonderful to know.
There ain't nobody ---any better---- because I'm cleverer than anyone I know–
Especially you people in the second row.
(spoken aside) What do they know?
I am terrific----- my heart's so happy----- and I'm filled with love and joy.
I am so real---- and though I try I can't conceal
The wonderful, wonderfulness----of -----me!

CUDOS, SANDY---YOU ARE INDEED TERRIFIC!

A POSITIVE APPROACH

> For myself, I am an optimist–it does not seem much use to be anything else.
>
> –Winston Churchill

People with a mental illness who have experienced one failure after another usually are extremely self-critical, are quick to put themselves down, have low self-esteem, and hold a negative outlook regarding their futures. Consequently, it is necessary that, from the beginning of the learning process, SEIR staff focus on helping students develop a positive attitude toward themselves and their chances for recovery. For this reason, eliminating the negative attitude that can interfere with the learning process is a priority. One way to accomplish this task is to teach students the practice of positive self-talk.[15] The importance of this technique is reflected in a statement by Brian Tracy (2007), author and professional speaker: "Your self-talk–determines the quality and tone of your emotional life," an important step to "becoming a highly effective person." Similarly, another writer stated:

> One of the most powerful influences on your attitude and personality is what you say to yourself. It is not what happens to you, but how you respond internally to what happens to you that determines your thoughts, feelings and your actions. By controlling your inner dialogue, or your "self talk," you can begin to assert control over every part of your life. (Love, 2009)

Truly, then, the role a positive attitude plays in goal achievement seems obvious, thus stressing the importance of introducing positive thinking into the lives of service users. To this end, this writer has incorporated into an anxiety-reduction desensitization process the development of a positive attitude Once again, a song from the forties sends a powerful message: in order to deal with the challenges of everyday life, be sure to "accentuate the positive" and "eliminate the negative." Indeed, these are words to live by for anyone confronted with adversity and seemingly unsurmountable circumstances.

ANXIETY: THE GOOD AND THE BAD

> Do not anticipate trouble or worry about what may never happen. Keep in the sunlight.
>
> –Benjamin Franklin

The process of reducing stress and learning to deal with performance anxiety can be, surprisingly, a positive experience if it offers frequent opportunities for success. However, students entering a SEIR program usually have a negative view of anxiety and the resulting stress, finding it difficult to understand how any level of anxiety could possibly have positive qualities. Further, their reasons for hesitating to appear before

15. Positive self-talk is anything said to oneself for encouragement or motivation or, put another way, one's constant internal conversation.

an audience are often precluded by anxieties stemming from sources that include:

- A fear of being judged.
- An exaggerated fear of memory loss.
- A fear of being labeled as "disabled."
- Concerns about being placed in an anxiety-producing situation away from the protective and relatively stress-free therapeutic environment.
- A reluctance to be in a position where others are depending upon them to perform well.

Resolve in advance that no matter what happens, you will not allow it to get you down.

Considering that individuals with the aforementioned challenges often, in addition, have low self-esteem and an exaggerated fear of failure, it will take patience, practice, and perseverance to overcome the anxieties associated with stage performance. Therefore, beginning with the first rehearsal, it is important to address any fears and anxieties by describing the process to be used in preparation for opening night. Once cast members understand how this process works to minimize their anxieties in a "user-friendly" approach, they will actually begin to look forward to their first performance.

A DESENSITIZATION PROCESS: SMALL TO LARGE AUDIENCES

Although the anxieties brought about by the stress of performance may be viewed as negative and counterproductive in the therapeutic sense, the positive aspects of having to deal with performance anxiety should be considered. As students place themselves in situations involving risk and the unknown, such as a stage performance, they should be guided and supported in their efforts to gain control of their anxieties and fears. It is only through learning new skills, gaining new insights, and taking risks that personal growth required to improve self-esteem and self-confidence can be realized. Knowing this, a "controlled risk" approach is strongly recommended where performers are guided

Neutralize any negative thoughts or emotions by speaking to yourself positively all the time.

through a series of "risky" experiences that ensure success. A process describing how to incorporate controlled risk into an anxiety-reduction method is presented below.

THE FIRST STEP

Early in the rehearsal process, preferably no later than the second session, introduce the topic of performance anxiety with a discussion that offers opportunities for cast members to express their concerns and anxieties about performing before an audience for the first time. For the reader who would like some assistance in beginning this discussion, here are some ideas in the form of the instructor's statements that may help to break the ice:

- To get this discussion started, I would like for us to talk about any concerns or anxieties anyone has about being on stage. Don't be afraid to speak up, for you are not alone in how you feel. Who would like to begin? (If members are hesitant to speak, staff can offer assistance with a question such as: Is anyone afraid they might forget their words?)
- Now let's talk about stress-resistant individuals and what makes them that way. Does anyone know why some people can handle stress better than others? In other words, what are the characteristics of people who are stress-resistant? (It may be helpful to write these answers on a board to help members answer the next question.) What do you think you can do to learn to deal more effectively with performance-related stress?
- How do you currently handle stress? How can performance experiences help you deal with performance-related stress in any situation? How can learning to deal with performance anxiety help you with stress in daily living?
- Has anyone in this group ever been in a show of any kind? How did you handle your performance anxiety?
- Do professional performers get stage fright?

- What is adrenaline? How can adrenaline have a positive effect on your performance?
- How can you support each other through stress-producing performance experiences?

At the conclusion of this discussion, explain to students how the process described below will help them handle their anxieties associated with performance.

Note #1: It is important to allow time (about 10 minutes) at the end of each rehearsal for students to process their feelings regarding the rehearsal experience and for staff to address student concerns, praise and thank the cast for their hard work, and offer any support and assurances that will keep the cast motivated and excited about their first performance.

PERFORMANCES

In preparing students for their first experience on stage, it is vitally important to be sure rehearsals and performances offer a graduated process that builds self-confidence, fosters optimism, and, most importantly, reduces fear of failure. To this end, described below are the types of performances and procedures this writer has found to be successful in preparing cast members for performances in a variety of venues. Divided into three categories, *In-Class Performances, Performances Before Small Audiences,* and the *Dress Rehearsal Performance,* these procedures offer performance experiences with one major purpose: gradually reducing performance anxiety.

Class Performances

Performing For Each Other

As early as the second week, begin dividing the class into two groups to have them perform for each other. Because students are just beginning to learn new songs and dances, this process can be introduced after one chorus of a song has been learned. For example, if the goal is to learn the first chorus of a song, students can be divided into two groups that sing for each other with observers listening to see whether they understand the words. By introducing this method as soon as any part of a song or dance is familiar, students can begin to (1) experience performing for others, (2) learn how to accept constructive criticism, (3) learn that perfection is not the goal, (4) understand that mistakes are part of the learning process, and (5) learn how to recover from mistakes so as not to bring attention to themselves. Due to its importance in preparing students for their initial performance before an audience, having groups perform for each other should be done as often as possible.

Look upon the inevitable setbacks that you face as being temporary, specific and external.

As students begin to perform for each other, it is important that they support each other with positive responses (i.e., applause and compliments). Then when staff feel they are ready, ask performers to critique each other with one or all of the following methods:

- **Self-Critique.** Ask each person to give one positive statement about his or her performance by saying: "What did you do well?" This process can be followed by asking: "How could you improve your performance?" *Avoid* comments that could be interpreted as critical (i.e., "What did you do wrong?" or "Did you make any mistakes?").
- **Group-Critique.** To prepare for this procedure, write where all can see the following questions: "Did you understand the words?" Did most of the performers hold their heads up?" "Did they dance in time to the music?" "Did anyone smile?" "Did dancers demonstrate good posture?" "Did they perform with energy and enthusiasm?" "Did they look at the audience?" Remind students that this is a group assessment and to avoid criticizing individuals.
- **Anonymous Critiques.** If staff feel it would be helpful to use an anonymous process rather than one that requires openly expressing an opinion before others, have students write their comments on paper, and then hand them to an instructor. Using this method provides staff with the option to screen out criticisms that may be hurtful.

Note #2: Introduce props and other costume pieces early in the rehearsal process (i.e., hats, canes and boas). It is amazing how just a few of these items can excite, motivate, and energize performers.

Video Recording

Video recording early in the rehearsal process offers opportunities for students to:

- Critique their performances.
- See how others see them.
- Realize the importance of smiling, looking at the audience, staying together and maintaining a high energy level.
- Check their progress and see how they are improving.
- Appreciate the results of their hard work.

Note #3: Be certain that students have signed a photo and video release form (Appendix B).

Note #4: Try to video all performances for feedback at the next rehearsal.

Performances Before Small Audiences

Stage 1: In-House

As soon as a few acts have been learned, a brief performance before a few staff members or other students is recommended. The acts do not have to be "show ready," but may be billed as a "work in progress." In fact, cue cards are recommended to lessen anxieties and boost self-confidence. This performance before the smallest of audiences is especially important because it is the first step in helping performers confront and handle the inevitable nervousness that accompanies any appearance before others.

> **Remember that it is impossible to learn and grow and become a successful person without adversity and difficulties.**

Note #5: This event also offers an opportunity to administer the pre and post self-evaluations (Appendix B).

Stage 2: Preview

About 6 weeks into rehearsals, a preview performance can be held for friends and family members. The audience should be small, and the performance can take place in the rehearsal facility. For this event, students should wear as much of their costuming as possible; however, no makeup or sets are necessary. To reduce fear of forgetting lyrics or dance steps, the use of cue charts is recommended.

Note #6: This event also offers an opportunity to administer the pre and post evaluations.

Stage 3: In the Community

Between the 9th and 11th weeks, a performance before a small community audience can be beneficial in preparing students for their first appearance before a large audience. This performance should be before a group that will be supportive and appreciative of the performers' efforts; for this reason, a hospital, retirement facility or senior center is recommended. This event is helpful not only to the performers but to the stage crew as well because "traveling" with a show requires a great deal of planning and preparation. It is not necessary to present the show in its entirety, but at least 30 minutes are suggested.

Note #7: These events also provide opportunities to administer the pre and post-performance evaluations.

Dress Rehearsal-Performance

Usually held 1 or 2 days before opening night, the dress rehearsal performance offers the opportunity for rehearsing at the show site before a larger audience. Invitations for this event may be extended to groups of individuals from special populations (physical, developmental, and psychiatric disabilities), senior citizens, and support groups (families, mental health organizations). This is also an excellent opportunity for the performers to invite families and friends. Moreover, it is important that, following this performance, the students and audience have a chance to socialize

Keep your thoughts on your goals and dreams, on the person you are becoming.

so the performers can hear from their friends and family members how well they performed and experience the feelings of satisfaction from a job well done.

Note #8: Be sure that everyone associated with the show receives a written schedule with a time line of the activities for opening night.

The Big Show!

Those who have experienced the excitement (and sometimes chaos) of an opening night know the importance of being organized down to every last detail. When producing a show involving people whose anxieties are very high, it is more important than ever that the process, from pre-show to post-show, proceeds as smoothly as possible. It is at this event that the role of the stage manager becomes especially important because he or she is responsible for seeing that each act is ready to enter on time and that staff are available to deal with any last-minute crises. To this end, the guidelines in Chapter 7 have been created to assist the reader in producing a show that will be a memorable event for both performers and their audience.

Note #9: Every effort should be made to make a video recording of this performance with complementary copies available to performers.

Case Example 7: "Ellen"

When Ellen joined Theatre Extraordinaire the company was 1 month from its annual public performance at a local performing arts center. For someone diagnosed with a severe anxiety disorder, it would seem that she was placing herself in an impossible situation, especially because she had a fear of appearing before an audience of any kind. But determined to overcome the challenge ahead and, despite her anxieties, she attended rehearsals right up to the day of dress rehearsal. However, it was then that she informed staff she was having second thoughts about performing. When offered the opportunity to help backstage rather than perform, she decided to think about it. After changing into her costume and participating in a dance warm-up session, she walked around the theatre doing deep breathing exercises and talking with fellow cast members. As a result, she found that others were as nervous as she. Encouraged by the support of her peers, Ellen told herself there was no turning back. Later, upon making her entrance for the opening number, she experienced "total panic," worsened by the sight of some friends in the front row. Then the applause began. Almost instantly Ellen felt her anxiety begin to decrease. Afterward she told the author that the unexpected and surprising support from the audience played a major role in getting her through the show. When asked how she felt about her performance, Ellen said she had "always felt like she was in a shell, but when performing she could feel parts of that shell falling away," stating further: "One of the biggest highlights of my life was walking out on that stage." At a later time, when interviewed by a local reporter, Ellen stated it was the staff giving her permission to not perform that relieved some of the anxiety she was experiencing. "They (staff) said, 'You know, you don't have to do this if you don't want to'–but I got on stage and I performed. I got hooked!" Today Ellen will tell anyone it was On Stage! that helped her learn to control her performance anxiety to the point where she now is able to speak in front of hundreds of people about her mental illness.

The Cast Party

Whether it is a picnic at a park, a potluck at a private home, or dinner at a restaurant, a cast party to celebrate a successful show opening is a must! When this event will take place depends on the number of performances scheduled; however, this writer recommends that it be held as soon as possible so cast members have the opportunity to celebrate their success and view a video of their performance. In the meantime, staff should be preparing to discuss the following at the next rehearsal:

- How performers are feeling now that the major event is over. Because some cast members may experience the "post-performance doldrums," a natural let-down after a big show is over, it is important to process these feelings, assuring the cast that it is not unusual to feel down after experiencing the "high" from such a successful event.
- The positive effects that the show experience has had on performers' lives. A plan for future activities that will help performers look forward to the next project.

In summary, the importance of an organized and structured approach to reducing performance anxiety is critical, especially for people with disabilities. By participating in simulated performances early in the rehearsal process, cast members can begin to desensitize themselves to the inevitable anxieties associated with performance and develop the confidence and coping mechanisms necessary for each succeeding performance experience.

Chapter 5

MUSIC, COGNITION, AND RECOVERY

ONE LIFE AT A TIME

Melanie was of preschool age when diagnosed with autism, a label that sent her to a mental health institution for children and from there to a state psychiatric hospital. Because atypical psychotropic drugs were not available at that time, she exhibited no signs of improvement for several years, spending her days sitting in a catatonic-like state and never leaving her ward. Due to her lack of progress, the medical team held little hope for her recovery, determining she would be hospitalized indefinitely. Then Clozaril, a new antipsychotic drug, was introduced as a breakthrough treatment for schizophrenia and, subsequently, given to Melanie. Still, it took several years of treatment before any signs of improvement became apparent. When she finally responded and began, for the first time, talking and interacting with others, there was, indeed, a call for celebration. However, having been institutionalized most of her life, she had no training in social skills and other coping mechanisms, significantly limiting her ability to move forward in her recovery.

It seemed, then, that little in Melanie's life would ever change–that is, until a new psychiatric technician, "Jonathan," was assigned to her ward and took an interest in her. He began by talking with Melanie in an attempt to establish a relationship, gradually seeing changes in her behavior. Then one day, to everyone's surprise, Melanie asked for an ice cream cone. While to the reader such a simple request may not seem like a monumental event, it was, indeed, a call for celebration, for here was a person who had been hospitalized for decades with no trips into the community. So Jonathan asked her if she would like to go into town with him to get the cone. At first Melanie refused the offer, so he asked her to think about it. When he returned the next day, Melanie had decided to accept his invitation. Still, there was one major step to take before this trip could be made: permission from the treatment team. Although hesitant at first, the team eventually gave its approval and the trip was on. Thus, for the first time in more than 20 years, Melanie left her ward and the hospital grounds and travelled with Jonathan into town. Much to everyone's surprise, the excursion was very successful as Melanie presented no problem behaviors while thoroughly enjoying her ice cream cone. This event marked the beginning of a journey that would eventually lead Melanie to the On Stage! recovery program.

Shortly thereafter, Jonathan transferred to a case management position at a residential treatment center in the community, thus suspending his work with Melanie. He had been working in his new job for about 3 months when a new treatment approach was introduced into the county's mental health system, one that provided intensive treatment for persons hospitalized with a severe mental illness. So when the treatment team asked for referrals to this new program, Jonathan recommended Melanie. After receiving the team's approval, he was authorized to spend time with Melanie as part of a plan to see if she could be considered for community placement. To begin this process, he invited Melanie to visit him at his workplace, hoping to interest her in living there. What followed was a series of five visits over 30 days, beginning with 2 hours and eventually resulting in an overnight stay. In the meantime, Jonathan heard about On Stage! and, knowing how she loved to sing, felt the program was a perfect fit for Melanie.

After observing how well Melanie was doing on her visits, Jonathan invited her to attend the summer session of the "Introduction to Musical Theatre" class sponsored by On Stage!. He felt that if Melanie could complete a short class of 6 weeks, it would indicate she had the potential for pursuing further activities that would support her recovery. Consequently, Melanie completed the class and then re-enrolled in the course again in the fall, this time for 12 weeks. Once again, she surprised everyone by her regular attendance and her determination to learn the dance routines. At the end of the course, a "Graduation Celebration" was held in which the class performed for a small audience and certificates of completion were distributed. It was at this event that Melanie gave a performance that to this day is still remembered, especially by those who thought Melanie would never leave the hospital.

It happened like this. It was a December event. The program had begun and all was going as planned when suddenly, quite spontaneously, Melanie walked to center stage, grabbed the microphone, and began singing and dancing to Jingle Bell Rock. Needless to say, everyone was surprised and excited to see Melanie, seemingly unafraid and confident, performing before an audience with complete abandon. What a joy! The audience, in awe of what they had witnessed, clapped and cheered as she completed her performance and accepted a Certificate of Completion from her instructors.

Melanie's On Stage! Outcomes

When Melanie was referred to On Stage!, she had not made the transition into community living. However, within 2 weeks of enrolling in the "Introduction to Musical Theatre" class, she was invited to live at the residential center. Fearful at first, she was hesitant to leave the safety of the hospital and those who had cared for her for so many years. However, 2 weeks later and 1 month after enrolling in the On Stage! class, she told Jonathan she would like to live at the residential facility. Although the treatment team approved her discharge, it was not without some naysayers who were convinced that Melanie would never be able to handle the transition. Yet, the changeover went very smoothly, with Melanie exhibiting none of the fears usually experienced by others during this process. Today, she continues to live at her community home and, to the amazement of all concerned, has never been re-hospitalized.

So what contributed to Melanie's successful recovery journey? In a subsequent discussion the author had with Jonathan, it was determined that Melanie's progress can be attributed to:

- The actions of Jonathan, whose advocacy for and relationship with Melanie was responsible for the hospital's special attention to this patient.
- Melanie's On Stage! experience, where she had, for the first time in her life, the opportunity to develop social skills, improve her self-confidence, learn to work with others, and express herself in a process that fostered her creativity through her love of music.

- The supportive environment of On Stage! that provided a safe place for Melanie to learn new skills, preparing her for transition into the community.
- The participation of Jonathan in the introductory class. (He actually danced with the class!) Because he was able to attend the rehearsals and was an active participant, he not only offered the support Melanie needed to stay motivated but also served as a role model for her and other students.

For those who still believe that people with the most severe of mental illnesses cannot be integrated into the community, remember Melanie and heed the valuable lesson in this story: *When the circumstances are right, all it takes is one person to change the life of someone just waiting for the chance to be all he or she can be.*

MUSIC, COGNITION AND RECOVERY

> –virtually for all of us, music has great power, whether or not we seek it out, or think of ourselves as particularly 'musical'. This propensity to music–this musicophilia'–shows itself in infancy, is manifest and central in every culture, and probably goes back to the beginnings of our species.
>
> –Oliver Sacks

MUSIC AND LEARNING

Story 7: Einstein and the Violin

When the parents of Albert Einstein were told to take their son out of school because trying to teach him was a waste of school resources, they knew their son was not "intellectually challenged." So instead of sending him to a vocational school, as suggested, they bought him a violin, an event that, according to Einstein, turned out to have a life-long influence on his career. In fact, a friend of Einstein said Einstein figured out his problems and equations by improvising on his violin. Specifically, Einstein expressed how he felt about music in the following quote: "If I were not a physicist, I would probably be a musician. I often think in music. I live my daydreams in music. I see my life in terms of music–I get most joy in life out of music" (O'Donnell, 1999).

Knowing of Einstein's interest in music, one can only imagine what his reaction would have been had he known exactly how his music was affecting the cognitive and emotional processes in his brain. Considering his own experience, it seems he would have been anxious to discover just how music helped him in his quest for solutions in the challenging world of physics. To this end, he may have been quite surprised to learn that:

- Music training in early childhood can enhance verbal, visual-spatial, and verbal-temporal skills (American Music Conference, 2007; Forgeard, Winner, Norton, & Schlaug; Neville et al., 2008; Rauscher, 2003), and can affect general auditory attention and memory in both children and adults (Stanford University Medical Center, 2007; Trainor, Shahin, & Roberts, 2009).
- "The brain grows in response to musical training the way a muscle responds to exercise" (Minton, 2008), thus contributing to enhanced plasticity of the brain. The importance of this factor in brain development and its relevance to cognitive rehabilitation is noted in an article by Hyde et al. (2009), when the authors suggest that "long-term intervention programs can facilitate neuroplasticity[16] in children, and could be of "particular relevance to children with developmental disorders and to adults with neurological diseases."
- Music affects the whole brain. According to neuroscientists, the brain has no "music center" (Institute for Music and Neurological Function, 2009; Sacks, 2007; Tramo, 2001), because no matter where they looked in the brain, "researchers have found evidence of the power of music to affect neural activity" (Minton, 2008). These findings are further supported by Levitin (2006) in his book, *This Is Your Brain On Music,* in which he states: "Music listening, performance and composition engages nearly every area of the brain that we have so far identified, and involves near-

16. Neuroplasticity or brain plasticity is the brain's natural ability to form new connections in order to compensate for injury or changes in one's environment.

ly every neural subsystem." It would seem, then, that as researchers continue to discover new ways that music affects cognition, the future offers endless possibilities for discovering innovative music interventions to aid in cognitive recovery.

- Music education heightens the ability to think ahead, a valuable skill in problem solving. According to a study conducted by the University of California at Irvine, "students who used (math) software and played the piano–were able to leap ahead several steps on problems in their heads," offering the possibility of a "potentially powerful teaching tool" (American Music Conference, 2007). Indeed, the benefits of the ability to think ahead can be applied in many aspects of daily living, especially in the area of performance where thinking ahead, whether in a dance routine or a classroom presentation, can mean success or failure.
- Baroque music, specifically that composed by Mozart, may have a significant effect on brain development and learning. However, there seems to be uncertainty among researchers regarding this issue (Margulis, 2008), although some studies have shown positive results in the enhancement of spatial-temporal reasoning (Jausovec, Jausovec, & Gerlic, 2006; Suda, Morimoto, Obata, Koizumi, & Maki, 2008). Addressing this dilemma, Rauscher (2000) conducted a study where the findings suggested that further research on this subject is warranted "not only for its theoretical importance, but also for its potential practical implications, especially in education." On a personal note, this author finds that when engaged in activities requiring intense concentration (such as writing) that the steady tempo, simplicity of harmonies, and soothing predictability of baroque music enhance the level of concentration on the task at hand.

Teaching music is not my main purpose. I want to make good citizens. If children hear fine music from the day of their birth and learn to play it, they develop sensitivity, discipline and endurance. They get a beautiful heart.
(Shinichi Suzuki)

- Music can be used to treat brain disorders, including traumatic brain injury, stroke, Parkinson's and Alzheimer's diseases, cerebral palsy, and autism. Treatment is administered by board-certified music therapists and by music therapists specializing in Neurologic Music Therapy. Accordingly, the results of using music in rehabilitating physical traumas and brain disorders have been significant, with a wide range of studies noting the important role that rhythm plays in the rehabilitation process (Music Therapy, 2009; Neurologic Music Therapy, 2009; O'Donnell, 1999; Rathbun, 2001; Schulman, 2008; Watson, 2009; Van de Winkle, Feys, & Weerdt, 2004). Furthermore, even music listening alone can "enhance cognitive recovery and prevent negative mood" during the early stages of a middle cerebral artery stroke (Sarkamo et al., 2008).

- Music can improve cognitive functioning in people with a serious mental illness, especially those with schizophrenia. (This issue is addressed in a later section of this chapter.)

Story 8: King George and the Power of Music

One shining example of the power of order in music is King George I of England. King George had problems with memory loss and stress management. He read from the Bible the story of King Saul and recognized that Saul had experienced the same type of problems that he was experiencing. George recognized that Saul overcame his problems by using special music. With this story in mind, King George asked George Frederick Handel to write some special music for him that would help him in the same way that music helped Saul. Handel wrote his *Water Music* for this purpose–One cannot deny the power of music. High school students who study music have higher grade point averages than those who don't. These students also develop faster physically. Student listening skills are also improved through music education–The top engineers from Silicon Valley are all musicians. Napoleon understood the enormous power of music. He summed it up by saying: "Give me control over he who shapes the music of a nation, and I care not who makes the laws" (O'Donnell, 1999).

In summary, the effects of music on learning and cognitive rehabilitation have heightened the interest of researchers, clinicians, and educators. Consequently, studies supported by organizations such as the

Institute for Music and Neurologic Function[17] and the Americans for the Arts[18] have revealed how music can enhance learning by improving attention, limiting distractions, and directly affecting changes in brain chemistry and structure. Knowing this, professionals involved in cognitive rehabilitation have implemented the use of music to improve cognition in individuals who have experienced a traumatic brain injury or disorder or are facing cognitive challenges due to a mental illness. Yet despite extensive research on the effect of music on cognitive recovery, there is little information on the role the performing arts can play in building cognitive skills in people with a serious mental illness. Therefore, it is the intent of this chapter to contribute to existing knowledge an innovative psychosocial approach to improving cognition. Although the conclusions presented here are based primarily on clinical observations, the author feels the effect the performing arts have on cognition warrants consideration for future research.

COGNITIVE SKILLS AND SERIOUS MENTAL ILLNESS

> New findings suggest that music can stimulate complex cognitive, affective and sensorimotor processes in the brain, whose functions can be generalized and transferred to non-musical therapeutic purposes.
>
> –Neurologic Music Therapy, 2009

Cognitive rehabilitation has been used to treat people with a wide range of neurological disorders for decades. The use of this approach is well documented, known for its effectiveness in improving a person's capacity to process and interpret information and improve functioning in all aspects of family and community. However, cognitive rehabilitation has yet to be recognized as a treatment of choice in mental health treatment, although, according to Silverstein and Wilkness (2004), it is

17. The Institute for Music and Neurologic Function works to advance research on the emerging scientific effort "to draw on music's power to help retrieve lost and compromised function." In this effort, the Institute "advances research collaborations with outstanding investigative scientists and biomedical researchers, and in clinical research with physicians, music therapists, musicians, and other professionals" (Institute for Music and Neurologic Function, 2009).

18. Americans for the Arts is a nonprofit organization "dedicated to representing and serving local communities and creating opportunities for every American to participate in and appreciate all forms of the arts" (Americans for the Arts, 2009).

"becoming an increasingly popular intervention–for people with schizophrenia," but the "evidence based on its effectiveness is not impressive."

Fortunately, the lack of evidence regarding its effectiveness has not discouraged the development of alternative cognitive rehabilitation approaches for people with a serious mental illness. Created to produce more successful outcomes than in the past, these alternatives include: giving more attention to psychosocial treatment and social learning-based behavioral rehabilitation,[19] considering environmental factors (structure and stability in housing), and paying more heed to the successful use of cognitive rehabilitation with traumatic brain injury (Brooks, 2008; Carter, 1999; Heinssen, Lieberman, & Kopelowicz, 2000; O'Carroll, 2000; Silverstein & Wilkness, 2004). Additionally, researchers have stressed the need to "move away from focusing rehabilitation efforts on isolated cognitive processes and toward efforts to integrate cognitive activity" (Silverstein & Wilkness, 2004), and to develop interventions that combine both cognitive and social rehabilitation approaches (Corrigan, Mueser, Bond, Drake, & Solomon, 2009). In other words, instead of focusing on the remediation of one cognitive skill, identify a social activity favored by the service user in which both cognitive and social skills are remediated simultaneously. This approach not only integrates cognitive and social processes but also addresses a critical issue: holding the person's interest for an extended period of time. For instance, a person with schizophrenia with a long-term memory deficit and low level of motivation may be willing to work on improving his or her memory if the learning process is incorporated into an activity of interest (i.e., a card game requiring retention of information or memorization of lines in a play). Thus, considering the research supporting its importance, integrating cognitive and social rehabilitation approaches justifies careful consideration when planning cognitive interventions.

According to Revheim and Medalia (2004), cognitive rehabilitation is important in affecting positive recovery outcomes and overall community functioning. Knowing this, it seems that more attention needs to be paid not only to improving cognition in general, but also to en-

---

19. Social learning-based rehabilitation (social skills training) "consists of learning activities utilizing behavioral techniques that enable persons with–disabling mental disorders to acquire independent living skills for improved function in their communities" (Kopelowicz, Liberman, & Zarate, 2006).

hancing social cognition[20] through skills training and psychosocial rehabilitation (Corrigan et al., 2009; Horan, Kern, Shokat-Fadai, Sergi, Wynn & Green, 2009; Kopelowicz, Liberman, & Zarate, 2006; Spaulding, Reed, Sullivan, Richardson, & Weiler, 1999; Vaskinn, Sundet, Hultman, Friis, & Andreassen, 2009). Furthering the importance of this issue are studies that have found up to 75% of individuals with schizophrenia were significantly affected by deficits in attention-concentration, memory, motor skills, executive function,[21] spatial awareness[22] and intelligence (Elvevag & Goldberg, 2000; Katz, 2005; O'Carroll, 2000; Palmer, 2000; Pradhan, Chakrabarti, Nehar & Mankotia, 2008). These findings indicate a critical need for paying more attention to the remediation of these deficiencies, particularly because other researchers claim cognitive impairment in people with schizophrenia is the core of this disorder (Bowie & Harvey, 2006; Elvevag & Goldberg, 2000; Herbert, Metzer, Park, & Kessler, 1999; Pradhan, Chakrabarti, Nehra, & Mankotia, 2008). Pursuing this further, it is known that the effect of poor cognition upon people with psychiatric disorders other than schizophrenia, can significantly interfere with recovery. In fact, several researchers found that: people with bipolar disorder exhibited cognitive challenges similar to those with schizophrenia, although to a lesser degree (Pradham, Chakrabarti, Nehra, & Mankotia, 2008); individuals with major depression can have difficulty in several areas of cognition, including memory, psychomotor functioning, attention and verbal fluency (Harvey, 2007; Vicebech, Clemmensen, Egander, Rasmussen, & Rosenberg, 2002); and people with severe anxiety disorders, i.e., obsessive-compulsive disorder, can be challenged with verbal and non-verbal memory deficits (Segalas, Alonso, Labad, Jaurrieta, Real, Jiminez, et al., 2008).

Knowing the prevalence of cognitive deficits across the spectrum of psychiatric disorders, the need for effective rehabilitation methods is apparent. Consequently, Corrigan et al. (2009), developed an innovative psychosocial approach to cognitive recovery that is described in their latest book. In the chapter on cognition, the authors stress the

---

20. Social cognition is a mental process describing how people process social information, specifically, perceiving and interpreting information, emotional information, emotional processing, and social perception.
21. Executive function describes the way information is controlled and processed, helping to connect past experience with present action when planning, organizing, creating, and performing.
22. Spatial awareness is an awareness of the body's position in space.

importance of the role cognitive skills play in recovery, emphasizing the need for research focusing on cognitive interventions leading to social integration (2009). While acknowledging that some research has suggested current methods have been effective, the authors express their concern regarding a critical aspect of any rehabilitation approach: the generalization of newly acquired skills to every day living:

> What research has failed to find is that improvement in these measures (attention, memory, executive function) is related to change in real-world phenomena linked to a person's life goals. We believe that the future promise of cognitive rehabilitation rests with this latter issue. As rehabilitation researchers and providers use the methods outlined here, they need to evaluate their impact on a person's ability to work, live independently, develop relationships, and perform other activities basic to key life goals." (Corrigan et al; 2009)

Clearly then, the evidence for seriously considering cognitive rehabilitation for individuals with a serious mental illness is compelling. Most importantly, since combining current methods with social skills training has proven to be effective, especially for those with schizophrenia, it would seem that every effort should be made to include this training in cognitive recovery programs. To this end, a SEIR program strives to provide interventions that address the issues raised by Corrigan et al. How the SEIR approach addresses this need is described in the following section.

COGNITIVE SKILLS, FUNCTIONS AND SEIR SKILL-BUILDING ACTIVITIES

> Science has not found a specific 'music center' in the brain because the ways in which the brain processes music is complex. We do know that music affects our neurological, psychological and physical functioning in such areas as learning, language processing, emotional expression, memory, physiological, and motor responses.
>
> –The Institute for Music and Neurological Function

In an article on cognitive impairment and traumatic brain injury (TBI), Gerry Brooks (2008), Director of Brain Injury Programs at the Northeast Center for Special Care stated: "Art, dance, music, theatre and writing workshops–may have a unique appeal. The arts are fun and engaging and can produce uniquely high levels of cognitive and physical challenges, personal satisfactions and self-esteem." This quote speaks to the important role the arts can play in improving cognition of individuals with TBI. Consequently, because the goals of cognitive rehabilitation for TBI are often similar to those for treating people with schizophrenia and other psychiatric disorders, should the arts not be considered as having the same or similar effect on people with cognitive challenges related to their mental illness? Researchers studying the effects of music on cognition would probably give an affirmative answer to this question, especially those practicing neurologic music therapy whose specialty is cognitive rehabilitation. In an article about this field of practice, it is stated: "New findings suggest that music can stimulate complex cognitive, affective and sensorimotor processes in the brain, whose functions can be generalized and transferred to non-musical therapeutic purposes" (Neurological Music Therapy, 2009). In accordance with these findings and the potential of the performing arts to promote cognition, this author proposes that performing arts activities can promote cognitive skill building in five areas: (1) attention/concentration, (2) memory, (3) executive functioning, (4) motor skills, and (5) spatial awareness.

Before proceeding further, it is important to remember that cognitive skills do not function in isolation but are integrated to perform a specific task. For example, putting a jigsaw puzzle together requires the ability to concentrate, select and pick up specific puzzle pieces, and use visual-spatial skills when placing a puzzle piece in its correct position. In the same way, learning and performing dance routines involves the integration of all five cognitive skills described above. With this in mind, it is not difficult to understand how a SEIR program, with its psychosocial-based approach, can play an important role in promoting cognitive recovery. Consequently, it is anticipated that the information in this section will generate some ideas for exploring the role that the performing arts can play in cognitive recovery. To this end, a section on

Music is motivating and fun, helping people feel good about themselves by promoting confidence, risk-taking, self-esteem and self-discipline.

Figure 5

Cognitive Skills, Functions, and SEIR Interventions

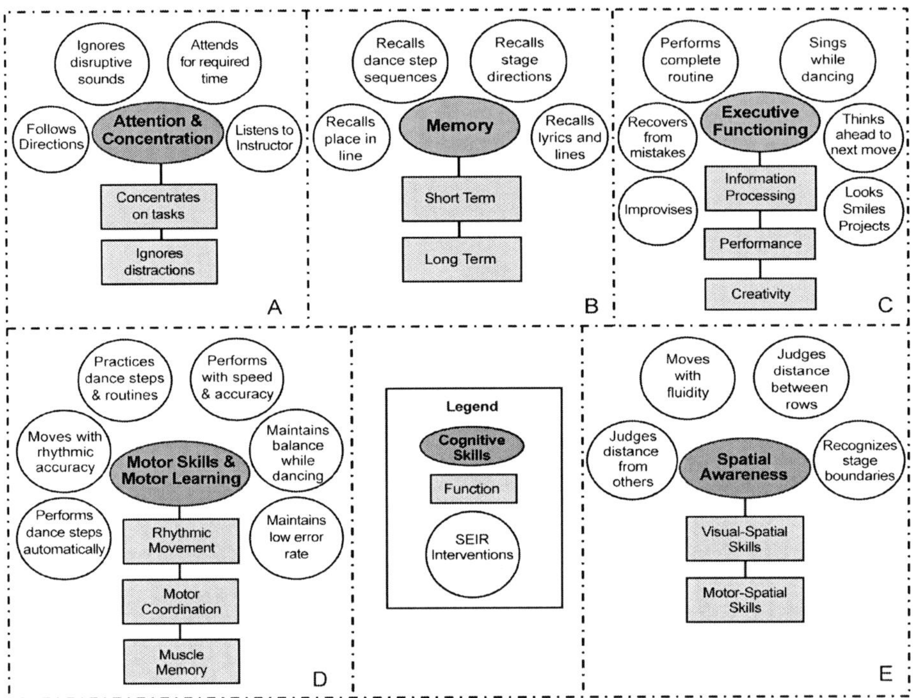

Figure 5. Cognitive skills, functions, and SEIR interventions.

each of the five cognitive skills identified in Figure 5 follows, along with nine "points to remember" found in the sidebars throughout the narrative (Americans for the Arts, 2009; Music Therapy, 2009; National Association of Independent Schools, 2009).

Attention and Concentration

When trying to define "attention" and/or "concentration," it will be found that these two words are often used interchangeably. For example, in general usage, "attention" is defined as the act of concentrating, whereas "concentration" is described as paying attention. However, some researchers in the mental health field have divided the term "attention" into several categories, as in *selective attention, sustained attention,* and *divided attention* (Elvevag & Goldberg, 2000), whereas others may combine attention with concentration. Because the author believes there is a distinct difference between "attention" and "concentration" when applied to people with psychiatric disabilities, she has chosen to use the definitions of Elvevag and Goldberg, reworded for the purpose of this discussion as follows:

- Attention (Selective): a conscious effort to focus the mind on a single object or thought for a brief amount of time.
- Concentration (Sustained Attention): a conscious effort to attend to a task for an extended amount of time.

Selective and Sustained Attention.

Of the cognitive deficits caused by a severe mental illness, three of these–attention, memory, and executive function–are recognized as presenting significant barriers to recovery. Accordingly, most researchers are in agreement that the remediation of attention deficits should be the first to be addressed, for both memory and executive function requires the ability to attend. Thus, this discussion focuses on remediating attention deficits in two categories: selective attention and sustained attention.

Inattention by someone with a psychiatric disorder can be caused not only from the chemical imbalances in the brain but also by external circumstances such as medication side effects and/or preoccupation with personal matters. To illustrate: A student with bi-polar disorder may exhibit symptoms associated with the manic phase of the illness (hyperactivity), a person with an anxiety disorder may find it impossible to concentrate due to extreme worry over an upcoming event; and an individual with major depression may lack the energy and motivation it takes to focus on any assignment. Then there is the student with schizophrenia whose difficulty with attention and concentration can be more disabling than people with other psychiatric disorders, thus diminishing involvement in many activities. Consequently, until they can increase their ability to attend, progress toward recovery will be extremely difficult.

Music promotes focus of attention and reduces distractions.

SEIR Interventions

Because the acquisition of attention skills is foundational to overall cognitive functioning, one of the primary goals of a SEIR program is to offer opportunities for the remediation of this most important skill. To this end, students become involved in activities focusing on two goals: increasing the ability to focus on an assigned task and reducing distractibility. These goals are achieved as students participate in classes and rehearsals where they learn to listen carefully to instructions and concentrate on following directions while ignoring distractions (Figure 5A). Further, for students interested in joining a SEIR musical theatre company but whose attention skills would interfere with their performance, enrollment in an "Introduction to Musical Theatre" class is recommended. This class can be especially helpful to those struggling with specific attention problems because the curriculum is divided into activities of 10 to 15 minutes in duration. For example, the frequent change from a brief seated activity to one of requiring movement can help students with limited attention spans successfully complete an assigned task. This achievement, while seemingly a minor one, can be an important step toward helping students develop the confidence and motivation needed to sustain interest and participation in the program. Finally, once they have completed the class and demonstrated an improvement in their attention and concentration skills, students have the opportunity to join the theatre company.

Case Example 8: "Ken"

Road Signs: Reflections of a Life

Loneliness is the vehicle you drive through life,
Which is the road leading in the direction of yourself.
The road signs are the dreams of your spirit,
Sometimes hard to read when you are going too fast.
Just slow down a little, stay on the road,
And soon you will see what the road signs really meant.
Then you remember the route for the next time
When it seems you end up starting all over again.

This verse above was written by Ken, a member of the On Stage! theatre family for 8 years. When the author met him for the first time, he was living in a group home and seemed to have progressed as far as possible in his recovery from schizophrenia. Struggling daily with voices and sounds in his head and the side effects of his medications, he had difficulty finding activities that would help him effectively cope with the symptoms of his disability. He did have one area of interest, however: He loved to sing. So when hearing about a new program called On Stage! and its performance opportunities, he enrolled in the "Introduction to Musical Theatre" class, the beginning of an exciting journey that would play a significant role in his recovery. Subsequently, within a short time, both staff and his family noticed changes in Ken's behavior. In addition to an improvement in self-confidence, his attention skills also began to improve, especially his ability to manage and cope with distractions from his voices. Aided by the characteristics of the music (rhythm and structure) that helped him to attend to his assigned role, Ken learned to focus on the task at hand, becoming less and less distracted by his hallucinations. His great sense of humor enabled him to laugh as he described the "wind going through my head." It was this humor plus a very positive attitude that made Ken an ideal candidate for membership in the On Stage! theatre company. When asked how On Stage! had made a difference in his life, he replied: "I get home every day from the rehearsals, and I think, 'Wow, this is great!" I'm doing something productive–My energy level is always really high."

Memory

It is a well-established fact that most people with schizophrenia are affected by a wide range of cognitive deficits. Of these, memory (short and long term) has been identified, not surprisingly, as one of the most important (O'Carroll, 2000). Accordingly, studies on the effects of remediation on memory impairment in people with schizophrenia have shown that cognitive rehabilitation can result in improved verbal memory that lasts over time (Fiszdon, Silverstein, Buchwald, Hull, & Smith, 2003) as well as overall

Music is organized sound whose rhythms have a powerful effect on cognition.

improvement in memory impairment (O'Carroll, 2000; Kurtz, Seltzer, Shagan, Thime, & Wexler, 2007). These studies and others have described several rehabilitation approaches utilized to improve memory functioning, including computer-assisted cognitive remediation (Kurtz et al., 2007), errorless-learning (Mulholland, O'Donoghue, Meenagh, & Rushe, 2008), psychosocial rehabilitation (Musser, Bond, Drake, & Sullivan, 2000; Corrigan, 2009) and occupational therapy (Katz, 2005). Additionally, O'Carroll (2000) reported that "patients who were receiving atypical antipsychotic medication appeared to benefit most from cognitive remediation, suggesting that such a combination treatment may be optimal," an idea that could further enhance memory functioning. Thus, it seems that an approach to cognitive remediation utilizing the performing arts, combined with one or more of the aforementioned interventions, could only heighten the chances for improving long- and short-term memory. In this regard, the author describes below the conditions and activities that support this premise.

SEIR Interventions

The author believes there are two elements of music that contribute to memory improvement in service users involved in performing arts activities. The first, *enhanced emotional well-being,* considers the role that music plays in reducing stress, thus helping students have fun while learning lyrics and dance routines. For example, in her SEIR programs, the author used vocal warm-ups to help students relax and have fun by combining body movements with vocal exercises performed to rhythmic and energetic music. Similarly, dance warm-ups were designed not only to energize students but to promote laughter and camaraderie as well. In all of these activities, performers were encouraged to be less self-critical, laugh at their mistakes, and practice eliminating negative self-talk. In particular, if some students were having difficulty with coordination in a hand jive routine, they were taught two important lessons: It takes practice to master a new skill, and the goal of any activity or performance is to do the best one can, not to obsess over being perfect. As students began learning these lessons, they started to relax and have fun. Moreover, for those with a fear that

> **Rhythm and repetition assist in internalizing sounds.**

there is not enough time to learn all that is required, anxieties were usually reduced when staff assured performers there was adequate time to learn, encouraging everyone to redirect their energies into achieving daily goals rather than worrying about the future. At the same time, performers were introduced to another crucial concept: There is no such thing as a mistake in performance. Thus, the stress from trying to be perfect is reduced, and the learning process made more enjoyable. After all, when people are having fun, it should not be surprising that memorization is no longer a formidable obstacle but a challenge to be met with a determination to succeed.

The second element of music enhancing learning and memory is the *effects of music on improved cognition* (Figure 5B). First to be considered is how short- and long-term memory are enhanced by a step-by-step learning approach focused on success. As each task is broken down into small, achievable steps, students are often surprised at how quickly they learn. Then as short-term memory improves, so does self-confidence, resulting in performers' believing in their ability to learn even greater amounts of material. Consequently, students find they are able to remember not only lyrics, lines, and dance routines, but positions on stage as well. Finally, motivated by their success and new-found confidence in their ability to memorize, performers will approach the next memory challenge knowing they will be successful and ready for the next performance.

Executive Functioning

Executive functioning, described in *Webster's Dictionary* as "the brain's ability to process feedback, interpret events and react appropriately to life's ups and downs," encompasses a wide range of skills, including planning, organizing, and paying attention to and remembering details (information processing). For many people with a psychiatric disability, the lack of skills required to function at this level can present a serious barrier to recovery. For example, a service user with schizophrenia who did not graduate from high school may wish to pursue obtaining a General Education Diploma (GED). However, unless he or she is able to organize a notebook, plan a schedule, or write a paper, attaining that diploma will be nearly impossible. Yet another person may desire to enroll in a vocational training program but is prevented from doing so because he or she has difficulty in following directions and retaining information. Thus, the persons in these examples face challenges requiring cognitive interventions to help them overcome the negative effects of these specific cognitive deficits.

SEIR Interventions

Service users who enroll in a SEIR musical theatre company are challenged with activities that involve an even higher level of cognitive functioning than those required in the aforementioned examples. As indicated in Figure 5C, the author proposes that in order to successfully execute a song and dance routine, performers must acquire skills in information processing, performance, and creativity. The same diagram identifies activities that develop the skills leading to improved functioning in these three areas, all requiring the ability to process information. Specifically, performers learn to: improvise (creativity), recover from mistakes (creativity), perform complete dance routines (performance), sing while dancing (performance), think ahead to the next move (planning), and look and smile at the audience while projecting their voices (performance). Once learned, performers will have gained the skills that not only lead to a successful performance but also can generalize to their everyday living activities.

Although asking a person with schizophrenia or another psychiatric disorder to learn all that is required to successfully perform a complex dance routine may seem an unrealistic request, it is not. Why? Because the SEIR rehearsal method with its success-oriented approach provides the support and time needed for each performer to practice and learn all that is required. During this process, performers are simultaneously developing several cognitive functions without having to think about any one function in particular. For example, performers who are working on improving their memory may be unaware that, while learning a four-step dance sequence, they are also improving their spatial and motor skills and ability to think ahead–all of this in one single activity that engages many of the cognitive skills incorporated into information processing. Similarly, other performers may be learning to

Music stimulates both hemispheres of the brain, encouraging bilateral activity and causing both intellectual and emotional responses.

recover from mistakes without calling attention to themselves, not realizing they are learning to improvise, a skill that prepares for unexpected incidents on or off the stage. Clearly then, a SEIR program with its innovative approach can play a significant role in improving these most important executive skills.

Of the three executive functions promoted by SEIR activities, information processing and performance are unquestionably the most challenging because a successful performance relies on the ability of the performer to effectively process information acquired from previously learned cognitive skills. For instance, dancers must recall (memory) lyrics and dance steps while recognizing the correct distance from each other within designated stage boundaries (spatial awareness). Then, while processing all of this information, they must remember to look at the audience, smile, and project their voices, challenging tasks for the experienced performer and significant ones for people with a serious mental illness. Yet despite all there is to learn, SEIR performers will succeed because the program's step-by-step learning approach allows them to experience frequent success. Subsequently, these successes give cast members the confidence they need to continue working toward a winning performance.

Music expresses and inspires a wide range of emotions and fosters creativity.

Finally, the third function developed in an SEIR performing arts activity is that of creativity, enhanced by improved self-confidence, recognition of talents and abilities, and development of improvisational skills. First, inexperienced SEIR students are given opportunities to develop the confidence and ability needed for self-expression, a quality necessary for connecting emotionally with their audiences. Next, those who feel they have no creative ability or are hesitant to share a given talent, due to a lack of self-confidence or fear of criticism, will find they are in a supportive environment where self-expression is fostered and encouraged. Last, performers learn to improvise and continue performing despite any missteps because improvisation and recovery from mistakes are two skills crucial to the success of any performance. Although it will take time, eventually performers learn that when on stage, "there is no such thing as a mistake."

Although research into the effects of music on remediation of executive function is not extensive, interest in this area of study seems to be broadening. In particular, a study by Thaut et al. (2009), used percussion instruments to improve executive function (mental flexibility) in brain-injured patients. According to these authors, it is possible that the changes in brain activity were influenced by "the inherent temporal structure in music and musical tasks (that provide) strong, self-regulatory and self-organizational constraints that cue and exercise reasoning, decision making, problem solving and comprehension processes in real time." Indeed, these findings provide a meaningful clue to the role that music and the performing arts can play in remediating executive functioning deficits. Thus, knowing the role they play in recovery, developing executive skills warrants the attention of those involved in planning cognitive interventions. These skills are critical to the success of a stage performance as well as the progress toward recovery.

Motor Skills and Motor Learning

Motor skills and motor learning are both cognitive skills basic to everyday normal functioning. The first, the ability to perform complex muscle and nerve acts producing movement, has two subcategories: fine motor skills utilized for fine motor movements (i.e., picking up a pencil) and gross motor skills required for executing gross motor movements (i.e., performance of jumping jacks). The second, motor learning, is defined by Fitts and Posner (1967) in a three-stage model. The first, the cognitive stage, "can be used to guide motor behavior" and is characterized by a high error rate. In the second, the associative stage, the person begins to experience a more successful performance. Finally, the autonomous stage involves movement that is automatic where the movements are consistent, coordinated, and smooth.

Although most people may find the execution of motor skills and motor learning relatively unchallenging, people with psychiatric disabilities, especially those with thought disorders, can have a great deal of difficulty performing the simplest movements. Consider, for example, the motor and planning skills involved in executing a dance sequence of more than two steps. In the first place, simply learning each step separately can be difficult for those with poor motor skills and motor coordination.[23] That challenge, coupled with the need to think ahead to the next step, can present a significant barrier to a successful

23. Motor coordination refers to the coordination of movements, usually between different subsequent parts of the same movement or movements of several body parts.

performance of the entire dance sequence. Certainly, considering the role that good motor skills and motor planning play in daily living, there should be no question as to the importance of including these skills in cognitive rehabilitation interventions.

SEIR Interventions

The origin and indicators of deficits in motor skills and motor planning have been identified in studies reporting that psychomotor planning deficits are often found early in people with schizophrenia (Grootens et al., 2009). Moreover, when diagnosing this disorder, motor coordination and the inability to perform more than two components in a motor sequence are indicative (Delevoye-Turrell, Giersch, Wing, & Danion, 2007; Schiffman et al., 2009). Knowing this, it may be helpful to consider the work of Schmidt and Weisberg (2000) when planning a cognitive rehabilitation intervention. These authors proposed that motor learning and motor performance can be divided into two distinctive processes: an *unobservable internal process* (motor learning) and *observable representation* (motor performance). How these two processes can be applied to the learning of a dance routine is illustrated in Figure 5. Specifically, when SEIR students are learning new dance steps, they will *practice* the moves repeatedly (observable behavior) in order to commit them to *memory* (unobservable behavior). Later on, *memorization* of the dance sequences will manifest itself in the *performance* of the new steps (observable behavior). Then, as these dance step sequences are learned, performers can focus mastering the ability to think ahead to the next move, an important motor planning skill strongly influencing the successful performance of the complete dance routine. These motor learning and motor performance processes are illustrated in Figure 6.

Combining song and movement significantly enhances learning.

When considering the complexity of the cognitive functions just described, it is not difficult to understand why some persons with a mental illness can require a lengthy step-by-step learning process to master a complete dance routine. For instance, a simple instruction such as "March in time to the music" can be difficult for a person with poor motor coordination who seems to be "marching to his or her own drum-

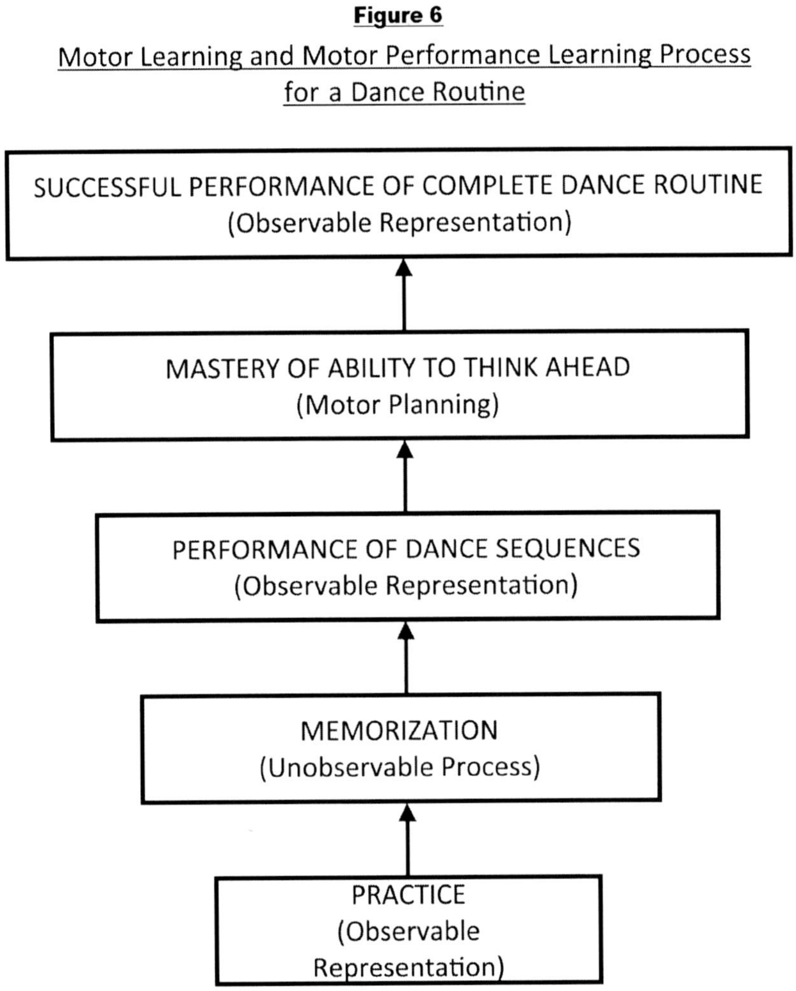

Figure 6. Motor learning and motor performance learning process for a dance routine.

mer." This task can be especially challenging to those with schizophrenia, who must simultaneously process listening to music and moving accurately to its rhythm. However, by using the SEIR learning approach, students can work toward developing, simultaneously, the three cognitive functions identified in Figure 5D: rhythmic accuracy, balance, and muscle memory. For example, by marching in place to a specific rhythm, students develop the first two of these functions (along with their listening skills) by moving to a rhythmic beat and maintaining their balance. Then, when learning dance sequences and routines, students develop the third function, muscle memory, a kinesthetic phenomenon occurring after repeated practice over an extended period of time. This function, achieved through practice regimens focusing on many repetitions of each dance sequence, results in performance at a mastery or an automatic level. Moreover, while performers are working diligently to master each routine, their learning is enhanced by the positive and supportive environment present in each and every SEIR activity.

Certainly, the success this writer has achieved in using her method for improving motor skills in people with a serious mental illness underscores the effectiveness of the SIER approach and the important role that music can play in promoting the development of motor skills and planning. Therefore, the author proposes that, when designing interventions to remediate deficits in these and other cognitive skills, the suggestions of Schmidt and Weisberg can serve as a reminder to keep the learning process focused on helping service users achieve success, one step at a time.

Spatial Awareness

> The connection between points in space or time can be simple or complex. It can be between oneself and the environment or between two or more objects outside of oneself.

In the previous quote, the authors were describing the meaning of "position-in-space" (Stockdale & Possin, 2009), a general term used to define spatial awareness. When further describing this cognitive function, the authors identified two types of spatial skills; visual-spatial and motor-spatial. The first, visual-spatial skills, is the ability to perceive the spatial relationship between objects or persons in one's field of vision. The second, motor-spatial skills, is the capability of moving the body accurately and smoothly through space. To illustrate, students in a high school marching band use their visual-spatial skills to judge the distance between themselves and others. At the same time, these performers employ the second type of spatial awareness, motor-spatial skills, as they move with fluidity from one step to the next. This example highlights the important role that spatial skills play in any activity requiring movement and knowledge of one's position in space. Knowing this, remediation of spatial deficits in persons with a mental illness warrants serious consideration when planning cognitive interventions.

So what type of behaviors would be exhibited in a person with deficits in spatial skills? In the light of this inquiry, consider these two instructions: "Please form two rows" and "Do the best you can to move smoothly from Step A to Step B." Both requests are simple enough, one would think. After all, what is so difficult about forming two lines or making a smooth transition from one step to the next? The answers to these two questions are found in understanding the struggles that people with schizophrenia encounter when trying to execute a dance routine. For instance, some performers with deficits in visual-spatial skills will find it difficult to visually judge the distance between themselves and those standing next to them. Moreover, there is a high probability that people with motor-spatial deficits will find it challenging to move effortlessly and gracefully from one move to the next. So, knowing that many persons with disabilities, especially those with schizophrenia, are affected with poor spatial skills, one can better understand how deficiencies in spatial awareness presented a significant challenge to SEIR dancers as they struggled to find order amid an environment that was both cognitively demanding and highly stressful.

SEIR Interventions

A SEIR program offers numerous activities promoting improvement in spatial awareness. Specifically, Figure 5E identifies four skills developed during the execution of a dance routine that aid in the remediation of two cognitive functions: visual-spatial and motor-spatial skills. Three of these, judging the distance from others, judging the distance between rows, and recognizing stage boundaries, contribute to the enhancement of visual-spatial skills. Then, during warm-up exercises, performers learn the fourth skill, moving with fluidity, as the rhythm of the music helps students develop the ability to smoothly transition from one move to the next. Later on, when rehearsing dance routines, performers have the opportunity to incorporate the skills learned in these exercises into dances that improve both their visual- and motor-spatial skills. There is no doubt, of course, that mastery of these skills takes time. However, suc-

Music is often based on patterns and mathematical relationships, giving it structure and form as well as predictability.

cess is possible when both performers and instructors have the patience and determination to persevere.

Summary

Cognitive deficits in people with a mental illness, especially those with schizophrenia, have been established as a serious deterrent to recovery. Knowing this, cognitive rehabilitation programs have been developed to remediate these deficits, the most effective seeming to be a psychosocial approach that includes social skills training. A SEIR program incorporates this method by offering many opportunities for cognitive skill-building along with activities that improve social skills. Specifically: attention and concentration are improved as the structure of music helps students focus and learn to ignore distractions; short- and long-term memory are developed in a step-by-step learning approach promoting success; executive skills are improved in activities requiring information processing and learning to perform many tasks simultaneously; motor skills and motor learning are ameliorated in exercises and dances focusing on improved coordination, fine and gross motor skills, and the ability to think ahead to the next move; and, finally, visual- and motor-visual spatial skills are enhanced in activities that teach students to move with fluidity and visually judge the distance between themselves and others. Further, while engaged in these cognitive-building activities, students develop their social skills in an environment promoting cooperation, camaraderie, peer support, self-esteem, and self-efficacy, all leading to an improved quality of life.

As researchers continue to explore innovative approaches to cognitive rehabilitation for people with psychiatric disorders, particular interest is being focused on the findings of neuroscientists who have studied the effects of music on the brain, demonstrating the potential for using music in cognitive recovery. These findings, along with the promising results from other research, will hopefully encourage the further pursuit of new approaches that not only emphasize cognitive recovery but include social skills training as well.

Chapter 6

STIGMA REDUCTION AND THE PERFORMING ARTS

ONE LIFE AT A TIME

"I want to be a producer"–I can still see and hear David as he stood center stage, belting out that song from *The Producers.* Or the time he joined another company member to sing the title song from *Cabaret.* Or his appearance as Joe the Bartender in a roaring 20s spoof as he sang *Set 'Em Up, Joe.* For, you see, David has many talents–actor, singer, and comedian. Put him on a stage and immediately you can see he is doing what he loves most, entertaining–a truly remarkable man who has overcome the many challenges he has faced as a person with schizophrenia.

David began to experience symptoms of his disorder when in elementary school and was hospitalized for the first and only time in 1973. As he struggled in his early school years to deal with academic challenges, he also had to endure bullying behavior from his peers. On top of everything, he was told he would never graduate from high school, "but I did!" "When someone told me I couldn't do something, I'd do it!" he asserted. This positive, can-do attitude proved to be a valuable asset as he faced daily the discrimination and stigma associated with his mental illness. Then he was told he would never work a day in his life–"but I did!" Accordingly, he tells of his first paying job in the 1980s as a paper carrier, and now how he works, and has for years, at the Spokane County Fair. When asked why he likes working at the fair so much, he says he enjoys seeing so many different kinds of people and that, after observing those with severe physical disabilities, he has learned a valuable lesson: "There is always someone a lot worse off than I am."

David was enrolled in Supported Education Enhancing Rehabilitation (SEER), a supported education program located on a local community college campus, when he heard about On Stage! in 1996. Needless to say, he did not hesitate to enroll in this new program, joining Theatre Extraordinaire, thus marking the beginning of a successful 10-year run with the company. He brought with him his performing experience that included appearances as a stand-up comedian in a local comedy club, membership in a theatre group called the *Open Door Players,* and partipation as a chorus member in *Three Penny Opera* at the Spokane Civic Theatre. However, when he enrolled in On Stage!, he had not performed for a long time and was far from the same person you would meet today.

Shy, introverted, and slow to learn, at On Stage! rehearsals, David would isolate himself from his peers by sitting at the far edge of a semicircle where he would busy himself writing in his notebook. (When asked what he was writing, he said he wrote science fiction stories as a hobby.) He would speak only when spoken to, seldom participating in group discussions. In addition to this lack of social skills, David did not take constructive criticism well, frequently reacting defensively and arguing with the instructor. He would sometimes arrive at a rehearsal angry and frustrated due to an incident on the bus or elsewhere, a behavior sometimes justified but frequently due to his paranoid thoughts. Additionally, he found it difficult to hold his head up and maintain good eye contact when dancing or singing. In contrast, he had some positive characteristics that helped him eventually integrate into the company: a good sense of humor, a friendly personality, a determination to learn, a high level of commitment–and a love of performing.

David's On Stage! Outcomes

Although recovery for David was a daily challenge as he struggled with the symptoms of his disorder, he worked hard to concentrate, stay focused, and improve his social skills. Yet from the beginning of his On Stage! experience, he proved to be an asset to the theatre company, due not only to his talent, but also to his work ethic and commitment to the program. His diligence really paid off. After a few months in the program, David began to demonstrate progress in his stage performance, behavior, and self-confidence. His determination to learn the many dance routines eventually resulted in his placement in the front line. Gradually his eye contact and posture improved, although remembering to keep his head up and look at his audience was always a challenge. He also began to joke with staff and peers, responded in discussions with humorous comments, initiated conversations, demonstrated insight into his and others behavior, reacted to constructive criticism without becoming defensive, and worked more cooperatively with others. Further, his tendency toward self-criticism changed from a resistance to try something new to "I can do that!", a modification in behavior resulting from an improved self-confidence and self-esteem. These changes were reflected in his comments that appeared in a newspaper article regarding an upcoming show in which he stated, "People might think, 'He can't do this.' I say, 'Yes, I can! Just sit back, and relax. You're here to have fun.'"

Overall, David made remarkable progress in his recovery during his tenure with On Stage!, progress that has generalized to his daily living activities 3 years after the discontinuation of the program. After leaving the theatre company, he became active once again in the Evergreen Club, a clubhouse that provides vocational training for people with a serious mental illness. Although prior to his On Stage! experience he was not enrolled in a specific training program, as of this writing he is working in the thrift store as a cashier. When asked how On Stage! helped him in his recovery, he stated he is less introverted, more social, and more interested in and concerned about other people. When reflecting on David's progress from his first rehearsal to his final performance, the lyrics from a show tune come to mind: *"It's not where you start, it's where you finish. It's not how you go, it's how you land!"*

A HISTORICAL PERSPECTIVE

> Individuals with serious mental illnesses do not have a "life adjustment problem" but rather a primary brain disease–They do not need to 'face the world' but rather to become part of the world.
>
> –Torrey, Erdman, Wolfe and Flynn, 1990

Story 9: Stigma Busting

It was curtain time at the eighth annual public performance of Theatre Extraordinaire. The place, the Bing Crosby Theatre in Spokane; the theme, *Fascinating Rhythm*; the excitement backstage, electric;

> the performers, nervous but energized. For at last that much-anticipated moment had finally arrived, ready or not. As the theme song began, the adrenalin was on full power when the cast "hit" the stage. The audience was amazed, especially those seeing this theatre company for the first time. Gone were those stigmatized ideas regarding people with psychiatric disabilities, stereotypes "blown away" by what was unfolding on that stage. Then, at the finale, amid thunderous applause and a standing ovation, cast members experienced once again the inevitable exhilaration that comes from yet another successful stage performance. Further adding to the cast's excitement of the moment was the knowledge that all those weeks of hard work had paid off in still another way: Many people in the audience would leave the theatre with a changed attitude and new perspective on how they would think about and relate to persons with a serious mental illness.

In an article on the relationship of stigma to self-esteem, the authors defined stigma as "–social-status loss and discrimination triggered by negative stereotypes that have become linked in a particular society to a particular human characteristic such as mental illness" (Link, Struening, Neese-Todd, Asmussen, & Phelan, 2001). This definition clearly describes the stigma that has been, for generations, a major barrier to recovery for people with psychiatric disabilities. Providing perspective to this issue is an article on mental illness in ancient Greece where Simon (1992) describes how stigma and mental illness have been connected for more than 2,000 years, and how these ancient attitudes and views can still be seen in Western culture today. Moving forward in history, Hinshaw and Cicchetti (2000) describe how, even as treatment became more humane, economic restrictions resulted in the establishment of asylums in the 16th and 17th centuries, where patients were treated as less than human and blamed for their afflictions. Then in the latter part of the 19th century, state institutions were built to accommodate the mentally ill with the intention of improving treatment; but again, lack of funding, government neglect, and stigma led to deplorable living conditions and mistreatment (Hinshaw & Cicchetti, 2000). Indeed, there seemed to be little hope for the residents of these institutions or anyone with a psychiatric disorder.

Then, fortunately for all concerned, there were reformers who strove diligently to change the direction of mental health treatment. One of these was Dorothea Dix, whose compassion for the mentally ill and tireless campaign for reform, beginning in the mid-19th century, resulted in the erection of many state hospitals and improvements in existing ones (Bowers & Hughes, 2009). Yet her efforts were later thwarted by unforeseen circumstances and the prejudices and stereotypes about mental illness that continue to persist even today. Therefore, it should not be surprising that these negative attitudes still exist due to their long-established roots (Knight, Wykes, & Hayward, 2006). Considering this historical perspective, it should not be difficult to understand why reducing a stigma so well engrained in the public psyche continues to be a major challenge. Furthermore, these stereotypes continue to persist despite the efforts of family and other advocacy groups to educate the public. In the meantime, service users struggle to regain self-respect, independence, and a place in society. So what is the answer? What strategies can be implemented that have not yet been tried?

Of course, there is no "magic bullet" or "fast fix" when it comes to changing long-established and persistent attitudes. However, in this writer's opinion, part of the answer lies in finding a way to let the general public know more about the potential and accomplishments of people with a mental illness. After all, how often is there a newspaper article or television story about a service user who is making a successful recovery by becoming employed or obtaining a college or vocational degree? Certainly, the answer is obvious: "very seldom." Nevertheless, changes in attitude are possible not only if the media could be persuaded to inform the public about the achievements of service users, but also if there were more opportunities for the public to interact with people with psychiatric disabilities in activities designed to eliminate stereotypes. (Gaebel & Baumann, 2003). Consequently, it seems that more attention should be paid to developing stigma-reduction programs that include both of these approaches. To this end, an example of how these approaches can be incorporated into a recovery program is included in this section. However, before proceeding, the author provides an overview of how the stigma associated with mental illness is perpetuated by the public, the media, mental health professionals, families, and, most important, service users.

THE PUBLIC AND THE MEDIA

> Media advocacy is a part of a strategy to exert pressure on those whose decisions influence an environment. It uses the mass media appropriately, aggressively and effectively to support the development of public . . . policies.
>
> –Wallack, Dorfman, Jernigan, & Themba, 1993

People with a mental illness are continually coping with a public whose misunderstanding of their brain disorders results in negative attitudes and behaviors (Berge & Ranney, 2005; Corrigan & Penn, 1999; Corrigan & Watson, 2002; Garske & McReynolds, 2005). Moreover, these negative perceptions can lead to the public perceiving service users as lazy, uneducated, unemployable, responsible for their own illness, and, perhaps the most devastating of all, people to be feared (Corrigan & Watson, 2002; Link, Struening, Rahav, Phelan, & Nuttbrock, 1997; Link, Phelan, Bresnahan, Stueve, & Pescosolido, 1999). Contributing significantly to these negative stereotypes is the media and the effects its portrayal of mental illness has on the public (McNulty, 2004) and, as a result, could possibly have on public policy.

Further underscoring the importance of the media's role in influencing the public's perception of mental illness, a survey conducted by the Robert Woods Johnson Foundation in 1990 identified the mass media as the most common source of public information about psychiatric illnesses (Wahl, 2003). Accordingly, at a symposium on stigma and discrimination, Wahl (2001) expressed his concern regarding how Americans "obtain their view of the world through movies, television and the news media," stating that "the perpetuation of–exaggerated stereotypes of mentally ill people reinforces culture-wide stigmatization." At this same event, Wahl (2001) emphasized that even though people with psychiatric disabilities commit violent acts at the same rate as the general population, "80 to 90 percent of people with a mental illness never commit a violent act."

It is important to understand that we are faced with recovering, not just from mental illness but also from the effects of being labeled mentally ill.
(Deegan, 1997)

Another negative consequence of the media's portrayal of people with a mental illness is the effect it can have on public policy. In an article on newspaper coverage of mental illness, Wahl, Wood, and Richards (2002) suggested that fears fueled by the media can lead to the perpetuation of stigma, lowered support for community care, employers' resistance to hire people with a mental illness, and easy permission for involuntary commitment. In the same study, the researchers found that relatively few stories are written on the accomplishments of service users, and when they do appear, the tendency is to emphasize dysfunction and disability. Considering the results of the aforementioned study and others, it should not be surprising that headlines sensationalizing any violent act by a "mentally ill person" often result in the assumption by the public that all people with a mental illness are violent only because they are labeled mentally ill (Mental Health Works, 2009; Lichtenstein & Peoples, 2003; Link, Phelan, Bresnohon, Stueve, & Pescosolido, 1999).

In further pursuit to identify ways in which the media perpetuates stereotypes, a study on themes and messages about mental illness in newspapers found dangerousness to be the most dominant theme, causing concerns about how the public views mental illness (Wahl, Wood, & Richards, 2002). Other researchers conducted surveys on how the words "schizophrenia" and "schizophrenic" are used in newspapers as metaphors when describing events and behaviors completely unrelated to a psychiatric disorder (i.e., "the weather is schizophrenic"), concluding that the misuse of this particular psychiatric terminology encourages stigmatization and can cause individuals to avoid seeking treatment (Chopra & Doody, 2007; Corrigan & Rusch, 2002; Duckworth, Halpern, Schutt, & Gillespie, 2003). Indeed, after seeing their opportunities for recovery obstructed not only by poor self-esteem but also by the stereotypes placed on them by the media and, consequently, the public (Wright, Gronfein, & Owens, 2000), it is not difficult to understand how service users can become discouraged and demoralized, feeling there is little hope for recovery.

ADVOCACY FOR CHANGE

> We look forward to the day when prevention and education, not metaphor and demonization, are the dominant messages carried to the public by the news media. (Duckworth et al., 2003)

All is not gloom and doom, however. Advocacy groups from both the public and private sector have been effective in challenging stereotypes and the negative attitudes so prevalent in today's society. For example, the National Alliance for the Mentally Ill (NAMI) has been successfully fighting the damaging stigma toward mental illness, making significant inroads educating media corporations (Corrigan & Penn, 1999; Lefley, 1989; NAMI, 2006). The result of NAMI's work is reflected in the production of films portraying people with a mental illness in a more positive light, a major breakthrough and a welcome change from movies of the past. Other national organizations focusing on public education and stigma reduction include the National Mental Health Association, the National Stigma Clearinghouse, and the Center for Mental Health Services, a government agency with an office on consumer empowerment (Corrigan & Penn, 1999).

In a unique approach to advocacy from the private sector, Connecticut Heritage Productions (CHP) used the performing arts to educate their audiences. With funding from a government agency along with a grant from a private foundation, CHP produced a series of one-act plays focused on educating people about recovery from mental illness and substance abuse (Connecticut Heritage Productions, 2007). This collaboration demonstrates how two organizations, although diverse in origin, can effectively work together to address the critical need to reduce the stigma associated with mental illness and related disorders. Additionally, grass-roots theatre companies comprised of service users have launched stigma-busting campaigns throughout the country and the world (Noble, 2005; Schizophrenia Daily New Blog, 2009). However, little is known about many innovative advocacy groups that are, no doubt, active throughout the country. In an effort to identify some of these, a survey was conducted resulting in the recognition of several organizations that have been successful in raising the public's awareness of mental illness and its realities (Estroff, Penn, & Toporek, 2004). One of these, the Central Iowa Players Stigma Busters Drama Troupe in Des Moines, Iowa, was recognized as exemplary in its efforts to reduce stigma:

> Performances consist of funny, dramatic, sometimes poignant, scenes covering a wide range of events from the players experiences as clients of the mental health system–We are a theatre group, not a therapy group. It just happens that some of the side effects are therapeutic. We work hard at perfecting our craft, mirroring the world as we see it, and as it sees us. Our results are powerful and real–We touch a lot of people–we put a face to mental illness. (Estroff, Penn, & Poperek, 2004)

Hopefully, surveys similar surveys will be conducted so more of these groups are identified, their efforts publicized, and training programs made available to help communities implement programs of their own.

Thus, the work continues with an ongoing effort to engage the media in public education campaigns. Although it can be difficult to interest editors and producers in writing or broadcasting positive stories about people with a mental illness, it is not impossible. For example, during the 7 years that this writer was executive director of Project Arts in Phoenix, Arizona, the program was featured in several newspaper articles and television broadcasts. These stories usually included interviews with service users who willingly shared their recovery experiences in an effort to reduce the stigma associated with their disorders. Additionally, the media in Salem, Oregon featured similar stories during the time the author's musical theatre company performed in the Salem-Portland area.

So what accounted for the media's interest in these programs? The author feels there were three primary reasons. First, no program of its kind existed in the Pacific Northwest. Second, the willingness of service users to disclose their disorders in a public forum was especially meaningful, giving readers/listeners opportunities to change their attitudes about mental illness. Finally, the way in which the performers were presented to the public was unique. Namely, whereas most theatre groups focus on educating the public by dramatizing mental health issues (i.e., stigma), the author's theatrical productions purposely avoid this approach. Consequently, the presentation of cast members in a normalized environment familiar to the public offered audiences the opportunity to witness the talents, strengths, and abilities of the performers. Frequently, after observing service users in performances with community volunteers, some attendees found their stereotyped attitudes changing significantly. As was so often heard following a performance: "I couldn't tell the volunteers from the other performers!"

A further example of how the media can play an active role in eliminating stereotypes is illustrated in the comments of a columnist for the *Spokesman Review* in Spokane. After visiting an On Stage! rehearsal, he wrote in a column titled "Talent, Courage a Must to Join Those On Stage!":

> Okay, I'll admit it. I went to the rehearsal expecting a train wreck. I was infected with some of the prejudice and fear many harbor toward the mentally ill. It's easy to marginalize these people, easier still to expect the worst. I was the one out to lunch. The dozen or so cast members gathered inside a Spokane church basement blew my boots off. They segued through a half-dozen song and dance numbers with heart, soul and quite a bit of polish. I wasn't embarrassed. I was moved. (Clark, 2003)

The responses of this reporter and others mentioned above illustrate how members of the press and the television industry have the opportunity to significantly change the attitudes of the public. The importance of this issue is addressed in an article by Lamb (2009), in which the author states: "–the strengths of persons with SMI must be perceived and valued–opportunities must be created to apply and make visible these competencies in ways that will reach the general public. By becoming more familiar with service users, reducing fear, and correcting misperceptions, stigma can be reduced." To this end, by portraying people with a mental illness in ways that highlights their achievements and progress toward recovery, the media could be a powerful force in eliminating the stereotypes and prejudices associated with psychiatric disorders.

From another perspective, an article appeared in a Spokane newspaper about a group of citizens working hard to see that the graves of patients buried long ago in a cemetery at Eastern State Hospital are identified with headstones, an effort to show "there is no shame to mental illness." One member of this group commented: "This is not about the dead. This is about the living" (Merryman, 2009), a message intended to emphasize the importance of eliminating long-held stereotypes and the shame so often experienced by service users and their families. Yet despite the efforts of this small group of citizens and many advocacy organizations, a great deal more needs to be done before stigma becomes less of a barrier to recovery.

PROFESSIONALS AND FAMILIES

> When you hear a mental health professional say that someone is low functioning, say to yourself, "That person is not low functioning. It's just that the mental health worker has failed to discover and value the gifts and special talents of that person." (Deegan, 1997)

Although the primary focus of stigma reduction is on educating the public, there are two other populations often not considered as problematic: professionals and families. For example, studies have found that too many professionals have stigmatizing attitudes toward their patients/clients and mental illness in general (Lauber, Anthony, Adkacic-Gross & Rossler, 2004; Lauber, Nordt, Braunschweig, & Rossler, 2006; Van Dorn, Swanson, Elbogen, & Swartz, 2005; Wahl, 1999). It is particularly disturbing that often these professionals do not understand the potential of their own clients, seeing them as less competent and incapable of reaching higher goals (i.e., attending college) (Wahl, 1999). Psychiatrists, in particular, have stigmatizing attitudes similar to the general public and should "at least improve (their) knowledge about stigma" (Lauber, Anthony, Adkacic-Gross, & Rossler, 2004). Overall, mental health professionals must improve their stigmatizing attitudes toward their clientele if they are going to significantly promote recovery in the people they serve (Corrigan, 2004; Gaebel & Baumann, 2003; Maio, 2004; Sadow, Ryer, & Webster, 2002). Clearly, then, knowing the role that mental health professionals could play in stigma reduction, it is time to give more attention to this issue when designing stigma-reduction campaigns (Link, Struening, Rahav, Phelan, & Nuttbrock, 1997).

Negative attitudes toward people with a serious mental illness affect not only the behavior of mental health professionals but families as well. Larson and Corrigan (2008), in an article on families and stigma, identified three stereotypes associated with family stigma: blame (poor parenting skills), shame (due to blame), and contamination (close association with stigmatized person). As a result of these conditions, family members experience decreased self-esteem, damaged family relationships, denial of the illness, and failure to seek help for ill family members due to "fear of stigmatization" (Wahl & Harman, 1989). Additionally, seeing their family members suffer from discrimination can further the frustration and sense of hopelessness already prevalent in the family unit. However, attitudes can change when families have the opportunity to observe their family members achieve success in a program that builds self-confidence, self-esteem and a sense of self-worth.

Story 10: "Project Culture": Talents Unplugged

It was in a most unlikely place for a stage production–a place with bars on the doors and windows and guards on duty 24 hours daily. It was within this restrictive environment that I agreed to produce a variety show with patients on the Psychiatric Secure Unit (PSU) in Oregon State Prison. With funding from Project Culture, a national effort to bring culture into the prison systems, it was my first task to convince the guards that the production of a show was indeed possible. I will never forget the initial meeting with the unit's employees, for the first question asked was: "How do you know there is enough talent on this unit to do a show?" I answered them by saying there were talents hidden in many of their patients that no one had ever seen because the opportunities to observe them were never presented. To demonstrate, I asked for the piano to be placed in the dayroom and the men assembled for our first meeting.

And so it began. As everyone gathered in the area of the piano, I began to play some popular tunes of the day. Watching carefully to see if any of the men were responding to the rhythm of the music, I noticed a young man leaning forward in his chair, listening intently. Soon he was at the edge of his seat, seeming to want to be nearer to the piano. When asked if he would like to play, his response was immediate and enthusiastic. Jumping from his chair, he sat at the keyboard and began playing. And play he did! His music was fast, intense, and filled with emotion, playing in the style of Jerry Lee Lewis, the famous rock n' roller from the 1950s. His performance created a feeling of excitement in his audience and, needless to say, a look of amazement on both employees and patients. From that day forward, there seemed to be no doubt in anyone's mind that something very exciting was happening, and that the show would go on!

MENTAL HEALTH SERVICE USERS

Individuals receiving mental health services can find their recovery efforts held back by not just one but three types of stigma. The first, general stigma, is the negative responses by the public toward any person with a mental illness, reactions that have "the potential to worsen the course of the illness" (Gaebel & Baumann, 2003; Gaebel, Zaske, & Baumann, 2006). The second, perceived stigma, is the belief by service users that, because they have a mental illness, they will be devaluated and discriminated against by most people and may even be too embarrassed to seek mental health treatment (Alonso et al., 2009; Knight, Wykes, & Hayward, 2006; Sirey et al., 2001). In other words, even though service users may not have directly experienced general stigma, they may believe, even expect, to be discriminated against just because of their mental illness. The third type, self or internalized-stigma, is the "devaluation, shame, secrecy, and withdrawal triggered by applying negative stereotypes to oneself" (Corrigan, 1998). Experiences from this type of stigma can result in many harmful effects that may include the following: a feeling of alienation from society, lowered self-esteem, unemployment, reduced psychiatric medication compliance, increased levels of positive symptoms, fewer social relationships, a sense of hopelessness, and a failure to seek treatment, all leading to significant interference with life goals and quality of life (Corrigan, 2004; Corrigan & Watson, 2002; Fung, Tsang, Corrigan, Lam, & Cheng, 2007; Hopper, 2007; Lysaker, Roe, & Yanos, 2007; Lysaker, Davis, Warman, Stasburger, & Beattie, 2007; Ritcher, Otilingam, & Grajales, 2003; Ritcher & Phelan, 2004). On the other hand, not all service users allow generalized stigma to inhibit their recovery. In fact, "some individuals are energized by prejudice and express righteous anger. Others neither experience lowered self-esteem nor become righteously angry; instead these individuals seem to ignore the effect of public prejudice altogether" (Corrigan, Mueser, Bond, Drake, & Solomon, 2009). It would seem, then, that because service users' own attitudes toward their disorders can play an important role in their chances for recovery (Corrigan & Rusch, 2002; Turkington & Siddle, 2000), a more aggressive approach is needed to help people with psychiatric disabilities deal with the debilitating effects of internalized stigma.

To summarize, people with a mental illness must confront daily the many negative results of stigma, whether from the public and the media, professionals and families, or from the effects of stigma upon themselves. Although the efforts of advocacy groups have yielded some significant results, there still remains a great deal to be done to eliminate the stereotypes and debunk the myths associated with mental illness. Consequently, it will take the efforts of individuals and groups at all levels, working together, to find innovative approaches to stigma reduction (Hinshaw & Cicchetti, 2000). To this end, the next section discusses briefly some interventions used to reduce stigma, along with a description of how three of the author's programs played a significant role in educating the public and others about mental illness.

STIGMA INTERVENTIONS

> Encouraging creative activities by users, such as art, theatre performances and poetry, and bringing these into the public arena, is a way of improving the attitudes of the public and enabling users to feel valued. (Leff & Warner, 2006)

Judging by the pervasive stigma that continues to be associated with mental illness, attempting to educate the public has yet to have a significant impact on eliminating stereotypes (McNulty, 2004). Thus, the struggle to find an effective way to reduce stigma continues. To this end, according to Larson and Corrigan (2008), advocacy groups have used three approaches–*protest, education,* and *contact*–in their efforts to educate the public. Of these three, personal contact was found to produce the most successful outcomes, especially when it:

1. Fostered interactions between persons with mental illness and the public.
2. Occurred in a setting where neither group is dominant over the other.
3. Involved cooperation and interdependence in working toward shared goals.
4. Involved informal contact among all participants, allowing everyone to become better acquainted.
5. Invalidated, through group interactions, negative stereotypes and beliefs about one another (Baron & Byrne, 1997; Larson & Corrigan, 2008).

Furthermore, it was found that the positive effects of personal contact are the most likely to maintain over time (Larson & Corrigan, 2008). Consequently, whether stigma is general, perceived, or internalized, innovative methods with a focus on personal contact are critically needed to destigmatize mental illness. To this end, it is the author's intent that the program examples described below and the information in Part Two will be helpful to those interested in starting similar public education performing arts programs where personal contact plays a significant role in reducing the stigma associated with mental illness.

PERFORMING ARTS INTERVENTIONS

> I've had several people tell me how much they enjoyed your production. It was definitely community involvement at its best!
>
> –Michael Smith, Manager of the Bing Crosby Theatre, commenting on an On Stage! production

When the author first began developing performing arts recovery programs, the primary intent was to offer service users experiences that would focus on improving self-confidence, an important first step toward recovery. However, as the author soon discovered, her programs offered a great deal more than originally intended. Not only did they provide a unique approach to recovery, but performances by her theatre companies proved to be an effective way to change the public's attitude toward mental illness by reducing stigma and eliminating stereotypes. How these changes occurred is described in the three performing arts recovery programs founded by the author. In each of these, the five conditions described earlier and evidenced to be the most effective in promoting stigma reduction (Baron & Byrne, 1997) worked in conjunction to achieve the outcomes described below:

1. **Fostering interactions.** "Contact is more effective when the participants are seen as equals, when contact is intimate (one on one), and when people work together in a cooperative rather than a competitive manner" (Estroff, Penn, & Toporek, 2004). This statement speaks to the benefits of positive interactions that are fostered during the production of any show requiring participants to interact with each other as cast members or backstage personnel. For example, in the On Stage! shows,

volunteers who were cast members rehearsed with service users, providing support and encouragement for those having difficulty learning their parts. Additionally, there was usually a stage left and a stage right manager staffed by a community volunteer who worked closely with cast members to be sure they were ready for their entrances. Working together in this way fostered interactions among all participants in a positive and productive manner.

2. **Promoting Equalization.** The success of any show involving volunteers would not have been possible if service users felt they were being dominated by someone from the "outside." Fortunately, this was never an issue in the author's shows, because her volunteers had no desire to "be in charge" or tell service users what to do. At the same time, service users were told to refrain from correcting or directing any cast member in order to avoid personal conflicts and disruption of the rehearsal process. On the other hand, production suggestions from participants were encouraged with the understanding that they were to be communicated to one of the co-directors, who, after considering all of the issues, would make the final decision as to whether the suggestions would be used. In the end, knowing that everyone would be treated equally helped a great deal in promoting and maintaining a positive work environment.

3. **Promoting Cooperation and Interdependence.** For many service users, learning to work as a member of a team can be challenging, especially if participants have had little or no opportunity to learn the skills needed to ensure the success of a group effort. Thus, in a performance environment that promotes personal contact among service users and volunteers, both groups can learn from one another. For example, as volunteers begin working with cast members, their preconceived negative perceptions of people with a mental illness begin to disappear. At the same time, cast members are learning that a successful performance depends upon the cooperation, flexibility, and patience of everyone associated with the production.

4. **Becoming Acquainted.** When promoting personal contact among service users and volunteers, it is important that every effort is made to create a cordial atmosphere, thus reducing some anxieties often present when strangers are getting to know each other. In SEIR productions, a special effort was made to see that new volunteers were introduced to each cast member prior to the beginning of any rehearsal. In addition, volunteers were encouraged to participate in a wrap-up circle as everyone shared their feelings about their recent rehearsal

experience. This activity was especially effective in "breaking the ice" and helping volunteers feel they were part of the "theatre family."

5. **Invalidating Stereotypes.** In addition to the goal of changing the public's attitudes toward people with psychiatric disabilities, it is equally as important for service users to change their attitudes toward those who may have, up to the present time, been the source of the stigma associated with mental illness. For many who have been victims of this stigma, learning to accept and trust members of the public can be difficult but not impossible. This is where personal contact can play a significant role in changing attitudes on both sides of the spectrum. For example, as preparation for any On Stage! production progressed, cast members found that volunteers performing in dance routines could make mistakes and laugh at themselves, were supportive of those struggling to learn their parts, and enjoyed performing with the company. After experiencing these positives interactions with volunteers, performers would begin to trust these community members who seemed to accept them as they were.

PROGRAM EXAMPLES

Although different from each other in several ways, all three of the programs presented below incorporated the five conditions, previously described, recommended for inclusion in stigma reduction programs. They were similar in other ways as well, because all had missions to promote recovery and educate the public about mental illness, were designed on a psychosocial rehabilitation/recovery model, and focused on recognizing and celebrating service user accomplishments. Of particular importance were the efforts of these organizations to reduce the stigma associated with mental illness with performances by their theatre companies for the public and special community events. The following description of each organization highlights the uniqueness of each and the activities that led to their success.

On Stage!

> I can say without reservation that On Stage! is one of the most impressive and innovative programs to individuals experiencing a mental illness.
>
> –Jeff Thomas, Executive Director, Family Service Spokane

Story 11: "It's In the Yellow Pages"

In 1996, after 12 years in Phoenix, I sold my home and car, had a huge moving sale, loaded myself and three cats on a plane, and returned to my home town of Davenport, Washington. At this point, I had not given much thought to finding a job, thinking it would be difficult to find work in my specialized field of mental health. Then one day while looking through the yellow pages, I found a listing for the Washington Institute for Mental Health Research and Training. Having no idea what this organization was about, I made an appointment with the director, Dr. Dennis Dyck, to see if he might be of some assistance in helping with my job search. After telling him of my experience and interest in implementing a musical theatre program for people with psychiatric disabilities, he became very interested. We talked about the possibility of applying for a research grant to fund a demonstration project in Spokane. Consequently, we received funding from Washington's state mental health division that launched On Stage!. Ever since, when asked how I happened to meet Dr. Dyck, I reply: "I found him in the yellow pages."

For 10 years, On Stage!, a unique recovery program of performing arts activities, served people with a mental illness in Spokane, Washington. Implemented in 1997 with a research grant from the Washington State Mental Health Division, Department of Social and Health Services, and administered by the Washington Institute for Mental Health Research and Training, On Stage! introduced to the community a new and exciting way to help service users on their road to recovery. The significant results of this research study, described in Chapter 1, laid the foundation for the program's successful "run" of 10 years, a remarkable record considering the ever-present funding challenges.

The On Stage! community outreach efforts were extensive. During its tenure, the organization's musical theatre company, Theatre Extraordinaire (TE), gave 98 performances to audiences totally more than 10,000, mostly in Spokane County.[24] These shows encompassed a wide variety of events, including mental health conferences, booster nights

24. Other classes were offered periodically, including those in wellness (Aerobics, Creativity, and Wellness), movement (Stretch and Tone, Dance, and Get Fit!), music (Music Fundamentals, Group Piano, Song Writing), and theatre (Play Reading).

at a local grange hall, church services, special events at a state hospital, an orientation for faculty at a community college, and mental health celebrations sponsored by the National Alliance for the Mentally Ill. The largest of these events was the annual show for the public at the Bing Crosby Theatre in downtown Spokane. These particular performances were designed to celebrate the achievements of the cast, while educating the public about mental illness. Of particular significance was the participation of the many volunteers who served as stage crew assistants, makeup artists, parent assistants, and lobby personnel. These individuals represented a wide range of community involvement, including students from local universities, colleges, high schools and elementary schools, staff from mental health agencies, and family members (Table 4). (It was not unusual to have a cast and crew numbering over 60!) Whether as performers, back stage assistants, greeters, or ushers, these wonderful, dedicated volunteers played an active role in the success of each production, sending a message to the community that the stereotypes and prejudices toward people with a mental illness are unjustified.

Of particular influence were the testimonials given by some cast members at the end of the company's annual shows. These personal success stories, as told in the example below, helped audiences understand that people with a mental illness have the talents and abilities to become contributing members of society if given enough support from community recovery programs.

Table 4
ON STAGE! CAST AND CREW ANALYSIS

Show Title Cast	*(Volunteers and Service Users) Crew*	*Community Volunteers*	*Community Organizations*	*(Funding and Donations)*
We've Come A Long Way, Baby!	19	8	4	7
Bootleggin' Blues	21	10	13	11
Living Free	44	19	47	16
Hats Off! Spokane	59	17	63	17
Steppin' Out	36	26	49	11
Fascinating Rhythms	36	22	44	10
Shine	25	19	32	9

Case Example 9: "Robin"
I came to On Stage! about 3 years ago after I had been diagnosed with bipolar disorder about 10 years ago. At the time I was not working, and I've been considered disabled for sometime now. I came to On Stage! at the urging of my therapist who wanted me to participate in a support group and I fought this with tooth and nail. I wanted nothing to do with a support group. I found an On Stage! pamphlet at the Women's Hearth and thought that would satisfy her. So I came to On Stage! to get my therapist off my back. And it has been an invaluable experience. It has helped me with time management skills. It helped me as far as having a commitment that I needed to go to three times a week to get me out of my house when things were really bad for me, and over the last 3 years I've grown tremendously, and now I have been able to go back to school. In 2 days I will be completing the Medical Assistant program at Apollo College and will move into my externship, completing that medical assistant program. So this will be my last Met show as an On Stage! member, but I hope to come back as a guest artist because next year I hope to be working full time. So I'm really excited about that." This amazing young woman did return for a guest appearance on a later show, bringing along a daughter who joined her in a duet. As of this writing, "Robin," now a mother of five, is still employed full time as a medical assistant.

Universities and Service Learning

> Service learning is a method of teaching, learning, and reflecting that combines academic classroom curriculum with meaningful service, frequently youth service, throughout the community. More specifically, it integrates meaningful community service with instruction and reflection to enrich the learning experience, teach civic responsibility, encourage lifelong civic engagement, and strengthen communities for the common good.

In its quest to educate the public, On Stage! reached out to as many public entities as possible, including local universities. For example, students from physical and occupational therapy programs at Eastern Washington University would complete practicums (field experiences) by working with students in the On Stage! program or by observing at rehearsals. These experiences were instrumental in changing university students' attitudes toward people with psychiatric disabilities. A physical therapy student reflected these changes by stating: "I think the biggest thing I've learned about myself–is that I should not have preconceived ideas about what people can accomplish." Another student who assisted with makeup prior to an On Stage! performance commented: "This (experience) made me realize that I shouldn't do something with a preconceived notion of what to expect because there's a good chance I could be wrong." Accordingly, the involvement of all university students with On Stage! had two major benefits. First, many of the negative attitudes toward people with a mental illness were reduced or eliminated. Second, the potential for educating others was enhanced as these students shared their experiences with others on their campuses and elsewhere.

A unique aspect of the On Stage! stigma-reduction campaign was the involvement of service learning students from Whitworth University in Spokane. Over several years, these students, under the direction of Dr. Rick Hornor, theatre department chair, taught classes to mental health service users in improvisation and mime. The results were astounding and are best described in excerpts from an article that appeared in Whitworth Today (2003), the university's magazine.

Story 12: University Students: Changing Attitudes

Many Whitworth students initially experience powerful anxiety and fear as they anticipate interacting with people coping with mental illness. Prior to their first workshop, Donna Douglass (On Stage! Program Director) meets with the students and Dr. Rick Hornor (Theatre Department Chair) to discuss the dynamics of mental illness and to help prepare them for the experience. "Having never worked with people coping with mental illness before, I really didn't know what to expect" (comments one student). "I had the stereotypical view that they are very weird and hard to communicate with–." (He later commented): "The people were wonderful–they were normal people who simply wanted a little love in their lives. We couldn't help but feel comfortable around them after only half an hour. Theatre strips away all barriers by its very nature of giving and receiving and playing together; it gave our group a wonderful atmosphere of community."

> Hornor–sees the transformation in his students and has experienced it himself. "By the end of the very first session, the students are saying, 'These are wonderful people who are kind and loving, and they want to learn.' That's significant. We move from ignorance to understanding, and therefore, from fear to acceptance." The experience is just as significant for On Stage! actors, Douglass says. "For our people battling the stigma associated with devastating disorders to experience acceptance from these Whitworth students is just incredible–They appreciated so much being treated no differently than anyone else. The Whitworth students show no fear, just acceptance, which establishes an immediate rapport between the two groups."
>
> According to Hornor, the On Stage! actors are the true teachers in the service-learning arrangement. "The people in On Stage! do more for us than we could ever do for them," he says. "They allow us to see their courage and to be a part of their really difficult lives, and to see them struggle, courageously, to move on rather than just give up." (One of Hornor's students summarized her experience by saying): "–I realized I can go into any situation with the idea that I don't know everything and be taught and helped by the people I am teaching."

In addition to teaching classes for On Stage!, Whitworth theatre students were involved in two of Theatre Extraordinaire's annual productions, in which all participants worked closely together in preparation for "the big show." This experience offered university students another opportunity to interact with service users in a normal, community environment where everyone worked together toward a common goal. The following statement by one service learning student seems to summarize the effect the On Stage! experience had on himself and his classmates: "I discovered that I need to stop trusting in stereotypes to shape my view of others and to seek to get to know people first."

Another approach involving college students and service users was reported by Twardzicki (2008) in an article on mental health stigma, social inclusion, and the performing arts. Although not identified as a service learning program, the goals of the theatre project described in this article are closely related to those utilized in a service learning approach–specifically, the focus on involving students in community activities promoting personal contact with people from special populations. In her article, Twardzicki describes how a 3-year partnership with a college and several community mental health agencies in Surrey, England, was successful in reducing the stigma associated with mental illness. The process involved several steps: recruitment of service users, informal meetings to discuss topics for sketches, development of sketches using music, drama, dance, and poetry contributed by service users and a final performance before an invited audience followed by a question-and-answer session among students, service users, and the audience. Consequently, everyone experienced the following benefits:

- Service users were introduced to activities that were therapeutic as well as enjoyable.
- College students gained experience working with a special population within a community environment.
- Audiences gained an appreciation of the power of the arts to challenge stigma; a recognition of the benefits of a partnership involving service users and students; and an increased understanding of mental health issues.

In summary, the Whitworth University service learning program and the unique approach developed in Surrey, England, underscore the importance of promoting personal contact between service users and community members in stigma-reduction campaigns. Moreover, special attention should be paid to the role the performing arts can play in educating the public, for the "stigma-free zone" of the theatre seems to provide an environment unequaled in its effectiveness to eradicate the myths, prejudices, and stereotypes associated with mental illness.

SEIR, Stigma, and Families

Story 13: It's a Family Show

When designing programs for On Stage! productions, one of the goals was to involve family members in either the show or backstage. A unique opportunity arose when three members of James' family volunteered to sing with him in *Fascinating Rhythms,* a show featuring family in several numbers. James was joined on stage by his father, mother, and sister as they sang and danced to "Side by Side." It was an amazing performance, especially because this fam-

> ily was performing together for the first time. Motivated and encouraged by the father, whose extensive experience in performing with a barbershop quartet helped to instill in his family the confidence they needed, this group sang their hearts out to an audience that applauded and cheered loudly as the family took their bows. What a joyful moment and incredible demonstration of how a loving, accepting family was supporting their brother/son on his road to recovery.

With most stigma-reduction programs focusing on educating the public, the negative effect that the mental illness of a family member can have on other family members may receive little attention. Yet how the family reacts to its afflicted son, daughter, husband, or wife can significantly affect the recovery of the person with a serious mental illness. Therefore, it is important that family members, along with others close to the family, are made aware of the talents and abilities of their loved ones. Then, with this awareness, they can offer the support needed to help their service users move forward in their recovery. To this end, the author's SEIR programs offered opportunities for service users to demonstrate their potential in a program where families can personally witness the achievements of their family members. How these performances directly affected the families of people with schizophrenia is reflected in the following observations by various family members.

"My daughter has been participating in this program for approximately 10 months–the program has helped dramatically with her social skills, self-esteem, ongoing time management struggles, and both musical and theatrical creativity. At first (our daughter)–was quite nervous about the idea of performing in front of the theatre troupe, let alone an audience–however, she is gradually conquering her fears and has worked her way up from the back (dance) row to the front. This is just amazing to our family and to her counselors—because it is so unlike the shy, introverted, easily confused person we all know." Another family member's renewed sense of hope is reflected in comments about her son: "On Stage! has given my son self-confidence, purpose, self-discipline, and an opportunity to socialize. He also enjoys being in an organization that tries to reduce the stigma associated with mental illness." Similarly, the parent of another cast member expressed her amazement at her son's progress: "Since being in On Stage!, (our son) has progressed not only in coordination of mind and body, but he has more purpose and can focus. We feel fortunate to have our son in this group and to see his life definitely improved." Further, in its ongoing efforts to work with the families of its cast members, every effort was made to include family members in the annual productions for the public, as in the following example.

Story 14: Let's Celebrate!

In the spring of 2002, community volunteers, mental health professionals, service users, and family members came together in an On Stage! show with a patriotic theme in recognition of the catastrophic event on 9/11/01. This event, billed as "Living Free," featured original songs focusing on unity and patriotism. In an opening number bringing the cast of 44 onto the stage, children from a local elementary school marched around the stage carrying American flags, danced to *We Are Family,* and joined everyone in singing *I'd Like to Teach the World to Sing.* To an applauding and cheering audience comprised of the public, mental health care givers, parents, family members, service users, and their friends, this performance established once again that people with a mental illness can contribute significantly to a given cause, demonstrating their ability to be productive members of the community in which they reside. This event concluded an all-day recovery workshop sponsored by a coalition whose mission was to see that "all service users have the opportunity to achieve their goals and dreams in a recovery journey that improves the quality of their lives and provides supports every step of the way."

Project Arts

Project Arts was a nonprofit organization with a much broader program than On Stage!. Located in Phoenix, Arizona, this psychosocial recovery program served adults with a serious mental illness throughout Maricopa County. Designed on an educational model, Project Arts offered classes in the visual arts (drawing, acrylics, and graphic arts), drama (comedy workshops and improvisation), and music (guitar). Other activities included music therapy and exercise groups and an Adult Basic Education program created specifically to serve people with a serious mental illness. Funding sources included corporate and private foundation grants, county mental health grants, and vocational rehabilitation referrals. In addition, the annual show for the public, *A Night on the Town,* raised a modest amount of dollars.

As the only program of its kind in the state, Project Arts introduced to the mental health community the effectiveness of activities in visual and performing arts on the recovery of adults with a serious mental illness. In keeping with its mission of stigma reduction and public education, events were held where performances by Theatre Extraordinaire and art work by Project Arts students were featured. Of particular significance was the attention Project Arts received from both the print and broadcast media, for this publicity helped greatly in the program's efforts to promote stigma reduction. When asked why the program created so much media interest, the author offered two reasons: the organization's innovative recovery approach and the presentation of people with psychiatric disabilities in a normalized environment where performers' achievements, not their mental illnesses, were the focus of attention–a far cry from the frequent portrayal of the mentally ill as violent criminals. Moreover, not only did the program's events reduce public stigma, but they also helped both mental health professionals and families change their attitudes about the potential of service users to achieve recovery.

Salem Creative Arts Center

Case Example 10: "Emily"

When I met Emily, she was living in a group home in Salem, Oregon and making little, if any, progress in her recovery. Diagnosed with major depression but intelligent and talented, she had no goals that would help her progress toward independence. During my first visit, I learned Emily had studied piano for several years. Upon hearing her play, I knew immediately she was accomplished enough to perform in the first production of Theatre Extraordinaire. When asked if she were interested in joining the theatre company, Laura was hesitant but agreed to attend the first rehearsal. What followed is a remarkable change that took place over a short time period, a transformation that began with her decision to play a piano solo on the company's first show.

After deciding to perform, Emily began practicing daily to prepare. Then after attending the company's first play rehearsal, she decided to join the chorus of the one-act musical. After her first successful performance, noticeable changes were observed in her behavior, particularly an increased energy level, an improved self-confidence, and an increased willingness to take risks. The latter was demonstrated when she accepted a role in a roaring 20s, play as a gangster's girlfriend, requiring her to wear a short flapper dress accessorized with a boa. Then, to the surprise of everyone, she agreed to perform a torch song titled *Hey, There, Big Boy!*. When performing this number in a dinner theatre show at a local restaurant, she further surprised all of us by walking into the audience and sitting on her psychiatrist's lap! With this one act, all of the benefits Emily received from her performing arts experiences were exhibited, highlighting her improved self-esteem and the confidence this extraverted behavior required. With this new-found belief in her ability to succeed, she enrolled in a local community college, where she eventually received a bachelor's degree in education, fulfilling her dream of becoming an elementary school teacher.

It was during her tenure as Director of Music Therapy at Willamette University (WU) that the author founded her first nonprofit organization, the Salem Creative Arts Center (SCAC) and Theatre Extraordinaire, her first musical theatre company for people with a serious mental illness. Comprised of adults living in group homes and WU music therapy students, the company gave its first performance in the university theatre after only 8 weeks of rehearsal. Thereafter, rehearsals continued as the cast learned new material and prepared for more shows, including a performance in Portland, a dinner theatre show in Salem, and a performance at the Western Regional Music Therapy Conference in Salem. Again, the uniqueness of the program got the attention of the local media, resulting in several newspaper stories and television interviews.

Theatre Extraordinaire's performances at conferences and other special events played a significant role in reducing stigma in general while helping family members realize the potential of people with a serious mental illness. This change in attitude is reflected in the following quotation from the president of a family advocacy organization, who, after attending a show, stated: "Interestingly, many of our members–were gratified at how good your show was and had not imagined what a wonderful job could be done with clients." In another example, the president of a mental health organization in Eugene, Oregon, commented: "The appearance of your troupe (at our mental health conference) aptly demonstrated to townspeople and clients how much can be achieved by dedicated workers who know how to 'bring out the most' in a group which often needs more encouragement and understanding than anything else."

Music Behind Bars

Although service learning programs were not yet a part of university and college curriculums in the late 1970s and early 1980s, WU students who participated in the SCAC theatre company received the same benefits as described in the On Stage! service learning program. In addition, some of these students were involved in another project that furthered their awareness of the hidden talents of people with a mental illness. Known as *Project Culture,* this program was a federal project funded by the Department of Corrections to introduce culture into the prison system. When the State of Oregon was selected to participate in this project, the author was employed to conduct a Music Therapy Workshop in the Psychiatric Secure Unit (PSU) in the Oregon State Penitentiary. The goal of this workshop was to produce a variety show with patients from PSU providing the entertainment. After 8 weeks of rehearsal and a few days prior to show time, an incident, told in the following story, occurred that will long be remembered by this writer and most certainly by everyone involved.

Story 15: Come Hear the Music

It was several days before show time. My WU music therapy students and I had been working for hours in the university's theatre workshop, painting scenery for the production. When we finally decided to quit for the night, one of the students, April Shimizu-Parker, said she had a surprise for me. Then, accompanied on guitar by Michael, a fellow music therapy student, she sang a song she had written for the cast of the PSU show, a song whose haunting melody and touching lyrics expressed so well how April felt about her experience in PSU. It is testimony to so many things-how sensitive April had become to the effects of prison life on the patients; how sad she felt, knowing she would never see them again; and how much she hoped her music would help to sooth the troubled feelings "you feel inside." As I listened to this song unfold, the tears began to fall, for I knew April had just given us a gift, a song that could not help but touch the heart of anyone who heard it. And so it was that "Come Hear the Music" came to be performed by April and Michael, in the performance at OSP. (Later on, this song was used as backgound music in a PBS documentary about the project.) I still have the videotape from that show, and whenever I hear April singing her wonderful composition, tears come to my eyes, and I'm back on that stage with April and Michael in a performance I shall long remember.

COME HEAR THE MUSIC
By April Shimizu Parker

Since you cannot see it now, I'll describe the view;
How the sun shines in the morning on the sparkling dew.
The wind plays a song through the Oregon trees,
And you can catch their fragrance on the breeze.
It saddens me you cannot see the starry skies at night.
You cannot dance in the aura of the golden, pale moonlight.
No one is beside you, just a cold and lifeless wall,
And the echoing of footsteps in the hall.

I've wished that I could change things, and so, perhaps, have you,
To change the past and make it over all again anew.
We know it's not that easy, but we can try–
To build the value in us money cannot buy.
You're more precious now than you may ever really know.
Lots of things can happen if you really want to grow.
The time is short, and I may never see you again;
So I'll thank you now for letting us be friends.

Chorus
Come with me–Come hear the music.
Come with me–Come take my hand.
Come with me–Come, let's make music.
A part of us to better understand.

Summary

The effects of the author's performing arts programs on reducing the stigma associated with mental illness have been demonstrated many times over. Accordingly, personal testimony from many sectors of the community have shown that public performances featuring people with psychiatric disabilities can significantly change the attitudes of the general public toward mental illness. These results can be attributed not only to the amazing commitment and dedication of the shows' cast members but also to the many devoted volunteers whose involvement made these productions possible. Indeed, these special people from the community would never forget the positive experiences they had as they became acquainted with each event's participants, witnessing for themselves the remarkable talents, enthusiasm, and dedication of everyone involved. Clearly then, the annual shows and other public events presented by the three programs described above demonstrated what the literature continues to emphasize: Personal contact is the most effective means of reducing stigma and eliminating stereotypes.

Part Two

GETTING STARTED

Chapter 7

THE MUSICAL THEATRE COMPANY

On Stage!
An Ode to Opening Night

Prologue
Houselights dimming, Voices whispering,
Raised baton, A sudden hush--

Overture
Trumpets sounding, Cellos singing,
Quickening hearts, Adrenalin rush–

Act I
Curtain rising! Scenery shining,
Hands applaud, The eye delights–

Act II
Enter dancers, Smartly stepping,
Costumes sparkling, Glowing lights–

Act III
Voices rising, Joy resounding,
Opening night, On stage at last!–

Epilogue
Curtain calls, Balloons and flowers,
Celebration! Joyful cast–

Reviews
Jubilation! Dreams abounding,
History turns another page–

Reflections
Curtain closed, One shining moment–
Memories of a night On Stage!

D. D.

Although the thought of implementing a new program can be exciting, energizing, and, yes, even exhilarating, these feelings can be dampened by uncertainty and frustration if there is no established process to follow and the outcome uncertain. Knowing this, the author provides information in this chapter that will guide the reader through the process of creating the first musical theatre production with a cast of people with psychiatric disabilities and related disorders. Included are suggestions on: recruiting and retaining cast members, organizing the first informational meeting, lowering production costs, and preparing for the first production. Also featured is a section on costuming and another on the importance of patience, practice, and perseverance during the rehearsal process.

Although this information can be utilized by mental health practitioners, it is specifically targeted toward community organizations and individuals with nonclinical backgrounds. For example, someone with knowledge in theatre but inexperienced in working with people with psychiatric disorders may be looking for resources that would help in the start-up process. Or perhaps there are people from an advocacy group interested in introducing theatre activities to the people they support. To this end, the author hopes that the information below, combined with that in earlier chapters, will inspire anyone interested in embarking on this new adventure, one that not only will be an exciting challenge, but also life-changing for all involved.

RECRUITMENT AND RETENTION OF CAST MEMBERS

When beginning a new venture, especially one involving musical productions with inexperienced participants, it is always a challenge to develop an approach in recruiting that will motivate students to enroll in the program. Furthermore, once they are enrolled, an even greater challenge is to keep students motivated and attending rehearsals regularly. Information in this section addresses both of these issues.

Recruitment

Although direct mail is one method that can be used to recruit cast members, there is no doubt that personal contact is by far the best approach for "selling" a new program. The effectiveness of this method was proven many times over when the author was in the process of establishing her theatre companies in Salem, Phoenix, and Spokane. As it turned out, the majority of students who attended the first rehearsal did so because of a personal contact either by phone or via a group meeting. So to help the reader plan a successful recruitment campaign, the following information describes in detail the recruitment methods utilized by the author: direct mail, personal contact, and phone follow-up.

Direct Mail. When creating information for a direct mailing, it is important to remember to allow enough time prior to the mailing date (see *Publicity Timeline* in *Publicity* section) for planning and preparation, and to package the information so it is brief, attractively presented, and designed to pique the reader's interest. Contents of this mailing should include:

- A cover letter that includes the (1) purpose of the program and the enrollment process; (2) eligibility requirements for enrollees; (3) place, date, and time of first rehearsal; (4) number of weeks in program (if known); (5) deadline for enrollment; (6) a request to schedule an informational meeting with interested students at their residences or at agencies; and (7) assurance that individuals attending this meeting are under no obligation to join the company and a phone number in case the addressee has any questions.
- A flyer for posting that provides a title of the program, who the population will serve, the start day and date, address of location of first informational meeting and a contact telephone number.
- An enrollment form to be completed by student or staff (see Appendix B).
- A self-addressed return envelope.

After applications are received, contact each student or agency by phone to confirm receipt of the mailer and to schedule a meeting with agencies and/or residences. If interested service users are not associated with a social service agency or special living facility, arrangements can be made to meet with these persons individually.

Recruitment Visits

After the mailers have had time to arrive at their destinations, call each residence and social service agency (if involved) to confirm receipt of the information. At the same time, request a date for program staff to talk with service users interested in knowing more about the new program. Once these arrangements have been made, a confirmation phone call to the facility 2 or 3 days prior to the visit is recommended.

During visits the following agenda is suggested:

- Describe the program and its purpose, being sure to announce that no prior performing arts experience is required for enrollment.
- Ask service users to share any background they may have in the performing arts (i.e., school plays, church choirs, variety shows, bands, music lessons, and how they felt about their experiences). (You probably will find that some individuals really enjoyed their performance activities while others may never forget how terrified they were to be on stage.)
- Ask participants who have had some performance experience to share any humorous situations they have encountered. Usually some funny stories can help the more anxious members of the group to relax and feel more comfortable about participating in the discussion. Also, there are two other benefits from hearing personal stories. First, service users get to know each other better, and second, you may gain some information that could be helpful when creating acts for your first production. To illustrate: The author recalls a patient in a maximum security facility who, when asked about his performing arts background, replied: "I was a carrot in a kindergarten play." Needless to say, this comment was especially humorous coming from a convicted felon whose fellow patients, trying to imagine this individual dressed as a carrot, burst into laughter. Consequently, other members of the group felt more comfortable in sharing their own stories, and the author learned some valuable information about her potential cast members.
- Play some music that will be included in the production.
- Demonstrate one or two of the dances being considered, using a hat and a cane to show how props are used. Hearing the music

and seeing examples of costumes and a few simple dance steps can be a great motivator.
- Ask for questions.
- Ask those interested in attending your informational meeting to complete an enrollment form.

Phone Follow-Up

Call those who have received mailers but were not involved in visits to find out who is planning to attend the initial meeting. Two days prior to the meeting call everyone on the list (agencies and/or individuals) to remind them of the time and place. Be sure to mention the refreshments!

THE INFORMATIONAL MEETING

Preparation

Prior to the first meeting:

- Meet with staff and volunteers to discuss the meeting agenda and to teach everyone a few steps in the dance routines.
- Try to have at least one dance choreographed for demonstration. For example, a simple routine to *Yankee Doodle Dandy* is a great song for beginners and provides an opportunity for participants to wear the skimmers (see Appendix A for a suggested dance routine). If possible, have another dance prepared to demonstrate how canes will be used.
- Assign responsibilities (i.e., refreshment coordinator, sign-in table).
- Ask everyone to report to the meeting site at least 30 minutes prior to start time to help with room set-up and other preparatory activities.

It is important that this initial meeting is well organized. To this end, the following preparations are recommended:

Staff and Volunteers. Be sure enough help is available to see that all runs smoothly. Specific duties should include:

- Two "greeters" at a sign-in table who will see that everyone signs in and receives a name tag. At the same time, ask each person to write the following information on a 3" × 5" card: name, address, and phone number; name of case manager and phone number (if applicable); and name and phone number of a person to contact in an emergency.
- Someone assigned to keep the refreshment table supplied and clear of clutter.
- Two or three people to help with activities.

Agenda. Print the program on a large poster board and display where all can see.

Supplies. Be prepared with pens, pencils, markers, clip board, yellow/white pad, name tags, sign-in forms, 3" × 5" cards, skimmers (hats), canes, song sheets, CD player, and CDs.

Sound Equipment

- **Piano:** If a piano will be used and the leader of the session will be leading the singing from the piano, place the instrument so it is part of the circle of chairs. If someone besides the leader is playing, the piano can be placed just outside the circle if desired.
- **Recorder:** Because music will be needed for the folk or line dances, be sure a recorder (tape or CD) is in place and ready to use.
- **Microphone:** It is often helpful to have a microphone and amplifier available for use by speakers in case some persons have hearing impairments or the event is held in a large room (a Karaoke machine works well for this purpose).
- **Song sheets:** For this initial session, song sheets (or books) with a variety of songs from different eras are recommended. If song sheets are used, have them prepared in a size 14 font because there are usually one or more service users whose eyesight is impaired due to side effects of medications or other medical issues.

Refreshments: Keep it simple with juices, sodas, bottled water, crackers/cookies and sugar-free items for those with diet restrictions. Create a festive atmosphere with a colorful table cloth, napkins and a center piece (optional). Ask everyone to finish their snacks before being seated, as food and beverages should not be allowed in the activity area.

Procedure

- Place greeters at the door about 30 minutes prior to start time with a list of enrollees and preparations as described above.
- Serve refreshments as soon as people begin to arrive.
- Arrange chairs in a circle. When everyone is seated, talk briefly about the program and go over the agenda.
- Distribute song sheets and do a sing-a-long of familiar tunes to break the ice and help everyone relax.
- Do one or two dances (i.e., circle folk dance, Virginia Reel, a Conga line).
- Demonstrate with staff a dance or two that will be used in show and show how canes can be used.
- Distribute skimmers[25] to all participants; then teach a few steps of a dance to those who would like to try.

Wrap-up

- Ask for questions.
- Distribute handouts describing date and time of first rehearsal.
- Pass around a clipboard with sign-up form for those who would like to enroll in the program.
- Sing one or two songs, up-beat and energetic.

THE FIRST THEATRE COMPANY

Launching a new musical theatre program, especially one for a special population, may seem daunting to the novice. However, it is possible with the right resources and guidance. So let's get started. When producing a show with people with disabilities, production costs are usually the first issue to be considered and the question asked: Can this be done with the limited funds available? Or, there is no funding at this time, so is it realistic to think that a project like this can be done? Be not

---

25. Skimmers are brimmed Styrofoam hats with bands (usually red) around the crown.

discouraged! How the "supposedly impossible" can become the "supposedly probable" is illustrated with two examples from the author's experience, beginning with her first theatre company in Salem, Oregon. The initial production of this new Salem company was presented in two acts: the first, a variety show, comprised of vocals, instrumentals, and poetry readings; and the second, a one-act musical play. (A special feature was the amazing performance by a young man with schizophrenia, who, to the accompaniment of a single guitarist, choreographed a routine using nunchakus!)[26] The costuming requirements for this production were minimal, consisting of a few accessories for the play and dark slacks and white shirts for the company's basic costume, all purchased from local thrift stores. Funds for costumes and snack were donated by the Salem Creative Arts Center Board. Other support was provided by Willamette University (space and printing services) and a local car dealership (loan of a van). The second organization, located in Phoenix, began with no funding, a board of directors, and a donated rehearsal space. Knowing the only way to "sell" her program to the mental health community was to produce a show for the public, the author, along with a choreographer and another music therapist, began 3 months of rehearsals. This effort culminated in the presentation of a show at a local community theatre to which the media was invited, resulting in a documentary on the project produced by the local PBS station. Consequently, Project Arts was awarded its first mental health contract with enough funding to hire part-time staff and lease space for a half-time day treatment program. These two program examples demonstrate how a vision can develop into a reality when the need is there, the timing is right, and the people involved strongly believe in their organization's mission and the ability of those they serve to be successful.

GETTING ORGANIZED

Before proceeding further, those interested in implementing this project should be aware that the personality characteristics of the leaders can play an important role in the program's success. For example,

---

26. Nunchakus is an Oriental hand weapon for defense against front assault, consisting of two foot-long hardwood sticks joined by a chain or thick cord that stretches to body width.

a positive attitude, good sense of humor, and a high energy level will go a long way in motivating all involved. In addition, the start-up process will require the organizers to have a high level of commitment, good leadership and organizational skills, and the ability to keep the cast motivated (especially during times when members are making mistakes and struggling to learn their parts). (See Appendix A: *Personality Characteristics of the Successful Teacher/Therapist.*) Although all of these qualifications may seem overwhelming, they really are not because they describe the requirements of any leader who is effective in his or her work. So the bottom line is this: with a strong determination to succeed and a "We can do it!" attitude, you, too, can be a producer!

So where do you begin? Initially, the author recommends that the project organizers create a document describing the project goals, especially those related to funding issues. This plan need not be complicated but should provide some direction for the project leaders with the following content recommended. The words enclosed in quotation marks are examples of how the document might be written.

- **A Project Name.** "This project will be called ________."
- **Statement of Purpose.** "The purpose of (name of project) is to establish within the community a musical theatre company for people with (name of disability or the term "disabilities")."
- **Eligibility.** "People (ages ___ to ___) with (name of disability) are eligible to participate. Participants must also be able to: arrange transportation to rehearsal site, function appropriately within a group, be willing to attend rehearsals regularly, and follow program rules."
- **Program Rules and Guidelines.** "A document stating program rules and guidelines will be created for distribution at the first rehearsal of the theatre company." It is important, early in the rehearsal process, to put into writing a description of expectations from cast members. Appendix A is an example of a format that may be used as written or adapted to the needs of the organization.
- **Staffing.** "Initially, the project will be staffed by volunteers unless funding is available to pay a project director. Immediate positions to be filled are a program coordinator, musical director, and a choreographer."

- **Funding.** "If no funds are available, the project will rely on donations from volunteers, families of participants, and local businesses. A fundraising committee will be created to consider ideas for fundraising events."
- **Timeline.** It is important to set a date for the first production even though it may need to be changed in the future. For example, a variety show may require only 4 to 6 weeks of rehearsals and is an excellent way to begin because participants will experience their first performance within a short time period. Of course, how quickly the cast learns their parts will depend on the population being served. "Rehearsals will begin on (date) at (location) and will continue for (number of weeks). The first performance is scheduled for (date) but is subject to change if necessary."
- **Publicity.** Putting someone in charge of coordinating the publicity for the first meeting of potential cast members is essential. "The publicity coordinator will see that information on the informational meeting is disseminated in a timely manner."

Although the creation of the above document is recommended, it will, of course, be up to the organizers of the new theatre company to decide whether or not using this process is the best course for them to follow. The important factor to consider is that no matter what method is used, an organized approach to a project such as this one will result in many benefits, the least of which is less stress on all involved.

Although the effort may seem daunting at first, the author affirms that starting a theatre company for people with psychiatric disabilities can be exciting, fun, and worth every minute of hard work. You will find this especially to be true when you begin to see how quickly the self-confidence and self-esteem of your cast improves. Moreover, there is nothing more exhilarating for these special performers than the applause and cheers heard from an accepting and appreciative audience. After all, that initial performance may be the first time that many performers realize success is possible and recovery no longer elusive.

THE FIRST PRODUCTION

The time for hard work has arrived. For not only does the cast have to memorize several songs and dances, but they also must develop the self-discipline it takes to produce a successful show. For example, they will have to learn the importance of following a practice and rehearsal schedule. Additionally, members must acquire the ability to discipline themselves in another way: by remaining silent during rehearsals and back stage. Consequently, this training pays off extremely well because when that curtain goes up, everyone will be well prepared to give the audience an evening (or afternoon) of unforgettable entertainment.

Opening Number. As discussed earlier, when planning song and dance routines comprised of the entire cast, immediate attention should be given to the opening number. Because this is the first act the audience will see, the music should be up-tempo, energetic, and strongly rhythmic. The dance routine can be simple, perhaps consisting of marching combined with a few uncomplicated dance steps. For example, in the author's first Salem production, the cast entered from the back of the theatre, using two aisles and marching to *Overture, Curtain, Lights.* When they reached the stage, a simple march routine was performed to an original song titled *We Can Do It,* concluding with the cast in a semi-circle at the front of the stage. On another occasion (in Phoenix), the show opened with the cast entering from the back of the theatre space, singing and marching to *I'm a Yankee Doodle Dandy.* Once on stage, they performed a simple dance routine to the same tune, and then segued into *Politics,* the opening number to a political satire. Clearly, then, a complex dance routine is not required to impress the first audience. What is necessary is attention to detail, with a focus on teaching performers to do the moves together, keeping lines straight, holding heads up, projecting voices, and smiling. (The latter can be especially challenging because often performers are concentrating so hard they forget to smile.)

Program Order. Another important detail in planning a show program is the order in which the acts appear. Specifically, there are two factors needing particular consideration in this process. First is the placement of numbers that involve the complete cast. When making decisions on this matter, the author recommends the following: a strong, energetic opening number that immediately engages the audience; an upbeat number in the middle that refocuses attention on the entire company; and a rousing finale that will leave the audience wanting more. The second factor is the placement of the not-so-strong solo or small-group acts. This can be a sensitive area requiring the director to consider the self-esteem and confidence level of the performers as well as the performance level of the act. So a rule of thumb that the author always tried to follow is this: avoid, if possible, placing a not-so-strong act immediately before a stronger one. For example, if Performer A with minimal vocal skills immediately follows an energetic performance by Performer B whose vocal skills and presentation style draw a loud applause, Performer A may feel embarrassed and discouraged that he or she did not receive the same audience response as Performer B. Therefore, placing Performer A before Performer B may prevent Performer A from feeling hurt and otherwise unhappy with his or her performance.

Case Example 11: "Maxine"

For several years, I worked with Maxine, a woman whose self-esteem and self-confidence initially were so low that she was constantly putting herself down, frequently stating she could not sing as well as some others in the company. When assured she was doing just fine, she would feel better for awhile, and then begin comparing herself to others again. Consequently, placing her before a strong performer could only reinforce how Maxine felt about herself, so every effort was made to see that she followed, rather than preceded, someone with strong performance skills. Later on, as her self-confidence improved and her comedic talents were discovered, it took less reassurance from staff to convince her that she could give a good performance. Although initially feeling she needed to be featured as a soloist, Maxine gradually began to realize that performing with one or two others could be a lot of fun, and that being in a group relieved some of her performance anxiety.

Song Selection

When selecting songs for inexperienced performers, there are two major factors to be considered: vocal range and rhythmic complexity. First, finding songs that are appropriate for an entire cast of beginners with limited vocal ability can be challenging especially because many tunes are written with vocal ranges reaching to the stratosphere! So in order to keep songs within the desired vocal range (not higher than one octave above middle C for the full cast), the author began writing show tunes and "songs of celebration" tailored to the vocal abilities of her cast members. Then there was the difficulty in finding songs written in "singable" keys. Although the range of some melodies was not a problem, the key in which they were written required the vocalist to sing notes that were much too high. Thus, the author, before she became computer literate, spent hours transposing songs by hand onto manuscript paper.

Fortunately, there are now computer programs that make transposing any song easy for those skilled in using the software. So hopefully, if the reader is not familiar with one of these software programs, a volunteer can be found to provide assistance.

Regarding the second factor, rhythmic complexity, it is important to remember that complex rhythms are not necessary for the production of an effective song and dance routine. In fact, a John Phillip Sousa march with a "clean and crisp" march routine can be just as effective as a song with syncopated rhythms and complex dance steps. Therefore, when selecting songs for a new theatre company, find tunes that are both strongly rhythmic and familiar. For example, patriotic songs like *Fourth of July Parade, It's a Grand Old Flag,* and *Yankee Doodle Dandy* offer both familiarity and steady marching rhythms. Then if the cast will not be singing as well as marching, of course there are an endless number of songs available.

PROGRAM GUIDES AND FORMS

To aid further in the organizational process of establishing a theatre company for people with disabilities, the following program guides and forms are included in the appendices.

Appendix A: Program Guides

1. Cane Construction Guide–An inexpensive alternative to purchasing dance canes.
2. Crisis Resolution Guide: Day of Performance–Appendix A.
3. Dance Routine–A suggested routine to *I'm a Yankee Doodle Dandy.*
4. Personality Characteristics of the Successful Teacher/Therapist–A detailed list of desirable characteristics for effective leaders, teachers, and therapists.
5. Program Boilerplate–A format to follow when designing printed programs.
6. Program Sample–A program from a major production.

7. Program Rules and Guidelines–After experiencing the confusion that results from failing to put into writing behaviors expected from students, the author strongly recommends that these program rules and guidelines (or adaptations thereof) be distributed on the first day of classes and rehearsals. Equally important is the process of reading each item out loud, allowing for questions and discussion on each. To counter the objections of someone who complains about having so many rules, the author has found that a discussion on why rules are necessary and the consequences that might occur if no guidelines are available can be helpful. This strategy usually is effective because it helps to reinforce the importance of each person taking responsibility for his or her behavior. Of course, if the reader feels the word "rules" will cause a problem, the term "guidelines" can be used instead.

Appendix B: Forms

1. Confidentiality Statement and Consent Form–This document describes in detail circumstances that require consent from cast members for taking photos or videos.
2. Member Enrollment Form–This form, completed by every cast member on enrollment, provides important information for staff.
3. Member Information Form–This form provides a permanent record for each cast member, including: the basics (name, address, phone, and emergency contact), costume sizes and assignments, and body measurements. There are two forms on each page sized be adhered to a 5" × 8"-inch card for placement in a file box.
4. Member Sign-In Form–Keeping a record of attendance is important, so having members sign in at each rehearsal helps greatly to verify presence. As backup, staff should have an attendance form for their own use, preferably placed on a clipboard for easy access.
5. Pre- and Post-Self-Evaluations–These instruments are provided for optional use. The author found them beneficial, especially before and after a major event, for performers often were surprised at the changes they saw on the post-evaluation form.
6. Theatre Company Contract–The use of this form is highly recommended for, unlike the general Program Rules and Guidelines, it clearly states what is expected of cast members

regarding behaviors and attitudes. The author suggests renewing this contract every 4 to 6 months as a way to refresh members' memories.

EXPECTING THE UNEXPECTED: THE CRISIS RESOLUTION GUIDE

Story 16: Be Ready for Anything!

The event was the annual conference of the Western Regional Music Therapy Association being held in Salem, Oregon. Theatre Extraordinaire, the SCAC musical theatre company, was to perform for conference attendees on the Willamette University campus. As curtain time drew near, the cast was assembled off stage, ready to enter for its opening number. Then, most unexpectedly, Ella, one of the cast members, told me she did not want to perform, and no one could change her mind. So she left the scene, returning to her group home. Now ordinarily, if a member were unable to perform in a dance routine or other musical number, the absence could easily be accommodated. However, in this case, Ella had a speaking roll in the play, so her leaving presented a bit of a problem. But have no fear–a student was right there to step into the role, thus preventing what could have been a very stressful situation. Consequently, the show did go on, and the performance was a success.

Ella's story is a good example of the importance of providing understudies or personnel able to step into a role at the last minute, especially in the production of a play. Further, it illustrates that no matter how diligently one prepares for any show involving a special population, something unexpected is bound to occur. So to assist the reader in preparing for the inevitable, a *Crisis Resolution Guide,* found in Appendix A, includes the many situations the author has encountered during her production experience. Of course, no matter what happens, the secret to dealing with any crisis is to remain calm, cool, and collected. So when the unexpected occurs, take three deep breaths, put on your "I've-got-everything-under-control" demeanor, and assure everyone there is no need to panic. For no matter what the situation may be, that curtain *will* go up and the show *must* and *will* go on!

THE "EXPERIENCED" THEATRE COMPANY

After a theatre company has had several months of training and produced its first show, staff can begin planning for the next production by selecting a theme song and creating a new opening number that includes dance routines with more complex dance steps and rhythms. The author always began this process by pouring over her collection of show music (including an extensive Sheet Music Magazine collection–a valuable resource, by the way) and scores from a local music store, searching for a song around which a show could be designed. Sometimes an appropriate tune would be found, but if not, writing a song to fit a specific theme was the next step, which brings to mind the following story.

Story 17: Hats Off!

It was the fall of 2001 and time to come up with a theme for the On Stage! 2002 annual public performance. I had always liked the idea of using "Hats Off" in the title, but I was struggling to find a song that fit this theme. Then one day at a rehearsal I happened to mention my dilemma, and what happened next is, to me, astounding. "Scott," a cast member with a long history of musical experience and a great baritone voice, offered to work on some lyrics over the weekend. Four days later, he returned with the results: lyrics to a yet-to-be-written song with a verse and two choruses. Even more remarkable was the perfect rhythm of the words–so perfect that when I began composing the music, only one word had to be changed. Of course it was expected that Scott would perform the song in the show, so as he and I rehearsed the music, Katherine began creating the dance routine to be performed as Scott sang. So we finally had our show title: *Hats Off, Spokane!*. All was progressing splendidly–until an unexpected turn of events. About 4 weeks prior to show time, Scott experienced a serious health crisis, making it impossible for him to perform. Needless to say, this circumstance, occurring so close to opening night, could have been a major setback. However, luck was on our side. Another member of the company, also a young man with boundless energy and an excellent voice, did not hesitate to step in for Scott. And to everyone's amazement, this number turned out to be one of the best we ever produced! My only regret is that Scott could not participate in the showcasing of his wonderful, creative work. So hats off to you, Scott–your contribution to the success of *Hats Off, Spokane!* will never be forgotten.

Hats Off, Spokane!

Hats off to you, Spokane–Hats off to you.
Hats off, my lilac friends–You've been so true.
Please do enjoy the show and put yourself at ease.
It is our fervent hope that parking was a breeze.

Hats off again, Spokane–You're oh, so fine.
Now watch us strut our stuff–Tonight's our time to shine.
So have a laugh, tap your toes, and give yourself some smiles,
While we say, Hats Off, Spokane; You are the tops, Spokane.
Hats off to you, Spokane, in On Stage! style.

Now that the theme was selected, the author would meet with her choreographer to discuss ideas for a medley of songs that could be included in the opening number. (At this point careful attention was given to the rhythms of each song to be sure they were not too complex.) Then, when the medley was in rough draft form, the first step of the learning process began: teaching the lyrics to the cast. Then, as the author worked on the vocals, Katherine Crow, the company's choreographer, began creating the dance routine, a process that was a joy to observe. With what seemed to be a natural ability, Ms. Crow incorporated the often limited dance skills of the performers into dance routines that were not complicated, yet made the dancers look great–like true professionals.

Every professional has a moment of going blank–What's important is the grace with which we recover. We have complete permission to perform in any way we can. –Katherine Crow

As the cast began working on the opening number, Ms. Crow and the author commenced to selecting two or three dance routines that would involve the entire cast. Because each large production number usually required about 4 months of rehearsals, song selection was completed as soon as possible. Smaller acts were developed as time progressed, including performances by soloists, small ensembles, and guest artists; an occasional sketch written by cast members and staff; and, periodically, an original one-act musical play. In Appendix A, the reader will find two examples of programs from these major productions.

SECRETS TO SUCCESS: PATIENCE, PRACTICE, AND PERSEVERANCE

Once the theme is selected and the opening number is ready, the hard work really begins. For not only does the cast have to memorize the songs and dances, but they also must learn the self-discipline it takes to produce a successful show. This effort requires not only weeks of practice, but also, for many, learning to control the frequent tendency to talk during rehearsals and back stage. To this end, the "silent treatment" described in Story 3 can be effective. However, peer pressure can be an even more efficient way of controlling this disruptive behavior because it is less time-consuming to execute. For example, with a simple gesture (forefinger to lips) by observant cast members, "offenders" can be quickly silenced, soon learning that their talking should cease. Consequently, this training pays off extremely well because when that curtain goes up, the cast will be focused and alert, well prepared to give its audience an evening (or afternoon) of memorable entertainment.

So what else does it take to produce a show comprised mostly of first-time performers who happen to have a mental illness? This question can be answered in three words: *Practice, Patience,* and *Perseverance.* Why these terms are important and how they are applied in show preparation is described in the following discussion, beginning with Word Number One, Practice.

Practice. For most cast members, finding the self-discipline necessary for practicing dance routines and songs at home can be especially difficult especially because many of them come from a daily routine of unproductive and unscheduled time. Therefore, spending some rehearsal time helping members plan how they will work practice into their daily lives can be helpful. Moreover, comments such as "I don't have time" or "I don't know where to start" can be addressed by offering some valuable information on time management. Then, to clarify the issue even further, the example of a practice schedule can be created, using a willing cast member as a model. Moreover, this discussion offers an excellent opportunity for staff to remind everyone not to set their expectations too high because learning new dance routines takes several weeks, a point that brings us to Word Number Two, Patience.

Patience. One consequence of a highly stressful life-style can be the lack of patience, whether experienced in a grocery store line or when trying to master a new skill. It should not be surprising, then, that many performers, whose life experiences have deprived them of the opportunity to develop the self-discipline and the patience required, find it particularly difficult to tolerate the time it takes to learn a dance routine, lines in a play, or lyrics to a song. Hence, it is important that one of the first items on the rehearsal agenda is a discussion of the process involved when learning a new skill. To illustrate, often personal experiences shared by staff can be helpful, examples that demonstrate how patience was involved when they were learning an instrument or studying to be a dancer. Accordingly, the author has been asked by many of her students how she became so skilled at the piano. Her answer was always, "My mother made me practice," usually followed by a description of a daily routine comprised of an hour of practice before and after school. Another approach is to ask whether any students had been through the process of learning to type, then asking whether they remember how both practice and patience were necessary as they learned a new skill. Subsequently, staff can describe how this same process is involved in learning dance routines, with the addition of Word Number Three, Perseverance.

Perseverance. Perseverance is defined as "activity maintained in spite of difficulties." In other words, it is the quality that enables us to keep moving forward despite setbacks and disappointments. In the following excerpt from his book, *Flow: Psychology of the Optimal Experience,* Mihaly Csikszentmihaly (1990) stresses the importance of this personal characteristic:

> We all know individuals who can transform hopeless situations into challenges to be overcome, just through the force of their personalities. This ability to persevere despite obstacles and setbacks is the quality people most admire in others, and justly so; it is probably the most important trait not only for succeeding in life, but for enjoying it as well.

Considering this statement and knowing how difficult it can be for people with a serious mental illness to find the motivation and energy needed to learn new skills, helping service users understand the importance of perseverance is critical if they are to achieve their recovery goals. Therefore, explaining how developing this trait in a performing arts activity can help them in their recovery efforts may provide the motivation needed to continue practicing. One way to communicate this information is to have students identify the skills learned in the performing arts program that could generalize to activities in their daily living. With this awareness, students may realize the importance of not giving up, despite mistakes, lapses in memory, or other temporary setbacks. Then after experiencing several successes, they will truly understand the importance of a "can-do" attitude and unrelenting perseverance.

Summary

Although creating a musical variety show with a cast of people with a serious mental illness may seem overwhelming to some, it need not be if there is an organized (and realistic) production plan and a methodical learning approach. Furthermore, keeping in mind that it can take 3 to 4 months to prepare for a major production, consideration should be given to the possibility that performers may become burned out from the lengthy rehearsal process. This is where periodic performances before small audiences become so important because they play a crucial role in keeping the cast motivated and morale high (Chapter 6). Furthermore, teaching performers the importance of good time management and following a practice schedule can help them avoid becoming overwhelmed by the amount of material they are asked to learn. With this information and an understanding of how practice, patience, and perseverance play an important role in the learning process, even individuals with no stage experience will find they have found a new way to celebrate life: by singing and dancing their way to recovery!

PUBLICITY AND PROGRAMS

Publicity

Preparing and disseminating publicity for any event can be time-consuming and labor-intensive. However, because most small organizations providing services to people with disabilities have neither the budget nor the staff to carry out an aggressive publicity campaign, there are a few basic, low-cost strategies that can be employed to ensure information on a special event is adequately disseminated. To this end, the author offers the timeline in Table 5 as a guide.

Table 5
PUBLICITY TIMELINE

Time Prior to Event	*Activity*
Six weeks	**Select** a publicity campaign coordinator (staff or volunteer). **Contact** organizations with newsletters to place ads for event in their publications and to determine deadlines for submission. **Assign** an individual to coordinate ticket sales, if applicable.
Four weeks	**Contact** local radio talk shows to request interviews. At the same time, ask if stations would consider recording a spot to be played periodically throughout the day. (Air time is free for public service announcements.) **Send** a press release to newspapers, radio, and television stations. **Ask** publicity coordinator to have someone design event flyer in two sizes: 8.5" × 11" (for posting) and half-sheets for distribution to individuals and groups. **Print** flyers and prepare envelopes for mailing.
Three weeks	**Distribute** flyers for posting by asking cast members to post them in the community or mailing to organizations. Remember: Information sent too early can be forgotten or ignored.
Two weeks	**Begin** designing the event program and *set a deadline* for printing sometime during the week before the performance.

For those who have never been involved in planning a publicity campaign, it is easy because of all the other tasks required, to wait too long to begin thinking about it. Procrastinating on this issue can result in negative consequences: low attendance at an event and a high stress level for those trying to implement a last-minute plan. Clearly then, pandemonium and high anxieties can be avoided by following one important rule: **Create a publicity campaign well in advance of the event!**

Programs

With all the details needing attention when producing a stage show, designing and printing programs may be low on a list of priorities. However, the program is an important component of the production process because performers often equate seeing their names in print with achievement and esteem. Further, the printed program provides a souvenier that can be shared with those unable to attend the show. It also serves as a permanent reminder of their performance, eliciting fond memories and good feelings as cast members reminisce about their unforgettable stage experience.

Regarding the program design, the type of event will determine this matter. For example, if the performance is held in-house and before a small audience, a program printed on an 8.5" × 11" sheet of paper may be appropriate. However, if a performance is held at a public event (i.e., a service club luncheon), it is important to take this opportunity to educate the audience about the organization's mission, goals, and purpose. These programs need not be elaborate or expensive to produce because they can be printed in black ink on white or colored paper. As a guide, in Appendix A, the reader will find a "boilerplate"[27] for a program that is printed on two sides and folded down the middle.

Can Confidentiality Promote Stigma?

One particular issue that might arise is how to print the names of performers on a document that will be distributed at a public event. Considering the confidentiality issues involved, the author usually used

27. A boilerplate is a standardized unit of writing that can be used over and over again without change.

first names with the last initial or first names only. However, later on in her On Stage! program, she introduced the cast to the idea of using full names instead. Although this diversion from the usual practice of concealing the identity of service users might be seen as unacceptable by many, this writer feels that the use of a name and an initial sends a message to the public that service users are ashamed or embarrassed by their illness, thus further promoting the stigma associated with mental illness. After expressing her feelings on the subject, she said that if performers are willing to fully disclose their identity, they are making a statement that says: "I am proud of who I am and of my accomplishments and am here to let you know people with a mental illness are no different from anyone else with an ongoing medical condition. So I am hoping that from this day forward you will see me as a person in recovery who has much to offer this community." So after discussing the positive effects of full disclosure with the On Stage! cast, members agreed unanimously to have their first and last names printed on event programs. Consequently, a document was prepared that gave On Stage! permission to print full names on all future programs, an act, in the opinion of this writer, that was a major step toward fulfilling the organization's mission to destigmatize mental illness.

COSTUMES

If there were one word to be used as a guide to a successful production, it would be "organization." This is especially true when two special circumstances are in play: not enough support staff and a cast of amateur performers with serious mental health disorders. Both conditions require special attention to detail, the first because too much responsibility for one person can result in extreme stress for everyone, and the second because most people with a mental illness have difficulty dealing with a disordered and chaotic environment. Therefore, for the sake of staff and performers alike, a production plan should include the planning of costumes and all details involved, including props and makeup.

It is important that costume design and planning is done early in the production process to allow adequate time for adaptations, changes, and unexpected cast substitutions. The following discussion is intended to help the reader be aware of potential problems that may occur when working with costumes, and to be better prepared for dealing with the attention to detail required to have everything ready on schedule.

In the author's experience, adequate funding was seldom available for costumes materials and construction. Therefore, a basic costume for both men and women was designed that could be easily constructed and adapted for a variety of show themes. With a seamstress or two donating services and a determination to search thrift stores and garage sales in all kinds of weather, the production staff always managed to provide costuming for every event. In this section, the reader will find ideas that have been successfully implemented in the author's shows, including: (1) basic costume designs, (2) costume organization, (3) costume construction, and (4) performance preparations.

Basic Costume Design

To simplify the costuming of a cast with a wide range of sizes, a basic costume of short-sleeved white shirts/blouses or colorful t-shirts with black pants, shoes, and socks is suggested. In addition, the following pieces may be used to add variety and interest to each production number:

- Vests: Color–red. A reversible vest of black and red provides added versatility to a wardrobe.
- Skirts (Optional): Style–reversible wrap-a-round; Color–navy blue or black with solid color fabric on reverse side.
- Hats: Styrofoam skimmers, enough for each dancer and extras to allow for breakage.
- Accessories:
  - Bow Ties: Red for men
  - Bows: For women to wear on blouses for added color and style
  - Canes: One for each dancer (see Appendix B for construction tips)
  - Gloves: White
  - Other: Boas, beads, headbands, feathers

The creative use of accessories and extra costume pieces can adapt the basic costume to almost any production number. This strategy is used to decrease the number of costume changes and is especially helpful in promoting quick transitions between numbers and reducing confusion when working in a backstage area that has limited space for costume changes. For example, a patriotic theme can be enhanced by red ribbons and bow ties; red, white, and blue striped paper around skimmers; and small American flags carried by the cast. Another example is to add a touch of Christmas with a white faux-pas fur trim on vests and a Santa Claus hat. Further, a 1950s theme can be portrayed with a poodle sewn onto the wraparound skirts and men in t-shirts with rolled-up sleeves. Thus, a show can be effectively costumed with a minimum of dollars and some creative shopping.

After the costumes have been designed, the next step is to plan for their construction by:

- Finding someone to construct vests (hopefully a volunteer).
- Asking cast members if they own any part of the basic costume (blouses, shirts, shoes, pants).
- Taking measurements of each student and recording information on Member Information form (Appendix B).
- Shopping at thrift stores and garage sales, remembering to take a tape measure and cast sizes. Watch for items that might be used in future shows.
- Purchasing black tennis shoes instead of dress shoes to keep costs down.

Costume Distribution

When costumes are ready for distribution, the author recommends the following:

- Assign a number to each item and write it with a permanent marker onto the costume pieces (when there is space on the piece). This method is a simple way to organize record-keeping and eliminates the confusion resulting when performers are trying to identify their costumes. An alternative is to write names on pieces of masking tape and adhere to costume pieces.
- Place each pair of dance shoes, if used, in a plastic bag with members' name attached.
- Hang each costume on hangers that have members' names where they are clearly visible. File folder labels can be used for this purpose by writing the name on one half of the label, and then wrap-

ping it around the neck of the hanger. Accessories can be placed in a plastic bag that hangs on a hanger.
- Have each member take as much responsibility as possible for putting costumes away after each rehearsal.

SETS AND PROPS

After producing many shows with a "low or no" budget, the author's production staff became very creative. From "dumpster dives" to donations from local businesses, the following materials were used to build sets that were both inexpensive and portable.

Flat Construction

Flats 3 or 4 feet wide and 6 feet high that are easily stored or transported can be constructed with two-by-fours and canvas. If funds are not available to purchase the canvas, white sheets can be used instead. Flats with two or three sections, rather than just one, are recommended because they can stand alone. The following construction tips are for a three-sectioned flat.

Supplies required

Two-by-fours, 18 feet for each flat; sizing for sheets or canvas; nails; staple gun; six hinges with screws; and acrylic house paint.

Assembly

1. Build three 3′ × 6′ sections by nailing together the two-by-fours.
2. Stretch canvas or sheets tightly across each frame and secure with staples.
3. Apply sizing to canvas or sheets with paint brush, allowing ample time for drying.
4. Paint designs onto flats, again allowing ample drying time.
5. Join three units together with hinges.

Set Design

To create a set for shows without a theme, the author has found the following method to be both simple and effective.

Mylar

For those unfamiliar with this material, it is shiny, metallic, and available in rolls of sheets in a variety of colors. When attached to a backdrop, the result is a glitter that adds "pazazz" to any set. To prepare the stage and/or audience area:

- Cut mylar into 2- or 3-inch-wide strips. (This will take a while, so be patient!)
- Attach strips to backdrop with safety pins to a curtain or with masking tape (lots of it!) if there is only a bare wall. Another option is to attach the strips to a light, thin strip of wood that can be suspended from the ceiling.
- Attach strips to walls and across entry ways to enhance a festive atmosphere.

Other Decorations

- Cut out large stars from cardboard, paint white, cover with spray glue and sprinkle with silver glitter.
- Attach stars to mylar strips with staples or masking tape. Stars may also be hung from ceiling and taped onto walls.
- Bring on the balloons! Balloons always add a festive touch to any occasion, so do not forget about them. When possible, have the name of the show and/or a logo printed on each balloon. Filled with helium, they can be placed in "bouquets" around the performance area and/or tied to chairs. (If balloons are allowed to float at ceiling level, be sure they are well inflated or they may suddenly drop on an unsuspected member of your audience–or float in front of your video camera!)

THEME SHOWS

Theme: Patriotic

Stage Set: General (Open stage)
Colors: Red, white, and blue

- Streamers–Hang strips of red, white, and blue crepe paper from ceiling at back of stage, vertically on side of stage walls, horizontally in front of stage, on walls in audience area, and around poles if available. If the area is small, drape strips across ceiling.

- Flags–It a large flag is available, it can be hung at back of stage in place of streamers. Place standing flags (if available) on either side of stage.
- Pictures–Attach large cardboard pictures of U.S. presidents to front of stage or on walls in audience area.
- Stars–Attach small cardboard stars covered with silver glitter to streamers.
- Table Decorations–If the audience is seated at tables:
  - *Place* a large cardboard star covered with glitter in the center of the table.
  - *Use* red, white and blue table clothes.
  - *Construct* centerpiece by cutting a 4- or 5-inch styrofoam ball in half. With rounded side of one half placed downward, insert small flags and metallic sparklers into ball. Fill in extra space with small bunches of red and blue tissue paper, attaching with straight pins. Throw confetti streamers and loose confetti randomly onto tablecloth.

Theme: 1950s

Stage Set: Soda Fountain
Colors: Pink, black, and white
Decorations

- Streamers–Hang pink and black or pink, black, and white streamers as backdrop, alternating strips of silver mylar with crepe paper.
- Stars–Add large glittered stars to mylar strips and small stars to crepe paper.

Set Design

The following items are suggested to enhance the 1950s set:

- Cars–Construct large cut-outs of 1950s cars (i.e., Mercury, Chevy, Hot Rod, 6 to 8 feet long, 2 1/2 to 3 feet high) from cardboard. Paint with bright colors (yellow, blue, red). Set against walls on stage or in front of stage, if raised. (At a fundraiser with a 1950s theme, one of these cars was an auction item that sold very quickly!)

- Juke Box–Construct from cardboard 5 feet high and 3 feet wide. Paint with bright colors and highlight with silver glitter. Place at side or back of stage.
- Banner–Construct a large banner from butcher paper with name of soda fountain painted in large letters. Highlight letters with silver glitter.
- Tables–Place small tables with chairs on stage to create atmosphere of soda fountain. Cast sits at tables until time to perform. Arrange tables at back and sides of stage to create a "dance floor."

Table Decorations (for tables in audience)

Pink tablecloths and the following centerpiece are suggested: Fill soda glasses with pink and white cotton balls topped with small red pom-poms to replicate sodas. Then place bouquets of pink, black and white helium balloons with long strings taped under soda glasses to create a festive atmosphere.

Theme: Roaring 20s

Stage Set: Speakeasy nightclub
Colors: Selected
Set Design

- Bar–Construct a simple bar from pieces of wood. Place bar at back of stage, either right or left. Place a few glasses on bar. Assign someone to serve as bartender.
- Tables/Chairs–Place small round or square tables around edge of stage for cast seating. Cover with red and white checked tablecloths. Arrange chairs around tables.
- Decorations–Use materials suggested earlier to cover back wall and audience area if desired.

Audience Seating

Depending on the size of the performance area, one of the following may be used as an audience seating arrangement.

- Theatre Seating–This is the traditional arrangement where chairs are placed in rows. Audiences are usually spectators and do not participate in the performance.
- Cabaret Seating–This arrangement is more informal and can allow for audience participation. For a 1950s show, the audience can be included as "customers" in the soda shop, sitting comfortably around small and large tables.

In summary, producing a show with any special population can be a challenge. However, if approached with a positive attitude, enthusiasm, and a well-organized plan, you can look forward to a successful production. Moreover, service users, volunteers, and the community as a whole will benefit not only from the performance but also from the effect your shows can have on reducing the stigma associated with mental illness. Hopefully, the information in this and earlier chapters will pique your interest and provide motivation to launch a theatre project in your community. After all, the message in that famous show tune cannot be denied: "There's no business like show business!"

APPENDICES

Appendix A

PROGRAM GUIDES

1. CANE CONSTRUCTION GUIDE

If funding is unavailable to purchase dance canes, they can easily be constructed with a 36" × 3/4" dowel, glassy latex, and white paint. Apply paint as follows:

1. Mark off 1 inch on one end of dowel and one and 1 1/2 inches on opposite end.
2. Apply masking tape to each end of dowel to cover the area where paint will be applied.
3. Apply two coats of black paint, allowing ample time for drying between coats.
4. Remove masking tape from both ends of dowel.
5. Apply masking tape at the top of black areas on both ends to prevent white paint from running into black.
6. Apply two coats of white paint to each end, again allowing ample drying time between coats.
7. When white paint is dry, remove tape and you're done!

2. CRISIS RESOLUTION GUIDE: DAY OF PERFORMANCE

INCIDENT	RESOLUTIONS	CRISIS PREVENTIONS
1. Illness or family emergency prevents one or more students from performing.	1A. Staff members are substituted for students. 1B. Cast members are "shuffled" to acommodate absences. (This solution requires a last-minute rehearsal.) 1C. If absentee has a major role, another cast or staff member is substituted.	1A. Have two or more staff ready to substitute in all presentations. 1B. Prepare student understudies for major roles. 1C. Ask students to notify staff immediately of an emergency. One or two hours can make a big difference in resolving the crisis and avoiding undue anxiety.
2. Cast member experiences extreme anxiety minutes before curtain and cannot perform. Individual may walk out.	2A. Same as 1A, B, and C. 2B. If student had part in a skit, give substitute the script to use on stage. 2C. Inform audience of changes and explain situation without disclosing performer's reason for not appearing. Use the phrase "is unable to perform."	2A. An ongoing process of reducing performance anxiety will usually prepare performers for the inevitable anxieties associated with a performance. 2B. If this situation does occur, assure anxious performer that it is ok for him or her not to perform, offering reassurance, not reprimand.

CRISIS RESOLUTION GUIDE: DAY OF PERFORMANCE–*Continued*

3. Cast member has transportation problem.	3A. send driver to transport cast member. 3B. Call another student with a car and request assistance.	3A. Have enough staff and volunteers available to transport if necessary. 3B. Arrange to have all students transported by van. 3C. Divide transport among staff and cast members who have vehicles. 3D. Check to be sure drivers' insurance covers transporting cast members. 3E. For cast members responsible for their own transport, remind them to allow ample time for travel.
4. The time for cast to report for performance has passed, and one or two students are absent.	4A. Ask other cast members if they know of absentee's whereabouts. 4B. Call cast member's residence. 4C. If student has no phone, send a driver to residence.	4A & B. Have addresses and phone numbers of all cast members available. 4C. Have drivers available.
5. Cast member forgets to take medication before leaving for performance.	5A. Call residence and ask if someone is available to deliver medication. 5B. If residence cannot deliver, send driver with cast member to pick up medication.	5A. Remind all cast members at last rehearsal to take their medications. Include this reminder in memo with schedule for day of performance. 5B. Have driver available.

continued

CRISIS RESOLUTION GUIDE: DAY OF PERFORMANCE–*Continued*

6. Cast member leaves part of costume at home.	6A. If cast members can describe to someone at residence exactly what and where items are located, call residence to see if items can be delivered. 6B. If necessary, send driver to pick up costume items.	6A. Require that all costume pieces provided by cast members be brought to a rehearsal prior to performance. If students must wear any items home, a reminder phone call on the day of performance is suggested. 6B. Have driver available.
7. A costume is torn.	7A. Give costumes to someone for immediate repair.	7A. Have basic sewing kit available at all times and a supply of hemming tape and safety pins. Even masking tape holds a hem in place in an emergency.

3. DANCE ROUTINE: *I'M A YANKEE DOODLE DANDY*

Starting Position: Down stage in one, two, or three lines. Feet together, arms at sides.

Instructions: Part A

Lyrics	Step	Counts	Arms/Hands	Feet
I'm a Yankee Doodle Dandy; A Yankee Doodle, do or die. A	A1	16	Swinging at sides	March in place: R L R L, etc.
Real live nephew of my Uncle Sam–	A2	8	L arm at side R arm at forehead in salute	Standing in place: **Counts 1–7:** Beginning with R foot, turn to R and walk in a complete small circle with 7 steps. **Count 8:** Face audience
Born on the Fourth of July I've–	A3	8	Hands on waist for 8 counts	**Count 1:** Kick R foot to L across body. **Count 2:** Step R foot in place next to left. **Count 3:** Kick L foot to R across body. **Count 4:** Step L foot in place next to R. **Counts 5 & 6:** Repeat counts 1 & 2 **Count 7:** Kick L foot to R across body. **Count 8:** Step L foot in place next to R.

continued

Instructions: Part B

Lyrics	Step	Count	Arms/Hands and Feet
			Standing in place:
Got a Yankee Doodle sweetheart;	B1	8	**Count 1** (on "got"): Throw L arm to L side so it is positioned away from body at 45 degree angle from floor. Turn palm toward front, fingers straight and spread wide (jazz hand position). R arms is held down at side. **Counts 2–4:** Hold position. **Count 5** (on "she's"): Throw R arm to R side in same position as L arm. **Counts 6–8:** Hold position.
			Place hands on knees; then bend knees with face looking at audience. Bounce up and down in "horseriding" motion as follows:
Yankee Doodle went to London just to ride the ponies.	B2	8	**Count 1:** Bend knees. **Count 2:** Partly straighten knees. **Count 3–8:** Repeat counts 1 & 2.
I am a Yankee Doodle boy.	B3	8	**Count 1:** Stand up straight. Place L arm down at side, at same time pointing to chest with R thumb. **Counts 2–6:** Hold position. **Counts 7–8:** Place R arm down at side.

4. PERSONALITY CHARACTERISTICS OF THE SUCCESSFUL TEACHER/THERAPIST

Communicates Effectively
- Has warm and friendly manner
- Speaks and writes clearly and concisely
- Presents new ideas and supports them
- Expresses agreement or disagreement without becoming defensive

Makes Thoughtful Decisions
- Avoids jumping to conclusions
- Seeks out, listens to, and considers ideas from others

Accepts Responsibility
- Does not project blame onto others
- Admits mistakes and learns from them
- Is dependable
- Manages time efficiently and effectively
- Follows through with commitments

Is Self-Confident
- Is comfortable speaking in front of others
- Is assertive
- Has good eye contact in conversations with others

Is an Effective Leader
- Motivates others
- Accepts and uses ideas from others
- Delegates authority
- Has good organizational skills

Is Non-Judgmental
- Accepts others as they are
- Accepts values of others
- Allows others to make their own decisions

Is Flexible
- Adapts to any situation
- Accepts change willingly

Has a Good Sense of Humor

- Is able to laugh at self
- Can see humor in difficult situations
- Helps others take themselves less seriously

Is Genuinely Concerned for Others

- Is sincere when offering praise
- Shows empathy toward others

Is Creative

- Explores and develops creative ideas
- Understands importance of helping others discover their creative abilities
- Assists others in developing creative problem-solving skills

Is Self-Aware

- Refrains from becoming emotionally involved with students
- Seeks help when unable to handle difficult or emotional situations
- Responds to hostility from others without becoming angry or defensive
- Remains calm in a crisis situation
- Is in control of emotions at all times

Has Positive Attitude

- Understands and teaches importance of positive thinking
- Encourages others to remain positive in difficult situations
- Is energetic and enthusiastic

5. PROGRAM BOILERPLATE

(Front Page)

Name of YourOrganization

Presents

NAME OF SHOW

Featuring

Name of Your Theatre Company
or Group

with

Name of Master of Ceremonies

Day, Month, Year
Time
Location
Address of Location

Proceeds benefit individuals with (Name of Special Population)

(Page 2)

PROGRAM

Welcome-------- MC/Dignitary/Program Director

Opening-- Cast
Title of Acts
Names of Featured Performers

Title of Solo---------------------- Name of Performer

Company Number------------------------------------Cast
Song Titles/Dances
Names of Soloists/Featured Performers

Guest Artist------------------------------------- Name
Song Title/Act

Title of Skit------------------------- Company Players

Duet/Solo/Small Ensemble------------------ Names
Song Titles

Finale-- Cast
Song Titles

INTERMISSION

(Page 3)

CAST

(List names alphabetically in two columns. Include staff and volunteers performing with the company.)

Name	Name
Name	Name
Name	Name
Name	Name
Name	Name

PRODUCTION

Director-- Name
Choreographer------------------------------------- Name
Costumes--- Name
Make-Up-- Name
Stage Manager------------------------------------- Name
Stage Assistants---------------------------------- Names
Lights/Sound--------------------------------------- Name
Sets-- Name
Publicity-- Name
Ushers--- Names
Videographer--------------------------------------- Name

(Page 4)

ABOUT YOUR ORGANIZATION

Include your organization's mission, purpose and goals and any information you feel would be of interest to your audience.

ACKNOWLEDGEMENTS

List all organizations and individuals that have provided significant support for this event.

We wish to extend our appreciation to everyone who has made this event possible.
Thank you for attending.

(Name of organization) is funded/supported by (names of organizations providing on-going support.

6. PROGRAM SAMPLE

(This program is designed to be printed in landscape and folded in half.)

PROGRAM

ACT I

Welcome---------------Director of
Mental Health Provider

Opening---Cast
Hats Off! Spokane
Lyrics by HN Music by D. Douglass
Lullaby of Broadway by Dubin and Warren

Swimming to the Other Side--Discovery School

Reaching For Our Star--------------------------Cast
Vocalists: LS and SW
Dancers: LC and JP
Written by D. Douglass

Musical Selections---------------------Celtic Nots

Selections from *Music Man*-------------------Cast
Seventy Six Trombones and *Good Night, Ladies*
Music and Lyrics by Meredith Wilson
Featuring
students from Discovery School and
Lewis and Clark High School marching band

Musical Selections---------------------Celtic Nots

Act I Finale--------------------------------------Cast
Everything's Coming Up Roses
by Sondheim & Styne
There's No Business Like Show Business
by I. Berlin
Now You Have Seen What We Can Do
by D. Douglass

INTERMISSION

ACT II

Selections from *Little Mary Sunshine*-------Cast
Lyrics and Music by Rick Besoyan
Forest Ranger Song
Performed by JP, PJ and SW
Playing Croquet, Swinging & How Do You Do?
Performed by the
"Ladies from Eastchester Finishing School"

Let the Rest of the Word Go By-----------------PA
Love Me with All Your Heart

Do Re Mi---Cast
Music by Rodgers and Hammerstein
Performed by PA, Discovery School
Children and Staff

Go With the Flo or
Tales from a Laundromat------On Stage! Players
Written by Cast and Staff
There is Nothin' Like a Dame from
South Pacific by Rodgers and Hammerstein
Anything You Can Do, I Can Do Better
From "Annie Get Your Gun" by Irving Berlin

Coleman's Cross-------------------------Celtic Nots
With Columbia Ballet Theatre Dancers

Ties and Tails-----------------------CL, JP and SL
We've Come a Long Way, Baby!---------------Cast
Music and Lyrics by D. Douglass

Finale--- Cast

*Awarding of Met Medals-------------------Staff

*At the time of this production, the theatre in which it was performed was known as the Metropolitan Center for the Performing Arts, later to be renamed the Bing Crosby Theatre. Thus, the term *Met Medals* was used to describe these awards, placed around the neck of each cast member by a local dignitary. Following the performance, the audience was invited to meet and greet cast members in the lobby of the theatre, a process that promoted the use of personal contact in reducing the stigma associated with mental illness.

7. PROGRAM RULES AND GUIDELINES

The rules and guidelines presented here are divided into two categories: the *Do's* and the *Don't's*. The reader is encouraged to adapt these items or add new ones to accommodate the requirements of a particular program.

Do's

1. Do arrive at least 15 minutes prior to class or rehearsal to allow time to hang up coats, use rest rooms, etc.
2. Do stay in the group until break time or the end of class unless it is absolutely necessary for you to leave. Even a brief absence can cause delays in the learning process.
3. Do attend classes and rehearsals regularly, notifying staff if you are ill or cannot attend for emergency reasons.
4. Do schedule doctor and other appointments around your class or rehearsal schedules.
5. Do support each other. If you see someone becoming discouraged, offer your support and encourage that person to keep trying.
6. Do be considerate of others.
7. Do ask questions if you do not understand something. In the learning process, there are no "dumb" questions.
8. Do be patient and prepared to do dance steps, routines, and songs many times. It is this process that helps you learn the required material.
9. Do give yourself credit for each small success.
10. Do maintain good personal hygiene.

Don't's

1. Don't be afraid to make mistakes. Try to think of mistakes as building blocks to learning.
2. Don't expect to learn everything on the first day. Learning dance routines and songs takes a great deal of practice, so try to avoid setting your expectations too high.
3. Don't interrupt your instructor when he or she is talking to the group or an individual. Wait patiently until the instructor is free.
4. Don't arrive late. After classes or rehearsals have begun, late arrivals are disruptive and cause delays in the learning process. We realize there are times when lateness cannot be avoided, but try your best!
5. Don't tell other students what to do! If you have suggestions or see things you feel should be changed, please tell an instructor. Too many

people giving directions only causes confusion and can lead to anger and hurt feelings.

Thank you for your cooperation and for enrolling in our performing arts program.

Appendix B

FORMS

1. CONFIDENTIALITY STATEMENT AND CONSENT FORM

(Name of Organization)

Name of Student________________________________

It is my understanding that my name may be used only with my written permission documented on a consent form provided by either (name of organization) or the media organization involved. Knowing this, I voluntarily and of my own free will hereby permit (name of organization) to:

1. **Videotape** rehearsals and performances to obtain feedback for the purpose of improving my performance and the performance of the theatre company.

DATED this _____ day of _____________, 20___

_______________________________ _______________________________

Student Signature Witness

2. To make **audio tape recordings** for the purpose of improving my performance.

DATED this _____ day of _____________, 20___

_______________________________ _______________________________

Student Signature Witness

3. To use **photographs, slides** and **video** or **audio tape recordings** made by (name of organization) and/or the print and broadcast media for the purpose of promoting (name of organization) performances.

DATED this _____ day of ____________, 20___

_______________________________	_______________________________
Student Signature	Witness

2. MEMBER ENROLLMENT FORM

Name_____________________________________ Date______________

Address_______________________________ Zip Code______________

CM/PCP______________________________ Phone________________

Significant Medical Problems (i.e., diabetes, epilepsy)

____

____

____

Medications ____

____

____

Emergency Contact

Name_________________________________ Phone________________

If there is any other information staff should know, please describe:

____

____

____

3. MEMBER INFORMATION FORM

(Two half-sheets per page)

Name____________________________________ Date______________

Address________________________________ Phone________________

__________________________________ Zip________ DOB_________

Emergency Contact____

COSTUME SIZES AND ASSIGNMENTS

Shirt/Blouse____#____ T-Shirt____ #____ Shoes_____#____ Hat____#____

Pants____#____ Socks____

MEASUREMENTS

Chest/Bust_____ Waist_____ Head____ Arm Length (shoulder to wrist)____

Neck_____ Pant Length (inside leg)_____ Pant Length (waist to shoe)_____

Skirt Length_____

Other ____

Name____________________________________ Date______________

Address________________________________ Phone________________

__________________________________ Zip________ DOB_________

Emergency Contact____

COSTUME SIZES AND ASSIGNMENTS

Shirt/Blouse____#____ T-Shirt____ #____ Shoes_____#____ Hat____#____

Pants____#____ Socks____

MEASUREMENTS

Chest/Bust_____ Waist_____ Head____ Arm Length (shoulder to wrist)____

Neck_____ Pant Length (inside leg)_____ Pant Length (waist to shoe)_____

Skirt Length_____

Other ____

4. MEMBER SIGN-IN FORM

NAME	DATE

5. PRE-PERFORMANCE SELF EVALUATION

Name____ Date_______________

Instructions: Read each statement carefully. Then underline the answer that best describes how you feel **at this moment**.

HOW DO YOU FEEL YOU WILL PERFORM?

1. My concentration will be good throughout the performance.
Strongly agree Agree Disagree Strongly disagree

2. I will feel no guilt if I make a mistake.
Strongly agree Agree Disagree Strongly disagree

3. I will be in control of my performance.
Strongly agree Agree Disagree Strongly disagree

4. My nervousness will probably be noticed by the audience.
Strongly agree Agree Disagree Strongly disagree

5. My interactions with the audience will be positive and make me feel good about my performance.
Strongly agree Agree Disagree Strongly disagree

6. I am confident I will give a good performance.
Strongly agree Agree Disagree Strongly disagree

7. My memory will be good.
Strongly agree Agree Disagree Strongly disagree

8. I will project my voice well.
Strongly agree Agree Disagree Strongly disagree

9. I will feel confident on stage.
Strongly agree Agree Disagree Strongly disagree

(PLEASE COMPLETE OTHER SIDE)

10. I will perform with energy.
Strongly agree Agree Disagree Strongly disagree

11. If I make a mistake I will recover quickly and keep going.
Strongly agree Agree Disagree Strongly disagree

12. My eye contact with the audience and my fellow performers will be good.
Strongly agree Agree Disagree Strongly disagree

13. The audience will understand my words when I sing or speak.
Strongly agree Agree Disagree Strongly disagree

14. I will smile at the audience and my fellow performers most of the time.
Strongly agree Agree Disagree Strongly disagree

15. I will hold my head up and my posture will be good.
Strongly agree Agree Disagree Strongly disagree

6. POST-PERFORMANCE SELF EVALUATION

Name______________________________________ Date_______________

INSTRUCTIONS: Read each statement carefully. Then underline the answer which best describes how you feel.

HOW DID YOU PERFORM?

1. My concentration was good throughout the performance.
   Strongly agree Agree Disagree Strongly disagree

2. I did not feel guilty if I made a mistake.
   Strongly agree Agree Disagree Strongly disagree

3. I was in control of my performance.
   Strongly agree Agree Disagree Strongly disagree

4. My nervousness was probably noticed by the audience.
   Strongly agree Agree Disagree Strongly disagree

5. My interactions with the audience were positive and made me feel good about my performance.
   Strongly agree Agree Disagree Strongly disagree

6. I am confident I gave a good performance.
   Strongly agree Agree Disagree Strongly disagree

7. My memory was good.
   Strongly agree Agree Disagree Strongly disagree

8. I projected my voice well.
   Strongly agree Agree Disagree Strongly disagree

9. I felt confident on stage.
   Strongly agree Agree Disagree Strongly disagree

(PLEASE COMPLETE OTHER SIDE)

10. I performed with energy.
Strongly agree Agree Disagree Strongly disagree

11. If I made a mistake, I recovered quickly and kept going.
Strongly agree Agree Disagree Strongly disagree

12. My eye contact with the audience and my fellow performers was good.
Strongly agree Agree Disagree Strongly disagree

13. The audience understood my words when I sang or spoke.
Strongly agree Agree Disagree Strongly disagree

14. I smiled at the audience and my fellow performers most of the time.
Strongly agree Agree Disagree Strongly disagree

15. I held my head up and my posture was good.
Strongly agree Agree Disagree Strongly disagree

WHAT DID YOU THINK OF THE PERFORMANCE OVERALL?

1. The performance flowed smoothly.
Strongly agree Agree Disagree Strongly disagree

2. The performance was better than I expected.
Strongly agree Agree Disagree Strongly disagree

3. The performance was energetic.
Strongly agree Agree Disagree Strongly disagree

4. Performance problems were handled well by all.
Strongly agree Agree Disagree Strongly disagree

5. Everyone backstage was quiet and cooperative.
Strongly agree Agree Disagree Strongly disagree

Taking into consideration all of the challenges we faced in preparing this production, do you feel this performance could have been improved?
___Yes ___No

If yes, what do you feel we could have done to improve it?

7. THEATRE COMPANY CONTRACT

CONTRACTUAL AGREEMENT BETWEEN THE CAST OF (Name of Theatre Company/Organization) AND STAFF

AS A(N) (Name of Company/Organization)
STAFF MEMBER, I AGREE TO:

1. Provide the instruction necessary for the productions presented by (Name of Organization).

2. Coordinate all aspects of the program required for successful musical theatre productions.

3. Help and support cast members in their efforts to perform at their maximum capacity and ability.

4. Base all casting and production decisions on each member's abilities, avoiding favoritism and other personal issues that might influence these decisions.

AS A CAST MEMBER OF (Name of Theatre Company) I AGREE TO:

1. Commit to participating in the theatre company for a minimum of 3 months.

2. Attend all scheduled rehearsals and performances. If I have a reason for being absent, I will notify my instructors in advance of that absence.

3. Participate in all activities to the best of my ability.

4. Alert my instructor if I am experiencing any health, behavioral, or other problems that might interfere with my level of participation and performance.

5. Manage my behavior at all times, remembering to be considerate of others.

6. Comply with my clinical team treatment plan.

7. Accept instruction willingly and refrain from telling others what to do.

8. Maintain a positive attitude toward my fellow cast members, staff, and my ability to be successful.

9. Be loyal to(name of organization), its staff and students, supporting my fellow cast members whenever possible and refraining from any behaviors that could undermine the success of the theatre company.

10. Recognize the authority of my instructors, realizing that they make the final decisions on any issue that deals directly with production activities.

11. Recognize that casting decisions made by my instructors are based on each member's abilities and by the fit of those abilities to the casting needs of the company.

12. Accept constructive criticism from my instructors, realizing that corrections and suggestions are targeted toward improving my performance and are not to be taken personally.

13. Conduct myself in a professional manner at all times, remembering that I represent not only (name of organization) but also (names of other organizations if applicable).

14. Be patient with myself, realizing that learning new skills takes practice, patience, and perseverance.

15. Work hard, have fun, and believe in myself!

My signature indicates that I understand, agree with, and intend to comply with this contract.

____________________________ ____________________________

Cast Member Staff

REFERENCES

Alonso, J., Buron, A., Rojas-Farreras, S., de Graaf, R., Josep, M. H., de Girolamo, G., Bruffaerts, R., Kovess, V., Matschinger, H., & Vilagut, G. (2009). Perceived stigma among individuals with common mental disorders. *Journal of Affective Disorders, 118*(1–3), 180–186.

Americans For The Arts. (2009). *Arts education and cognitive development.* Retrieved on September 17, 2009, from http://www.artsusa.org/pdf/get_involved/advocacy/research/2009/artsed_cogdev09.pdf.

American Music Conference. (2007). *Music making: Music and the brain.* Retrieved on February 4, 2009, from www.amc-music.com/musicmaking/brain/irvine.htm.

Anderson, G. (2007). *Developing a stress-resistant personality.* Retrieved on June 24, 2009, from http://angertrends.blogspot.com/2007/08/developing-stress-resistant-personality.html.

Anthony, W., Cohen, M., Farkas, M., & Gagne, C. (2004). *Psychiatric Rehabilitation.* Boston, MA: Center for Psychiatric Rehabilitation.

Anthony, W. A. (1992). A revolution in vision (Editorial). *Innovations & Research, 1*(4).

Atkinson, P. A., Martin, C. R., & Rankin, J. (2009). Resilience revisited. *Journal of Psychiatric Mental Health Nursing, 16*(2), 137–145.

Bandura, A. (1977). *Social learning theory.* Upper Saddle River, NJ: Prentice Hall, Inc.

Baron, R. A., & Byrne, D. (1997). *Social psychology.* Boston: Allyn and Bacon.

Barondes, S. H. (2003a). *Better than Prozac: Creating the new generation of psychiatric drugs.* New York: Oxford University Press.

Barondes, S. H. (2003b). *A talk with Samuel Barondes, M. D. The Edge.* Retrieved on January 24, 2009, from http://www.edge.org/3rd_culture/barondes_index .html.

Berge, M., & Ranney, M. (2005). Self-esteem and stigma among persons with schizophrenia: Implications for mental health. *Care Management Journal, 6*(3), 139–144.

Bipolar World. (2009). *History of mental illness and early treatment in a nutshell.* Retrieved on September 8, 2009, from http://www.bipolarworld.net/Bipolar%20Disorder/History/mental_illness.htm.

Blankertz, L. (2001). Cognitive components of self esteem for individuals with severe mental illness. *American Journal of Orthopsychiatry, 71*(4), 457–465.

Boeree, G. (2006) *Albert Bandura.* Retrieved June 23, 2008, from http://webspace.ship.edu/cgboer/bandura.html.

Bowers, J. D., & Hughes, P. (Eds.). (2009). Dorothea Dix. *Universal International Historical Society.* Retrieved on May 4, 2009, from http://www25.uua.org/uuhs

/duub/articles/dorotheadix.html.

Bowie, C. R., & Harvey, P. D. (2006). Treatment of cognitive deficits in schizophrenia. *Current Opinion in Investigational Drugs, 7*(7), 608–613.

Brooks, G. (2008). Cognitive impairment and cognitive rehabilitation after traumatic brain injury. *Outcomes: Newsletter of the Northeast Center for Special Care.* Retrieved on February 10, 2009, from http://www.northeastcenter.com/information-bulletin-cognitive-impairment-and-cognitive-rehabilitation-after-traumatic-brain-injury.htm.

Carter, C. S. (1999, Summer). The importance of cognitive disability in schizophrenia. *Insight: Newsletter of the Services for the Treatment of Early Psychosis (STEP) Program, 1*(2). Retrieved on February 9, 2009, from http://www.wpic.pitt.edu/research/psychosis-insight/insight/read2.pdf.

Chopra, A. K., & Doody, G. A. (2007). Schizophrenia, an illness and a metaphor: Analysis of the use of the term "schizophrenia" in the UK national newspapers. *Journal of the Royal Society of Medicine, 100*(9), 423–426.

Clark, D. (2003, May 6). Talent, courage a must to join those On Stage. *Spokesman Review,* Spokane, WA, p. B1 & B8.

Connecticut Heritage Productions. (2007). *Acts of recovery.* Retrieved on March 4, 2010, from http://chproductions.org/node/10.

Cook, J. A., & Wright, E. R. (1995). Medical sociology and the study of severe mental Illness: Reflections on past accomplishments and directions for future research. *Journal of Health and Social Behavior, 35* (special edition), 95–114.

Corrigan, P. W. (1998). The impact of stigma on severe mental illness. *Cognitive and Behavioral Practice, 5*(2), 201–222.

Corrigan, P. W., & Penn, D. L. (1999). Lessons from social psychology on discrediting psychiatric stigma. *American Psychologist, 54*(9), 765–776.

Corrigan, P. W., & Rusch, N. (2002). Mental illness stereotypes and clinical care: Do people avoid treatment because of stigma? *Psychiatric Rehabilitation Skills, 6*(3), 312–334.

Corrigan, P. W., & Watson, A. C. (2002). The paradox of self-stigma and mental illness. *Clinical Psychology: Science and Practice, 9*(1), 35–53.

Corrigan, P. (2004). How stigma interferes with mental health care. *American Psychologist, 59*(7), 614–625.

Corrigan, P. W., Mueser, K. T., Bond, G. R., Drake, R. E., & Solomon, P. (2009). *Principles and practices of psychiatric rehabilitation: An empirical approach* (p. 34). New York: The Guilford Press.

Csikszentmihalyi, M. (1990). *Flow.* New York: Harper & Row.

Deegan, P. E. (1997). Recovery and empowerment for people with psychiatric disabilities. *Social Work in Health Care, 25*(3), 11–24.

Delevoye-Turrell, Y., Giersch, A., Wing, A. M., & Danion, J. (2007). Motor fluency deficits in the sequencing of actions in schizophrenia. *Journal of Abnormal Psychology, 116*(1), 56–64.

Douglass, D., Martineau, D., & Dyck, D. (1997). *On Stage!: A study on the effect of the performing arts on the rehabilitation of adults with severe and persistent mental illness.* Unpublished manuscript, Washington State University Spokane, Washington

Institute for Mental Health Research and Training, Spokane, WA.
Duckworth, K., Halpern, J. H., Schutt, R. K., & Gillespie, C. (2003). Use of schizophrenia as a metaphor in US newspapers. *Psychiatric Services, 54,* 1402–1404.
Elvevag, B., & Goldberg, T. E. (2000). Cognitive impairment in schizophrenia is the core of the disorder. *Critical Review in Neurobiology, 14*(1), 1–21.
Estroff, S. E., Penn, D. L., & Toporek, J. R. (2004). From stigma to discrimination: An analysis of community efforts to reduce the negative consequences of having a psychiatric disorder and label. *Schizophrenia Bulletin, 30*(3), 493–509.
Fisher, D., & Ahern, L. (2009). *People can recover from mental illness. National Empowerment Center.* Retrieved on September 6, 2009, from http://www.power2u.org/articles/recovery/people_can.html.
Fiszdon, J. M., Silverstein, S. M., Buchwald, J., Hull, J. W., & Smith, T. E. (2003). Verbal memory in schizophrenia: Sex differences over repeated assessments. *Schizophrenia Research, 61*(2–3), 235–243.
Fitts, P. M., & Posner, M. I. (1967). *Human performance.* Belmont, CA: Brooks/Cole.
Forgeard, M., Winner E., & Schlaug, G. (2008). Practicing a musical instrument in childhood is associated with enhanced verbal ability and nonverbal reasoning. *PLoS One, 3*(10), e3566.
Fung, K. M. T., Tsang, H. W. H., Corrigan, P. W., Lam, C. S., & Cheng, W. (2007). Measuring self-stigma of mental illness in China and its implications for recovery. *International Journal of Social Psychiatry, 53*(5), 408–418.
Gaebel, W., & Baumann, A. E. (2003). Interventions to reduce the stigma associated with severe mental illness: Experiences from the Open the Doors program in Germany. *Canadian Journal of Psychiatry, 48,* 657–662.
Gaebel, W., Zaske, H., & Baumann, E. (2006). The relationship between mental illness severity and stigma. *Acta Psychiatrica Scandinavica, 113*(s429), 41–45.
Garske, G. G., & McReynolds, C. J. (2005). Psychiatric rehabilitation: A means of de-stigmatizing severe mental illness. *Journal of Applied Rehabilitation Counseling, 36,* 28–34.
Grootens, K. P., Vermeeren, L., Verkes, R. J., Buitelaar, J. K. Sabbe, V. G. C., van Veelen, N., Kahn, R. S., & Hulstijn, W. (2009). Psychomotor planning is deficient in recent-onset schizophrenia. *Schizophrenia Research, 107*(2–3), 294–302.
Gureje, O., Harvey, C., & Herman, H. (2004). Self-esteem in patients who have recovered from psychosis: profile and relationship to quality of life. *The Australian and New Zealand Journal of Psychiatry, 38*(5), 334–338.
Hall, P. L., & Tarrier, N. (2003). The cognitive-behavioral treatment of low self-esteem in psychotic patients: A pilot study. *Behavior Research and Therapy, 41*(3), 317–332.
Harvey, P. D. (2007). Cognitive impairment in major depression and bipolar disorders. *Psychiatry, 4*(1), 12–14.
Heinssen, R. K., Liberman, R. P., & Kopelowicz, A. (2000). Psychosocial skills training for schizophrenia: Lessons from the laboratory. *Schizophrenia Bulletin, 26*(1), 21–46.
Herbert, Y., Metzer, H.Y., Park, S., & Kessler, R. (1999). Cognition, schizophrenia and the atypical antipsychotic drugs. *Commentary from the Procedures of the National*

Academy of Sciences, 96(24), 13591–13593.

Hinshaw, S. P., & Cicchetti, D. (2000). Stigma and mental disorder: Conceptions of illness, public attitudes, personal disclosure and social policy. *Development and Psychopathology, 12*(4), 555–598.

Holahan, C. J., & Moos, R. H. (1985). Life stress and health: Personality, coping and-family support in stress resistance. *Journal of Personality and Social Psychology, 49*(3), 739–747).

Hopper, K. (2007). Rethinking social recovery in schizophrenia: What capabilities approach might offer. *Social Science and Medicine, 65*(5), 868–879.

Horan, H. P., Kern, R. S., Shokat-Fadai, K., Sergi, J. J., Wynn, J. K., &, Green, M. F. (2009). Social cognitive skills training in schizophrenia: An initial efficacy study of stabilized outpatients. *Schizophrenia Research, 107*(1), 47–54.

Hyde, K. L., Lerch, J., Norton, A., Forgeard, M., Winner, E., Evans, A. C., & Schlaug, G. (2009). The effects of musical training on structural brain development development. *The Neurosciences and Music III: Disorders and Plasticity: Annals of the New York Academy of Sciences, 1169,* 182–186.

Institute for Music and Neurological Functioning. (2009). *The importance of music and brain research.* Retrieved on September 15, 2009, from http://www.bethabe.org /Resource_Center97.html.

Jausovec, N., Jausovec, K., & Gerlic, I. (2006). The influence of Mozart's music on brain activity in the process of learning. *Clinical Neurophysiology, 117*(12), 2703–2714.

Karatizias, T., Gumley, A., Power, K., & O'Grady, M. (2007). Illness appraisals and self-esteem as correlates of anxiety and affective comorbid disorders in schizophrenia. *Comprehensive Psychiatry, 48*(4), 371–375.

Katz, N. (Ed.). (2005). *Cognition and occupation across the life span.* Bethesda, MD: Aota Press.

Knight, M. T. D., Wykes, T., & Hayward, P. (2006). Group treatment of perceived stigma and self-esteem in schizophrenia: A waiting list trial of efficacy. *Behavioral and Cognitive Psychotherapy, 34*(3), 305–318.

Kobasa, S. C., & Puccetti, M. C. (1983). Personality and social resources in stress resistance. *Journal of Personality and Social Psychology, 45*(4), 839–850.

Kobasa, S. C., Maddi, S. R., & Courington, S. (1981). Personality and constitution as mediators in the stress-illness relationship. *Journal of Health and Social Behavior, 22*(December), 368–378).

Kopelowicz, A., Liberman, R. P., & Zarate, R. (2006). Recent advances in social skills training for schizophrenia. *Schizophrenia Bulletin, 32*(Supplement 1), S12–S23.

Kunikata, H., Mino, Y., & Nakajima, K. (2005). Quality of life of schizophrenic patients living in the community: The relationships with self-esteem. *Psychiatric and Clinical Neurosciences, 59,* 163–169.

Kurtz, M. M., Seltzer, J. C., Shagan, D. Thime, W. R., & Wexler, B. E. (2007). Computer-assisted cognitive remediation in schizophrenia: What is the active ingredient? *Schizophrenia Research, 89*(1–3), 251–260.

Lamb, J. (2009). Creating change: Using the arts to help stop the stigma of mental

illness and foster social integration. *Journal of Holistic Nursing, 27*(1), 57–65.
Landis, T. J. (2009). *Stress management and relaxation.* Retrieved on June 26, 2009, from http://progdata.umflint.edu/LANDIS/HCR%20107%20Overheads.ppt.
Larson, J. E., & Corrigan, P. (2008). The stigma of families with mental illness. *Academic Psychiatry, 32*(2), 887–91.
Lauber, C., Anthony, M., Aidacic-Gross, V., & Rossler, W. (2004). What about psychiatrists' attitude to mentally ill people? *European Psychiatry, 19*(7), 423–427.
Lauber, C., Nordt, C., Braunschweig, C., & Rossler, W. (2006). Do mental health professionals stigmatize their patients? *Acta Psychiatra Scandanavia, 113* (Suppl. 429), 51–59.
Leary, M. R. (1999). Making sense of self-esteem. *Current Directions in Psychological Science, 8*(1), 32–35.
Leff, J., & Warner, R. (2006). *Social inclusion of people with mental illness.* Cambridge University Press: New York.
Lefley, H. P. (1989). Family burden and family stigma in major mental illness. *American Psychologist, 44*(3), 556–560.
Levin, A. (2001). Violence and mental illness: Media keep myths alive. *Psychiatric News, 6*(9), 10.
Levitin, D. J. (2006). *This is your brain on music: The science of a human obsession.* New York: Plume.
Liberman, R. P., & Phipps, C. C. (1987). Innovative techniques for the chronically mentally ill. In W. W. Menninger & G. Hannah (Eds.), *The chronically mentally ill patient.* Washington DC: American Psychiatric Press.
Lichtenstein, B., & Peoples, J. (Producers). (2003). *The face of mental illness* [Film]. Produced by 47th Street for Public Broadcasting Service (PBS). Retrieved on April 30, 2009, from www. pbs.org/pov/pov2003/west47thstreet/special_face .html.
Link, B. G., Phelan, J. C., Bresnahan, M., Stueve, A., & Pescosolido, B. (1999). Public conceptions of mental illness: Labels, causes, dangerousness and social distance. *American Journal of Public Health, 89*(9), 1328–1333.
Link, B. G., Struening, E. L., Nees-Tood, S., Asmussen, S., & Phelan, J. C. (2001). The consequences of stigma for the self-esteem of people with mental illness. *Psychiatric Services, 52*(12), 1621–1626.
Link, B. G., Struening, E. L., Rahav, M., Phelan, J. C., & Nuttbrock, L. (1997). On stigma and its consequences: Evidence from a longitudinal study of men with dual diagnoses of mental illness and substance abuse. *Journal of Health and Social Behavior, 38*(2), 177–190.
Love, J. (2009). *Positive self-talk.* Retrieved on July 8, 2009, from http://ezinearticles .com/?Positive-Self-Talk&id=30657.
Lysaker, P. H., Davis, L. W., Warman, D. M., Strasburger, A., & Beattie, N. (2007). Stigma, social function and symptoms in schizophrenia and schizoaffective disorder: Associations across 6 months. *Psychiatry Research, 149*(1), 89–95.
Lysaker, P. H., Roe, D., & Yanos, P. T. (2007). Toward understanding the insight paradox: Internalized stigma moderates the association between insight and social functioning, hope, and self-esteem among people with schizophrenia spectrum

disorders. *Schizophrenia Bulletin, 33*(1), 192–199.

MacKain, S. L., & Wallace, C. J. (1989). *Evaluation of Social and independent living skills models.* Los Angeles: Clinical Research Center for Schizophrenia and Psychiatric Rehabilitation.

Macinnes, D. L. (2006). Self-esteem and self-acceptance: An examination into their relationship and their effect on psychological health. *Journal of Psychiatric and Mental Health Nursing, 13,* 483–489.

Maio, H. A. (2004). Evidence? *Psychiatric Rehabilitation Journal, 28*(2), 197–199.

Mann, M., Hosman, C. M., Schaalma, H. P., & de Vries, N. K. (2004). Self-esteem in a broad-spectrum approach for mental health promotion. *Health Education Research, 19*(4), 357–72.

Margulis, E. H. (2008). *Debunking the "Mozart effect."* Retrieved on September 20, 2009, from http://www.therapytimes.com/content=0302J84C489EAE8440A040441.

Markowitz, F. E. (2001). Modeling processes in recovery from mental illness: Relationships between symptoms, life satisfaction, and self-concept. *Journal of Health and Social Behavior, 42*(1), 64–79.

McNulty, J. P. (2004). Mental illness, society, stigma and research (Commentary). *Schizophrenia Bulletin, 30*(3), 573–575.

Meltzer, H. Y., Park, S., & Kessler, R. (1999). Cognition, schizophrenia and the atypical antipsychotic drugs. *Procedures of the National Academy of Sciences,* November 23, 13591–13593.

Menninger Foundation. (1982). Guide to the order sheet. *Bulletin of the Menninger Clinic, 46*(1), 1–101.

Mental Health Works. (2009). *Stigma and mental illness* [Fact sheet]. Retrieved on April 30, 2009, from http://www.mentalhealthworks.ca/facts/sheets/stigma.asp.

Merryman, K. (2009, April 26). Patients' graves get markers. Spokane, WA: *The Spokesman Review.*

Meyers, S. (2009). *What is a stress-resistant person?* Retrieved on June 24, 2009, from http://www.extension.umn.edu/distribution/familydevelopment/components/7269bs.html.

Miller, D. M. (2009). *The correlation between sense of humor and mental health.* Retrieved on June 22, 2009, from http://clearinghouse.missouriwestern.edu/manuscripts/405.php.

Minton, B. L. (2008). *Music shown to facilitate the development of neurons in the brain.* Retrieved on December 28, 2009, from www.naturalnews.com/024286_the_brain_mood_genes.html.

Mobray, C. T., Bybee, D., & Shriner, W. (1996). Characteristics of participants in a supported education program for adults with psychiatric disabilities. *Psychiatric Services, 47*(12), 1371–1377.

Mulholland, C. C., O'Donoghue, D., Meenagh, C., & Rushe, T. M. (2008). Errorless learning and memory performance in schizophrenia. *Psychiatry Research, 159*(1–2), 180–188.

Music Therapy. (2009). *Treatment of Cerebral Palsy.* Retrieved on September 16, 2009, from http://www.originsofcerebralpalsy.com/05-treatment/02-musictherapy.html.

National Alliance on Mental Illness. (2006). *Stigma busting works!* Retrieved on May 1, 2009, from http://www.care2.com/c2c/groups/disc.html?gpp=35638&pst=620728.

National Alliance on Mental Illness. (2008). *About recovery.* Retrieved on August 6, 2008, from http://www.nami.org/Template.cfm?Section=About_Recovery&Template=/TaggedPage/TaggedPageDisplay.cfm&TPLID=23&ContentID=34759.

National Association of Independent Schools. (2009). *Enduring understandings.* Retrieved on September 17, 2009, from http://admin.nais.org/files/Word/09 AC_Curriculum%20Connections3.doc.

Neurologic Music Therapy. (2009). *Clinical implementations.* Retrieved on September 17, 2009, from http://www.wfnr.co.uk/pdf/nmt-wfnr.doc.

Neville, H., Andersson, A., Bagdade, O., Bell, T., Currin, J., Fanning, J., Klein, S., Lauinger, B., Pakulak, E., Paulsen, D., Sabourin, L., Stevens, C., Sundborg, S., & Yamada, Y. (2008). *Effects of music training on brain and cognitive development in underprivileged 3- to 5-year-olds, preliminary results.* Retrieved on September 20, 2009, from http//www.dana.org/news/publications/detail.aspx?id=10752.

New Theatre Productions. (Australia). (2009). *Imperfectly sane-delusions of splendor. Schizophrenia Daily News Blog,* 2007, May 15. Retrieved on May 25, 2009, from http://www.schizophrenia.com/sznews/archives/005078.html.

Nidamboor, R. (2010). *Music is the language of the soul.* Retrieved on March 8, 2010, from http://tinpan.fortunecity.com/harrison/624/musicand soul.htm.

Noble, S. E. (2005). Mental illness through popular theatre: Performing (in)sanely). *New Directions for Adult and Continuing Education, 107*(Fall), 45–53.

O'Carroll, R. (2000). Cognitive impairment in schizophrenia. *Advances in Psychiatric Treatment, 6,* 161–168.

O'Donnell, L. (1999). *Music and the brain.* Retrieved on February 4, 2009, from http://www.cerebromente. org.br/n15/mente/musica.html.

Ormrod, J. E. (1999). Social learning theory. Retrieved on July 15, 2008, from teachnet.edb.utexas.edu/~lynda_abbott/social.html.

Pajares, F., & Schunk, D. (2001). Self-beliefs and school success: Self-efficacy, self-concept and school achievement. In R. Riding & S. Raynor (Eds.), *Perception* (pp. 239–266). London: Ablex Publishing.

Palmer, A. (2000). *20th century history of treatment of mental illness: A review.* Retrieved on August 22, 2008, from http://web.archive.org/web/20040710022826/http://www.mentalhealthworld.org/29ap.html.

Pradhan, B. D., Chakrabarti, S., Nehra, R., & Mankotia, A. (2008). Cognitive functions in bipolar affective disorder and schizophrenia: Comparison. *Psychiatry and Clinical Neurosciences, 62*(5), 515–525.

Rathbun, J. A. (2001). *Not the same old song.* Retrieved on September 18, 2009, from http://www.rehabpub.com/features/112001/2.asp.

Rauscher, F. H. (2000). *Is the Mozart effect "debunked"?* Retrieved on September 22, 2009, from http://www.uwash.edu/psychology/rausher/Debunk.pdf.

Rauscher, F. H. (2003). Can music instruction affect children's cognitive development? *ERIC Clearinghouse on Early Education and Parenting.* Retrieved on

September 20, 2009, from http://www.ericdigests.org/2004-3/cognitive.html.

Ravnkilde, B., Videbech, P., Clemmensen, K., Egander, A., Rasmussen, N. A., & Rosenberg, R. (2002). Cognitive deficits in major depression. *Scandinavian Journal of Psychology, 43*(3), 239–251.

Rethink. (2009). *Recovery from serious mental illness.* Retrieved on September 10, 2009, from http://www.enotalone.com/article/3106.html.

Revheim, N., & Medalia, A. (2004). Verbal memory, problem-solving skills and community status in schizophrenia. *Schizophrenia Research, 68*(2), 149–158.

Ritcher, J. B., Otilingam, P. G., & Grajales, M. (2003). Internalized stigma of mental illness: Psychometric properties of a new measure. *Psychiatry Research, 121*(1), 31–49.

Ritcher, J. B., & Phelan, J. C. (2004). Internalized stigma predicts erosion of morale among psychiatric outpatients. *Psychiatry Research, 129*(3), 257–265.

Rodgers, M. L., Norell, D. M., Roll, J. M., & Dyck, D. G. (2007). An overview of mental health recovery. *Primary Psychiatry, 14*(12), 76–85.

Roe, D. (2003). A prospective study on the relationship between self-esteem and functioning during the first year after being hospitalized for psychosis. *The Journal of Nervous and Mental Diseases, 191*(1), 45–49.

Rogers, E. S., Anthony, W., & Lyass, A. (2004). The nature and dimensions of social support among individuals with severe mental illnesses. *Community Mental Health Journal, 40*(5), 437–450.

Rutter, M. (2007). Resilience, competence, and coping. *Child Abuse and Neglect, 31*(3), 205–209.

Sacks, O. (2007). *Musicophilia.* New York: Vintage Books.

Sadow, D., Ryder, M., & Webster, D. (2002). Is education of health professionals encouraging stigma towards the mentally ill? *Journal of Mental Health, 11*(6), 657–665.

Sarkamo, T., Tervaniemi, M., Laitinen, S., Forsblom, A., Soinila, S., Mikkonen, M., Autti, T., Silvennoinen, H. M., Erkkila, J., Laine, M., Peretz, I., & Hietanen, M. (2008). Music listening enhances cognitive recovery and mood after middle cerebral artery stroke. *Brain, 131*(3), 866–876.

Schiffman, J., Sorensen, J. J., Maeda, J., Mortensen, E. L., Victoroff, J., Hayashi, K., Michelsen, N. M., Ekstrom, M., & Mednick, S. (2009). Childhood motor coordination and adult schizophrenia spectrum disorders. *American Journal of Psychiatry, 166*(9), 1041–1047.

Schmidt, R. A., & Wrisberg, C. A. (2000). *Motor learning and performance: A problem-based learning approach* (2nd ed.). Champaign, IL: Human Kinetics.

Schulman, M. (2008). *Music as medicine for the brain.* Retrieved on February 4, 2009, from http://www.usnews.com/health-news/family-health/brain-and-behavior/articles/2008/07/17/music-as-medicine-for-the-brain.html.

Seaward, B. L. (2004). *Managing stress: Strategies for health and well-being* (Chapter 6). Sudbury, MA: Jones and Bartlett.

Second Step Players. (2009). *Artreach.* Retrieved on May 25, 2009, from www.artreachheals.org/secondstep.html.

Segalas, C., Alonso, P., Labad, J., Jaurrieta, N., Real, E., Jimenez, S., Menchon, J. M.,

& Vallejo, J. (2008). Verbal and nonverbal memory processing in patients with obsessive-compulsive disorder: Its relationship to clinical variables. *Neuropsychology, 22*(2), 262–272.

Seligman, M. E. P., & Csikszentmihalyi, M. (2000). Positive psychology: An introduction. *American Psychologist, 55*(1), 5–14.

Sells, D., Marit, B., Marin, I., Mezzina, R., Topor, A., & Davidson, L. (2006). Arenas of recovery for persons with severe mental illness. *American Journal of Psychiatric Rehabilitation, 9,* 3–16.

Shahar, G., & Davidson, L. (2003). Depressive symptoms erode self-esteem in severe mental illness: A three-wave, cross-lagged study. *Journal of Consulting and Clinical Psychology, 71*(5), 890–900.

Shulman, M. (2008). Music as medicine for the brain. *U. S. News and World Report.* Retrieved on February 4, 2009, from http://health.usnews.com/articles/health/brain-and-behavior/2008/07/17/music-as-medicine-for-the-brain.html.

Silverstein, S. M., & Wilkniss, S. M. (2004). At issue: The future of cognitive rehabilitation of schizophrenia. *Schizophrenia Bulletin, 30*(4), 679–692.

Simon, B. (1992). Shame, stigma and mental illness in ancient Greece. In P. J. Fink, & A. Tasman (Eds.), *Stigma and mental illness* (pp. 29–39). Washington, DC: American Psychiatric Press.

Sirey, J. A., Bruce, M. L., Alexopoulos, G. S., Perlick, D. A., Raue, P., Friedman, S. J., & Meyers, B. S. (2001). Perceived stigma as a predictor of treatment discontinuation in young and older outpatients with depression. *American Journal of Psychiatry, 158*(3), 479–481.

Sorgaard, K. W., Heikkila, J., Hansson, L., Vinding, H. R., Bjarnason, O., Bengtson-Tops, A., Merinder, L., Nilsson, L., Sandlund, M., & Middelboe, T. (2002). Self-esteem in persons with schizophrenia: A Nordic multicentre study. *Journal of Mental Health, 11*(4), 405–415.

Spaulding, W. D., Reed, D., Sullivan, M., Richardson, C., & Weiler, M. (1999). Effects of cognitive treatment in psychiatric rehabilitation. *Schizophrenia Bulletin, 25*(4), 657–676.

Stanford University Medical Center. (2007). Music moves brain to pay attention, study finds. *Science Daily.* Retrieved on February 4, 2009, from http://www.sciencedaily.com/releases/2007/08/070801122226.htm.

Stockdale, C., & Possin, C. (2009). *Spatial relations and learning.* Retrieved on April 3, 2009, from http://www. newhorizons.org/spneeds/inclusion/teaching/stockdale.html.

Stuart, H. (2006). Media portrayal of mental illness and its treatments: What effect does it have on people with mental illness? *CNS Drugs, 20*(2), 99–106.

Student Affairs, TCU. (2009). *The stress-resistant personality.* Retrieved on January 4, 2010, from http://www.counseling.tcu.edu/stressresistant_personality.asp.

Suda, M., Morimoto, K., Obata, A., Koizumi, H., & Maki, A. (2008). Cortical responses to Mozart's sonata enhance spatial-reasoning ability. *Neurological Research, 30*(9), 885–888.

Thaut, M. H., Gardiner, J. C., Holmberg, D., Horwitz, J., Kent, L., Andrews, G., Donelan, B., & McIntosh, G. R. (Eds.). (2009). Neurologic music therapy improves executive function and emotional adjustment in traumatic brain injury rehabilitation. *The Neurosciences and Music III–Disorders and Plasticity: Annals of the New York Academy of Sciences, 1169,* 406–416.

Thesen, J. (2001). Being a psychiatric patient in the community-reclassified as the stigmatized "other." *Scandinavian Journal of Public Health, 29*(4), 248–255.

Torrey, E. F., Erdman, K., Wolfe, S. M., & Flynn, L. M. (1990). *Care of the seriously mentally ill: A rating of state programs* (3rd ed.). Washington, DC: Public Citizen Health Research and the Alliance for the Mentally Ill.

Torrey, W. C., Mueser, K. T., McHugo, G. H., & Drake, R. E. (2000). Self-esteem as an outcome measure in studies of vocational rehabilitation for adults with severe mental illness. *Psychiatric Services, 51*(2), 229–233.

Tracy, B. (2007). *The power of positive self-talk.* Retrieved on June 16, 2010, from http://www.advisortoday.com/200704/selftalk.html.

Trainor, L. J., Shahin, A. J., & Roberts, L. E. (2009). Understanding the benefits of musical training. *The Neurosciences and Music III–Disorders and Plasticity: Annals of the New York Academy of Sciences, 1169,* 133–142.

Tramo, M. J. (2001). Music of the hemispheres. *Science, 291*(5501), 54–56.

Tugade, M. M., & Fredrickson, B. L. (2004). Resilient individuals use positive emotions to bounce back from negative emotional experiences. *Journal of Personality and Social Psychology, 86*(2), 320–333.

Turkington, D., & Siddle, R. (2000). Improving understanding and coping in people with schizophrenia by changing attitudes. *Psychiatric Rehabilitation Skills, 4*(2), 300–320.

Tusaie, K., Puskar, K., & Sereika, S. M. (2007). A predictive and moderating model of psychosocial resilience in adolescents. *Journal of Nursing Scholarship, 39*(1), 54–60.

Twardzicki, M. (2008). Challenging stigma around mental illness and promoting social inclusion using the performing arts. *Journal of the Royal Society for the Promotion of Health, 128*(2), 68–72.

Van de Winckel, A., Feys, H., & De Weerdt, W. (2004). Cognitive and behavioural effects of music-based exercises in patients with dementia. *Clinical Rehabilitation, 18,* 253–260.

Van Dorn, R. A., Swanson, J. W., Elbogen, E. B., & Swartz, M. S. (2005). A comparison of stigmatizing attitudes toward persons with schizophrenia in four stakeholder groups: Perceived likelihood of violence and desire for social distance. *Psychiatry, 68*(2), 152–163.

Vaskinn, A., Sundet, K., Hultman, C. M., Friis, S., & Andreassen, O. A. (2009). Social problem-solving in high-functioning schizophrenia: Specific deficits in sending skills. *Psychiatry Research, 165*(3), 215–223.

Wahl, O. F. (1999). Mental health consumers' experience of stigma. *Schizophrenia Bulletin, 25*(3), 467–478.

Wahl, O. F. (2001). *Spring to action: A National Mental Health Symposium to Address Discrimination and Stigma.* Retrieved on April 21, 2009, from http://www.zoominfo.com/people/Wahl_Otto_8828142.aspx.

Wahl, O. F. (2003). News media portrayal of mental illness: Implications for public

policy. *American Behavioral Scientist, 46*(12), 1594–1600.
Wahl, O. F., & Harman, C. R. (1989). Family views of stigma. *American Journal of Psychiatric Rehabilitation, 15*(1), 131–139.
Wahl, O. F., Wood, A., & Richards, R. (2002). Newspaper coverage of mental illness: Is it changing? *Psychiatric Rehabilitation Skills, 6*(1), 9–31.
Walker, J. E. (1981). The social context of modeling. *Social Behavior and Personality, 9*(2), 129–137.
Wallack, L., Dorfman, L. E., Jernigan, D. J., & Themba, M. (1993). *Media advocacy and public health: Power for prevention.* Thousand Oaks, CA: Sage.
Watson, C. (2009). Rhythm for rehabilitation: Music therapy as part of the stroke rehabilitation team. *Carolina Center for Music Therapy.* Retrieved on September 23, 2009, from http:www.med.unc.edu/phyrehab/files/Rhythm_for_Rehabilitation .pdf.
Wright, E. R., Gronfein, W. P., & Owens, T. J. (2000). Deinstitutionalization, social rejection, and the self-esteem of former mental patients. *Journal of Health and Social Behavior, 41*(1), 68–90.

INDEX

A

Acquainted, becoming, 135–136
Advocacy groups, 127–129
Anger, 38–39
Anonymous critique, 88
Anthony, William A., 14
Anxiety
  desensitization, 85–87
  negative attitude, 84–85
  and performances, 87–93
  positive attitude, 83–84
  reducing, 81–83
Assertive community treatment, 16
Attention and concentration, 106–109
Attitude, 63

B

Bandura, Albert, 52–53
Behaviors (SEIR model), 59–60

C

Case manager interviews, 28–29
Cast members, 154–157
  see also Musical theatre
Central Iowa Players Stigma Busters Drama Troupe, 127–128
Change, 61
Clozaril, 12
Clubhouses, 16
Cognitive behavioral therapy (CBT), 16, 19
Cognitive skills
  attention, 107–109
  concentration, 106–107
  executive functioning, 111–112
  memory, 109–110
  and mental illness, 101–104
  motor learning, 114–115
  and SEIR model, 104–119
  spatial awareness, 117–118
"Come Hear the Music," 148
Community Mental Health Center Act (1963), 12–13
Confidence, 62
Confinement, 5–6
Connecticut Heritage Productions (CHP), 127
Cooperation and interdependence, 135
Costumes
  basic design, 176–177
  distribution, 177–178
  musical theatre, 175–178
  see also Sets and props
Creativity, 47–48
Crisis resolution
  musical theatre, 167
  program guide, 186–188
Criticism, 62

D

Dance routine, 189–190
Desensitization, 85–87
Dix, Dorothea, 124
Douglass, Donna, 23, 30, 140

E

Einstein, Albert, 97–98
Emotions, 62–63
Employment, 38
Equalization, 135

Executive functioning, 111–114

F

"Flow," 21
Focus groups, 27–28
Forms
  confidentiality statement, 197–198
  consent, 197–198
  members
    enrollment, 199
    information, 200
    sign-in, 201
  self-evaluation
    post-performance, 204–205
    pre-performance, 202–203
  theatre company contract, 206–207
  see also Program guides
Fun and enjoyment, 38

G

George I, 100
Goals
creativity, 47–48
  interpersonal skills, 44–45
  risk-taking, 49–50
  SEIR model, 40–51
    evaluation, 63–65
  self-confidence, 41–43
  self-discipline, 45–47
  self-presentation skills, 48–49
  social skills, 50–51
  team-building skills, 43–44
Group critique, 88
A Guide to the Order Sheet, xix

H

"Hats Off, Spokane!" 169
Hoffman, Albert, 10
Hornor, Rick, 140–141

I

"I Am Terrific," 83
Institutionalization, 12–14
Integrative aspects, 39
Interactions, fostering, 134–135
Interpersonal skills, 44–45
Interventions
  attitude, 63
  change, 61
  confidence, 62
  criticism, 62
  effective, 60–63
  emotions, 62–63
  performing arts, 134–136
  responsibility, 62
  risk-taking, 61–62
  social networks, 61
  stigma, 133–134

L

Laborit, Henri, 10
LSD, 10

M

Memory, 109–111
Mental health practices
  confinement, 5–6
  deinstitutionalization, 12–14
  history and research, 5–10
    ancient theories, 5–6
    evolution of treatment, 6–8
    psychotropic drugs, 8–10
  innovations, theory, 16
  and reducing stigma, 132–133
  see also Interventions
Mental illness
  and cognitive skills, 101–104
  need statement, 22–23
Mental institutions, 5–7
"Miracle drug." see Promethazine
Modeling
  imitation, 55–56
  observational, 54
  performance, 55
  symbolic, 56
  vicarious, 56
  see also Process
Motor skills and motor learning, 114–117
Multi-family education, 16
Music
  and learning, 97–101
  and recovery, 94–97
Musical theatre
  cast members, 154–157
  company
    contract (form), 206–207

"experienced," 168–170
first, 159–160
informational meeting, 157–159
costumes, 175–178
crisis resolution, 167
first production, 162–165
getting organized, 160–162
program guides, 165–167
programs (printed), 173–175
publicity, 173–175
refreshments, 158–159
sets and props, 178–179
song selection, 164–165
sound equipment, 158
and success, 170–172
theme shows, 179–182

N

National Alliance for the Mentally Ill (NAMI), xxiii, 15, 127

O

Observational learning, 53–54
see also Social learning theory
On Stage! xix, 36, 153
Oregon State Penitentiary, 147–148

P

Performances
and anxiety, 87–93
cast party, 92–93
class, 87–89
critiques, 88
dress rehearsal, 90–91
small audiences, 89–90
video recording, 89
Performing arts
and healing, 21–22
mental illness, 22–29
primary findings, 31
interventions, 134–136
and reducing stigma, 120–122
universities and service learning, 139–142
see also Musical theatre
Personalities
stress-resistant, 70–74
teacher/therapist, 191–192
Pharmaceuticals
antipsychotic drugs, 8, 11–12
promethazine, 10–12
psychotropic drugs, 8–10
Phenobarbital, 8-9
Policy, implications of, 31–32
Process
modeling, 54–56
imitation, 55–56
observational, 54
performance, 55
symbolic, 56
vicarious, 56
SEIR model, 51–59
self-efficacy, 57–59
self-regulation, 57
social learning theory, 51–54
observational learning, 53–54
principles, 52–53
stage performance, 56–57
Program guides
cane construction, 185
crisis resolution, 186–188
dance routine, 189–190
musical theatre, 165–167
rules and guidelines, 195–196
see also Forms; Musical theatre
Programs (printed)
boilerplate, 193
musical theatre, 173–175
sample, 194
Project Arts, xix, 36, 144–145
Promethazine, 10–12
Public and media, 125–126
Publicity, 173–175

R

Recovery
history and research, 14–15
model
history and development, 33-35
history and research, 15–17
and music, 94–97
and schizophrenia, 17–18
SEIR model, 35–36
and self-esteem (SEIR), 35–36
wheel, 63–65
see also SEIR model
"Reflections of a Life," 108
Resilience, 75–78
Respirine, 11

Responsibility, 62
Risk-taking, 49–50, 61–62
  see also Goals
Role shifting, 38
Routines, meaningful, 38

S

Salem Creative Arts Center (SCAC), xix, 36–37, 145–148
Schizophrenia, 17–18
SEIR model
  components
    behaviors, 59–60
    goals, 40–51
    process, 51–59
  design of, 37–39, 40f
  evaluation, 63–65
  and families, 142–144
  history and development, 35–37
  interventions, 108, 110–119
  structure, 39–60
    behaviors, 59–60
    goals, 40–51
    process, 51–59
  themes, 37–39
Self-confidence, 41–43
Self-critique, 88
Self-discipline, 45–47
Self-efficacy, 57–59
  see also Process
Self-esteem
  literature, 18–20
  and recovery (SEIR), 35–36
    as theme, 38
  see also SEIR model
Self-presentation skills, 48–49
Self-regulation, 57
  see also Process
Sets and props
  flat construction, 178
  musical theatre, 178–179
  set design, 178–179
  see also Costumes
Social and independent living skill modules, 23
Social learning theory
  background, 51–54
  modeling, 54–55
    imitation, 55–56
    performance, 55
    symbolic, 56
    vicarious, 56
  observational learning, 53–54
  principles, 52–53
  self-efficacy, 57–59
  self-regulation, 57
  stage performance, 56–57
Social networks, 61
Social skills, 50–51
Sound equipment, 158
Spatial awareness, 117–119
Staff and volunteers, 157–158
Stage performance, 56–57
  see also Process; Social learning theory
Stereotypes, 136
Stigma
  interventions, 133–134
  public and media, 125–126
  reducing
    advocacy groups, 127–129
    history and development, 122–124
    mental health services, 132–133
    and performing arts, 120–122
    professionals and families, 130–131
    programs, 136–148
Stress, coping with, 78–80
Stress reduction
  history and development, 66–69
  and resilience, 75–78
  stress-resistant personalities, 70–74
  "ten commandments," 70–80
Supported education, 16
Supported Education Enhancing Rehabilitation (SEER), 121

T

Team-building skills, 43–44
Theatre Extraordinaire, 33, 137
Theme shows
1950s, 180–181
  musical theatre, 179–182
  patriotic, 179–180
Roaring '20s, 181–182
Thorazine, 10–11
Traumatic brain injury (TBI), 104–105

U

Understanding and acceptance, 37

V

Video recording, 89

W

"Warehousing," 7
Washington Institute of Mental Health Research and Training (WIMIRT), xxiv
"A Whole Lot Better," 68–69
Work placement, 27
Work Readiness Skill Assessment (WRSA) wheel, 24–27